FOR THE
IB DIPLOMA

Mathematics
Study and Revision Guide

SL and HL

Ferenc Beleznay

HODDER
EDUCATION

Orders: please contact Bookpoint Ltd, 130 Park Drive, Milton Park, Abingdon, Oxon OX14 4SE. Telephone: (44) 01235 827720. Fax: (44) 01235 400454. Email education@bookpoint.co.uk Lines are open from 9 a.m. to 5 p.m., Monday to Saturday, with a 24-hour message answering service. You can also order through our website: www.hoddereducation.com

ISBN: 978 1 4718 6848 1

© Ferenc Beleznay 2016

First published in 2016 by

Hodder Education,

An Hachette UK Company

Carmelite House

50 Victoria Embankment

London EC4Y 0DZ

www.hoddereducation.com

Impression number 10 9 8 7 6 5 4 3 2 1

Year   2019 2018 2017 2016

Cover photo © Oscar Gutierrez/istock.com

Illustrations by Aptara Inc.

Typeset in GaudyStd, 10/12 pts by Aptara Inc.

Printed in Spain

A catalogue record for this title is available from the British Library.

Contents

Contents

How to use this revision guide

Welcome to the *Mathematics for the IB Diploma Study and Revision Guide*.

This book will help you plan your revision and work through it in a methodical way. It follows the *Mathematics* syllabus topic by topic, with revision exam practice to help you check your understanding.

■ Features to help you succeed

Key definition
Definitions of the key concepts you need to know for the exam.

IB SYLLABUS
IB syllabus boxes refers to specific points in the IB syllabus and features of the exam.

USING A CALCULATOR
These notes explain how using a graphing display calculator (GDC) can help you, as well as the difference between questions on the calculator and non-calculator papers.

CROSS REFERENCE
Cross reference boxes highlight the connections between concepts to help you and provide page references.

Example
Examples can help understanding by putting the definitions and claims into context and showing you how to answer questions.

Note
Notes give extra information and highlight the most important points to help you understand the concepts.

You can keep track of your revision by ticking off each topic heading in the book. There is also a checklist at the end of the book. Use this checklist to record progress as you revise. Tick each box when you have:

■ revised and understood a topic

■ used the Practice questions and checked your answers using the Answers and Detailed solutions.

Use this book as the cornerstone of your revision. Don't hesitate to write in it and personalise your notes. Use a highlighter to identify any areas that need further work. You may find it useful to add your own notes as you work through each topic.

The first half of the book covers the key concepts in six Topics. It includes definitions of the concepts and statements of the claims you should know by the time you take the exam. The order of the topics follows the syllabus to help you check you have covered everything. For reference, the relevant syllabus section numbers are included next to the section titles. With the exception of the two variable statistics, every concept of the SL syllabus is also in the HL syllabus. If there is no indication next to a concept, then it is relevant to both SL and HL students. The parts of the syllabus that only HL students need to know are clearly marked.

In some cases the definitions are precise (for example, those in the trigonometry topic), but often the formal definition would go beyond the level of the course (for example, for some calculus concepts). Some claims are stated in their most general form, but other claims (mostly in the calculus topic), are used only with some limitation. Some topics (such as trigonometry, for example) are treated in a quite rigorous way in the syllabus. In others (such as calculus and probability), we rely on an intuitive approach. The precise mathematical treatment often would be quite tedious, and would hide the aim of the course, namely the introduction of the basic concepts of several important areas of mathematics. This guide makes a clear distinction between definition and claim, which is crucial in learning mathematics. The definitions give the starting points for logically correct reasoning, either formal or informal. In some cases, the limitations of our approach are also highlighted. For example, when dealing with exponential expressions, we define a^x for rational exponents, but use the index laws for any real exponents (after only justifying these laws for natural number exponents).

Each chapter also has a list of useful past paper questions to check your knowledge on real exam questions.

The second half of the book helps you put everything you have learned into practice for the exam. It contains thirty longer questions, like the ones that appear on part B of the exams. Most of these have parts that ask for pattern recognition, generalisation. If you want to do well in the examination you need to think beyond routine applications of the concepts and rules. You need to be able to apply methods in unfamiliar settings and to see connections between concepts. Thinking about these questions can help understanding. The syllabus content that the question checks is given for all questions. Some questions are accessible to both SL and HL students, some use concepts that are only in the HL syllabus, and in some questions the first part is accessible to both SL and HL students, but the last part goes beyond the SL expectation. Interested SL students of course can have a go and try these parts as it can only help understanding. For all the questions, the numerical answers are included in a separate section.

In addition, hints are included in a Hints section following the Practice questions. These can be useful for those who only need a little help to start working on the solution. The hints also highlight the fact that a plan is always a good starting point for problem solving. Before starting to work on the solution, it can be helpful to think about what hint you would give to a fellow student about the question. If you see what the question tries to check and can give advice on how to approach it, then you are on the right track for solving the question.

As well as the numerical answers, detailed solutions are given in a separate section. These give the correct answer and show the best method for working through the question. It is useful to read these solutions even if you could solve the question, as you may have used a different method. Some exam advice is also given in margin notes next to the solutions. In any case, please try to solve the question yourself or follow the hint before you turn to the detailed solution. If you try to do the question yourself first, you will have a much better understanding of the solution even if you could not get to the correct answer.

There is also a section with further investigation ideas related to the Practice questions. Thinking about these problems can aid understanding, even though they go beyond what will be asked in the exam. At the same time, these ideas are useful as they encourage you to ask questions yourself, and not to simply answer questions asked by others. This type of thinking is useful when you are searching for an appropriate topic for your exploration.

The last part of this guide contains information about past paper questions. The tables list the syllabus topics, and next to each topic shows the question number(s) that checks the understanding of that topic in each past paper. The questions are not included; past papers can be purchased from the IB. However, if you want to practice a specific topic, or see what types of questions usually appear on exams with regard to a topic, this reference might help your search. Since the syllabus has changed, starting with the examinations in 2014, there are some topics in past papers that are no longer part of the syllabus. Questions from these topics are also included in these tables.

Getting to know the exam

Exam paper	Duration	Format	Topics	Weighting
Paper 1 (SL)	1.5 hours	Short-response and extended-response questions Non-calculator	All	40%
Paper 2 (SL)	1.5 hours	Short-response and extended-response questions Calculator	All	40%
Paper 1 (HL)	2 hours	Short-response and extended-response questions Non-calculator	All	30%
Paper 2 (HL)	2 hours	Short-response and extended-response questions Calculator	All	30%
Paper 3 (HL)	1 hour	Extended-response	1 of the 4 options	20%

SL students will sit two papers at the end of your Mathematics course – Paper 1 and Paper 2, worth 40% each. The other assessed part of the course is the Internal Assessment (worth 20%) which is marked by your teacher.

HL students will sit three papers: Paper 1 and Paper 2, worth 30% each, and an additional Paper 3 (worth 20%) which covers one of the four options. (This revision guide does not cover the option topics appearing on Paper 3 of the HL exam.) HL students also have an Internal Assessment (worth 20%) which is marked by your teacher.

Here is some general advice for the exams:

- Make sure you have learned the command terms (e.g. find, state, suggest, hence, draw, show). There is a tendency to focus on the content in a question rather than the command term, but if you do not address what the command term is asking of you then you will not be awarded marks. Your teachers have access to the IB list of command terms and their explanations.

- On both Paper 1 and Paper 2 of the exam, you will have short-response questions (part A) and extended-response questions (part B) to answer. For the short-response questions, space will be provided next to the question in the question booklet for the answer. If you run out of room, you can continue in the separate answer booklet, but you need to clearly indicate next to the question that you continued your work elsewhere. For the extended-response questions, any work next to the question in the question booklet will not be marked. You have to write all your work in the separate answer booklet, clearly indicating the question number.

- Plan your time carefully before the exams.

- At the start of the exam, you will have five minutes to read the paper without writing anything. Use this time to look at the questions and decide which ones you want to answer first. You don't have to work on the questions in the order they are presented in the paper.

Countdown to the exams

4–8 weeks to go

- Start by looking at the syllabus and make sure you know exactly what you need to revise.
- Look carefully at the checklist in this book and use it to help organise your class notes and to make sure you have covered everything.
- Work out a realistic revision plan that breaks down the material you need to revise into manageable pieces. Each session should be around 25–40 minutes with breaks in between. The plan should include time for relaxation.
- Read through the relevant sections of this book and refer to the key definitions, notes and examples.
- Tick off the topics that you feel confident about, and highlight the ones that need further work.
- Look at past papers. They are one of the best ways to check knowledge and practise exam skills. They will also help you identify areas that need further work.
- Try different revision methods, for example summary notes, mind maps and flash cards.
- Make notes of any problem areas as you revise, and ask a teacher to go over them in class.

My exams

Paper 1

Date:....................................

Time:....................................

Location:...............................

Paper 2

Date:....................................

Time:....................................

Location:...............................

Paper 3 (HL only)

Date:....................................

Time:....................................

Location:...............................

One week to go

- Aim to fit in at least one more timed practice of entire past papers, comparing your work closely with the mark scheme.
- Examine the checklist carefully to make sure you haven't missed any of the topics.
- Tackle any final problems by getting help from your teacher or talking them over with a friend.

The day before the examination

- Look through this book one final time. Look carefully through the information about Paper 1 and Paper 2 to remind yourself what to expect in both papers.
- Check the time and place of the exams.
- Make sure you have all the equipment you need (e.g. extra pens, a watch, tissues). Make sure you have a calculator for your Paper 2 exam (and also Paper 3 for HL students).
- Allow some time to relax and have an early night so you are refreshed and ready for the exams.

Topic **1** Algebra

1.1 Sequences and series (SL 1.1, HL 1.1)

In this section we consider sequences of numbers: $u_1, u_2, u_3, \ldots$ We will look at the concept of the limit of a sequence later in Topic 6 Calculus. We are concentrating on two simple rules to construct sequences and discuss the properties and applications of the resulting arithmetic and geometric sequences. One way of defining these, and more general types of sequences (for example, the Fibonacci sequence), is the method of recursion.

> **USING A CALCULATOR**
> Sequences can be generated and displayed in several ways. Graphic display calculators (GDCs) have built-in applications to work with sequences.

Recursive sequences

A sequence is defined recursively if one or more (initial) terms are specified and the later terms are expressed using previous terms (using so-called recurrence relations).

> **CROSS REFERENCE**
> See also: the discrete mathematics option. **(HL)**

Example
The recursive definition, $u_1 = 2$, $u_{n+1} = 2u_n + 1$ $(n \geq 1)$ defines the sequence 2, 5, 11, 23, …

Arithmetic sequences

Key definition
A sequence $u_1, u_2, u_3, \ldots$ is **arithmetic**, if there is a constant d, such that $u_{n+1} = u_n + d$ for all $n \in \mathbb{Z}^+$. The constant d is called the common difference of the sequence.

> **Note**
> The common difference is the difference between consecutive terms of an arithmetic sequence.

▇ Claims

- $u_n = u_1 + (n - 1)d$

- $u_1 + u_2 + \ldots + u_n = S_n = \dfrac{n}{2}(u_1 + u_n) = \dfrac{n}{2}(2u_1 + (n - 1)d)$

> **IB SYLLABUS**
> The formulae for the general term of an arithmetic sequence and the sum of a finite arithmetic series are in the IB Mathematics SL and HL formula booklets.

Geometric sequences

Key definition
A sequence $u_1, u_2, u_3, \ldots$ is **geometric**, if there is a constant r, such that $u_{n+1} = ru_n$ for all $n \in \mathbb{Z}^+$. The constant r is called the common ratio of the sequence.

> **Note**
> The common ratio is the ratio of consecutive terms of a geometric sequence.

Claims

- $u_n = u_1 r^{n-1}$

- $u_1 + u_2 + \ldots + u_n = S_n = u_1 \dfrac{r^n - 1}{r - 1} = u_1 \dfrac{1 - r^n}{1 - r}$, for $r \neq 1$

- $u_1 + u_2 + u_3 + \ldots = S_\infty = u_1 \dfrac{1}{1 - r}$, for $|r| < 1$

> **IB SYLLABUS**
>
> The formulae for the general term of a geometric sequence and the sum of a finite and infinite geometric series are in the IB Mathematics SL and HL formula booklets.

> **Note**
>
> Note the important conditions, $r \neq 1$ and $|r| < 1$.

Applications

Population growth and compound interest are important applications of geometric sequences.

For compound interest, the formula for the future value of an investment is

$Fv = Pv\left(1 + \dfrac{r}{100k}\right)^{kn}$, where Fv is the future value, Pv is the initial (present value) of the investment, r is the interest rate as a percentage, n is the number of years and k is the number of compounding periods in a year.

> **IB SYLLABUS**
>
> Worded questions involving population growth, finance, etc come up in exams. Note that this formula for the future value of an investment is not in the IB Mathematics SL and HL formula booklets.

> **USING A CALCULATOR**
>
> GDCs have built-in finance applications that can be helpful.

Sigma notation

Revised ☐

The following is a compact notation for sums of members of sequences:

$u_k + u_{k+1} + \ldots + u_n = \displaystyle\sum_{j=k}^{n} u_j.$

> **Example**
>
> $\displaystyle\sum_{j=3}^{6} j^2 = 3^2 + 4^2 + 5^2 + 6^2 = 86$

1.2 Exponents and logarithms (SL 1.2, HL 1.2)

Revised ☐

Exponential expressions

Revised ☐

> **Key definitions**
>
> - For $n \in \mathbb{Z}^+$, a^n is a shorthand notation for $\underbrace{aa \ldots a}_{n}$. In this case the base can be any real number, $a \in \mathbb{R}$.
> - For $n \in \mathbb{Z}^+$, $a^{-n} = \dfrac{1}{a^n}$. In this case we need to restrict the base a bit, so $a \neq 0$.
> - For $a \neq 0$, $a^0 = 1$. Although in some books $0^0 = 1$, here we leave 0^0 undefined.
> - For $x \in \mathbb{Q}$, $x = \dfrac{p}{q}$ with $p, q \in \mathbb{Z}$, $q > 0$, $a^x = \sqrt[q]{a^p}$. Although for some p- and q-values this definition can work for negative or zero values of a, in general we need to restrict the base to positive values: $a > 0$.
> - We will use exponential expressions for a positive base and any real exponent, but the definition is beyond the scope of this course. A possible approach is to approximate real numbers with rational numbers and define a^x using these values.

> **Note**
>
> We define exponential expressions of the form a^x in steps, starting with positive integer exponents and extending the definition to negative integer, 0 and rational exponents.

> **Example**
>
> $8^{\frac{2}{3}} = \sqrt[3]{8^2} = \sqrt[3]{64} = 4$

> **CROSS REFERENCE**
>
> See also: the exponential function, $x \mapsto a^x$ on page 15.

■ Laws of exponents

- $a^{x+y} = a^x a^y$
- $a^{x-y} = \dfrac{a^x}{a^y}$
- $a^{xy} = (a^x)^y = (a^y)^x$
- $(ab)^x = a^x b^x$
- $\left(\dfrac{a}{b}\right)^x = \dfrac{a^x}{b^x}$

> **Note**
>
> These index laws are easy to check for positive integer exponents. It is not so easy to check, but they are still true, for any real exponent with the restriction that the base is a positive real number.

> **IB SYLLABUS**
>
> These index laws are not in the IB Mathematics SL and HL formula booklets.

Logarithms

Revised ■

Key definition

The relationship (between the numbers $a > 0$, $a \neq 1$, $b > 0$ and c), $\log_a b = c$ is defined by $a^c = b$.

We will use $\log b$ as a shorthand notation for $\log_{10} b$. It should be noted that in other sources $\log b$ may not denote the base 10 logarithm.

> **Example**
>
> Since $3^2 = 9$, $\log_3 9 = 2$.

> **IB SYLLABUS**
>
> In this course, $\log_{10} b = \log b$.

■ Laws of logarithms

- $\log_a xy = \log_a x + \log_a y$, $x, y > 0$
- $\log_a \dfrac{x}{y} = \log_a x - \log_a y$, $x, y > 0$
- $\log_a x^y = y \log_a x$, $x > 0$
- $\log_a b = \dfrac{\log_d b}{\log_d a}$

> **Examples**
>
> $\log_2 6 = \log_2 2 + \log_2 3 = 1 + \log_2 3$
>
> $\log 0.2 = \log 2 - \log 10 = \log 2 - 1$
>
> $\log_5 125 = \log_5 5^3 = 3\log_5 5 = 3$
>
> Also, using the change of base law,
>
> $\log_{27} 81 = \dfrac{\log_3 81}{\log_3 27} = \dfrac{4}{3}$

> **IB SYLLABUS**
>
> The laws of logarithms are in the IB Mathematics SL formula booklet, but the IB Mathematics HL formula booklet only contains the change of base law.

1.3 Binomial theorem (SL 1.3, HL 1.3)

Revised ■

The coefficients of the expansions of $(a + b)^n$ (where $n \in \mathbb{N}$) can be found using Pascal's triangle:

$$
\begin{array}{ccccccccccc}
 & & & & & 1 & & & & & \\
 & & & & 1 & & 1 & & & & \\
 & & & 1 & & 2 & & 1 & & & \\
 & & 1 & & 3 & & 3 & & 1 & & \\
 & 1 & & 4 & & 6 & & 4 & & 1 & \\
\ldots & & \ldots & & \ldots & & \ldots & & \ldots & & \ldots
\end{array}
$$

The general formula for the binomial expansion is:

$$(a + b)^n = a^n + \binom{n}{1} a^{n-1} b^1 + \binom{n}{2} a^{n-2} b^2 + \ldots + \binom{n}{k} a^{n-k} b^k + \ldots + b^n,$$

where the binomial coefficients can also be found using the formula

$$\binom{n}{k} = \frac{n!}{(n-k)!\,k!}.$$

Another notation for the coefficients is $^nC_k = \binom{n}{k}$.

> **Note**
>
> Using sigma notation,
>
> $(a + b)^n = \displaystyle\sum_{k=0}^{n} \binom{n}{k} a^{n-k} b^k$

> **Note**
>
> This coefficient is usually read as 'n choose k'.

USING A CALCULATOR

Besides using the Pascal triangle or the formula, GDCs have built-in applications to find binomial coefficients. In exams all three ways of finding these binomial coefficients can be checked.

Examples
$(a + b)^2 = a^2 + 2ab + b^2$
$(a + b)^3 = a^3 + 3a^2b + 3ab^2 + b^3$
$(a + b)^4 = a^4 + 4a^3b + 6a^2b^2 + 4ab^3 + b^4$
...

1.4 Polynomials (HL 2.5)

Revised ☐

In this section we will look at some properties of real polynomials (expressions of the form $P(x) = a_n x^n + a_{n-1} x^{n-1} + \ldots + a_1 x + a_0$, where $a_k \in \mathbb{R}$, $a_n \neq 0$), and polynomial equations (of the form $P(x) = 0$ for some polynomial $P(x)$). The largest exponent, n, is called the degree of the polynomial.

Note

We assume here that $a_k \in \mathbb{R}$ for all $0 \leq k \leq n$, but all our claims are true for polynomials with complex coefficients.

CROSS REFERENCE

See also: complex roots of real polynomials (page 7) and polynomial functions (page 14).

Key definitions
- Polynomials can be added, subtracted and multiplied using normal algebraic operations (opening brackets, grouping like terms, etc).
- With division we need to be a bit more careful. For two polynomials $P(x)$ and $S(x)$:
  - $\dfrac{P(x)}{S(x)}$ in general is not a polynomial; it is called a **rational expression**.
  - If $S(x) \neq 0$ and $P(x) = S(x)Q(x) + R(x)$ such that $Q(x)$ and $R(x)$ are also polynomials, where the degree of $R(x)$ is less than the degree of $S(x)$, then $Q(x)$ is called the quotient when $P(x)$ is divided by $S(x)$, and $R(x)$ is the remainder.
    - We can use long division to find the quotient and the remainder.
    - Note that if $S(x)$ is a linear polynomial, then $R(x)$ is a degree 0 polynomial, so it is a constant, $R(x) = R$.
- The polynomial $S(x)$ is a **factor** of the polynomial $P(x)$ if there is a polynomial $Q(x)$ such that $P(x) = S(x)Q(x)$.
- The number a is a root of the polynomial $P(x)$ if $P(a) = 0$ (i.e. if a is a solution of the polynomial equation $P(x) = 0$).

Example
$\dfrac{x^3 - x^2 - x + 2}{x^2 + 1}$ is not a polynomial.
$x^3 - x^2 - x + 2 = (x^2 + 1)(x - 1) - 2x + 3$
When $P(x) = x^3 - x^2 - x + 2$ is divided by $S(x) = x^2 + 1$, the quotient is $Q(x) = x - 1$ and the remainder is $R(x) = -2x + 3$.
Hence
$\dfrac{x^3 - x^2 - x + 2}{x^2 + 1} = x - 1 + \dfrac{-2x + 3}{x^2 + 1}$

CROSS REFERENCE

See also: the x-intercepts of the graph of $y = P(x)$ (page 14).

■ Claims

■ **Remainder theorem.** If $S(x) = ax + b$ is a linear polynomial ($a \neq 0$) and $Q(x)$ is the quotient and R is the remainder when $P(x)$ is divided by $S(x)$, then

$$R = P\left(-\frac{b}{a}\right).$$

■ **Factor theorem.** If the linear polynomial $S(x) = ax + b$ is a factor of $P(x)$, then $P\left(-\dfrac{b}{a}\right) = 0$. Conversely, if $P(c) = 0$, then $(x - c)$ is a factor of $P(x)$.

Example
When $x^2 - x + 1$ is divided by $2x + 3$, the remainder is
$\left(-\dfrac{3}{2}\right)^2 - \left(-\dfrac{3}{2}\right) + 1 = 4.75$

Note

It can be the case that $(x - c)^2$ is also a factor of $P(x)$. In this case we say that $(x - c)$ is a repeated factor.

- For a polynomial $P(x) = a_n x^n + a_{n-1} x^{n-1} + \ldots + a_1 x + a_0$, where $a_n \neq 0$ and $a_k \in R$:

  □ For $n \geq 1$, there is a linear or quadratic factor of $P(x)$.

  □ For $n \geq 1$, $P(x)$ can be written as a product of linear and quadratic factors with real coefficients.

  □ There are no more than n real roots of $P(x)$.

  □ If $P(x)$ is the product of linear factors, say
  $P(x) = a_n(x - \alpha_1)(x - \alpha_2) \ldots (x - \alpha_n)$,
  then

  – the sum of the roots is:
  $$\sum_{k=1}^{n} \alpha_k = \alpha_1 + \alpha_2 + \ldots + \alpha_n = \frac{-a_{n-1}}{a_n}$$

  – the product of the roots is:
  $$\prod_{k=1}^{n} \alpha_k = \alpha_1 \alpha_2 \ldots \alpha_n = \frac{(-1)^n a_0}{a_n}.$$

> **CROSS REFERENCE**
>
> For polynomials with complex coefficients, see the fundamental theorem of algebra on page 7.

> **USING A CALCULATOR**
>
> In simpler cases, roots of polynomials can be found algebraically. GDCs also have built-in applications to find approximate values.

> **Note**
>
> These are two of Vieta's (or Viète's) formulae.
>
> There are other relationships between roots and coefficients, but these are beyond the syllabus.
>
> For example if α_1, α_2, α_3 are three solutions of $a_3 x^3 + a_2 x^2 + a_1 x + a_0 = 0$, then $\alpha_1 \alpha_2 + \alpha_2 \alpha_3 + \alpha_3 \alpha_1 = \frac{a_1}{a_3}$.

1.5 Proof by mathematical induction (HL 1.4)

Revised ▢

The principle of mathematical induction (informal statement)

We have infinitely many statements indexed by the positive integers, $P_1, P_2, \ldots$, such that

- P_1 is true, and
- whenever P_k is true for some $k \in \mathbb{Z}^+$, then P_{k+1} is also true.

From these we can conclude that P_n is true for all positive integers $n \in \mathbb{Z}^+$.

> **Note**
>
> The principle of mathematical induction can be illustrated by the domino effect (where one initial action leads to another and another). We accept it intuitively but we do not attempt to prove it. It is one of the Peano axioms (a formal way of studying the natural numbers). Axioms are building blocks that are used without proof.

Steps to follow

To prove statements $P_1, P_2, \ldots$ using mathematical induction:

- Prove P_1, the first statement.

- Assuming P_k (the induction hypothesis), prove P_{k+1}. In other words, prove the implication $P_k \Rightarrow P_{k+1}$. (This is the induction step.)

- Write a concluding statement. For example: Since P_1 is true, and for all $k \in \mathbb{Z}^+$, P_k implies P_{k+1}, therefore by the principle of mathematical induction, P_n is true for all positive integers $n \in \mathbb{Z}^+$.

> **IB SYLLABUS**
>
> In exams, proofs using mathematical induction can be asked for in relation to a wide variety of topics, including complex numbers, calculus, sequences and divisibility.

1.6 Complex numbers (HL 1.5, 1.6, 1.7, 1.8)

Cartesian form of complex numbers

Key definitions

- An expression of the form $a + b$i (where $a, b \in$ R and i is the imaginary unit with property $i^2 = -1$) is called the **Cartesian form** of a complex number. a is the real part, b is the imaginary part of $a + b$i. Real numbers are associated with numbers of the form $a + 0$i.

- Two complex numbers, $z = a + b$i and $w = c + d$i are the same, if $a = c$ and $b = d$.

- For $z = a + b$i, the complex number $z^* = a + (-b)$i $= a - b$i is the complex conjugate of z.

- In some texts the complex conjugate of z is denoted by $\bar{z}$.

- For $z = a + b$i and $w = c + d$i:
  - $z \pm w = (a \pm c) + (b \pm d)$i
  - $zw = (ac - bd) + (ad + bc)$i
  - if $w \neq 0$, then $\dfrac{z}{w} = \dfrac{ac + bd}{c^2 + d^2} + \dfrac{bc - ad}{c^2 + d^2}$ i

USING A CALCULATOR

GDCs can work with complex numbers in Cartesian form.

Note

Solving equations involving complex numbers sometimes involves comparing real and imaginary parts of the two sides.

CROSS REFERENCE

For important properties of conjugates, see the section on complex roots of real polynomials (page 7).

Note

We can add, subtract, multiply and divide complex numbers like real algebraic expressions of i, simplifying the result using the identity $i^2 = -1$.

Polar form of complex numbers

▦ Key concepts

- Complex numbers can be represented as points in a Cartesian coordinate system (Argand diagram), where the two coordinates are the real and the imaginary parts of the complex number.

- The modulus–argument (or polar) form describes the complex number using its modulus, r (the distance of the point in the Argand diagram from the origin), and its argument, θ (the angle between the line segment connecting the point and the origin, and the positive real axis, measured counterclockwise).

- Two useful notations for complex numbers in polar form are $r\operatorname{cis}\theta = re^{i\theta}$.

- Note that we only use $re^{i\theta}$ (known as Euler's form of the complex number) as a convenient notation that helps us remember some of the following claims. Exponentiation involving complex numbers is beyond the syllabus.

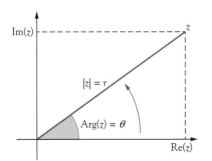

Note

The equality $e^{i\pi} + 1 = 0$ is called Euler's identity.

▮ Claims

- Conversion between polar and cartesian form. For $z = a + bi = r\operatorname{cis}\theta$:
  - ☐ $|z| = r = \sqrt{a^2 + b^2}$ and $\tan\theta = \dfrac{b}{a}$ if $\theta \neq \dfrac{\pi}{2} + k\pi$ and $a \neq 0$
  - ☐ $\operatorname{Re}(z) = a = r\cos\theta$ and $\operatorname{Im}(z) = b = r\sin\theta$
  - ☐ $z = r\cos\theta + ir\sin\theta = r(\cos\theta + i\sin\theta)$
- For $z_1 = r_1\operatorname{cis}\theta_1$ and $z_2 = r_2\operatorname{cis}\theta_2$:
  - ☐ $z_1 z_2 = (r_1 r_2)\operatorname{cis}(\theta_1 + \theta_2)$
  - ☐ $\dfrac{z_1}{z_2} = \dfrac{r_1}{r_2}\operatorname{cis}(\theta_1 - \theta_2)$

> **Note**
>
> Although $\tan\theta = \dfrac{b}{a}$, $\tan^{-1}\dfrac{b}{a}$ only gives an argument if the complex number is in the first or fourth quadrant of the Argand diagram.

> **Note**
>
> It is easier to multiply and divide complex numbers in polar form than in Cartesian form.

> **CROSS REFERENCE**
>
> The connection between these identities and the compound angle formulae is important (see page 20).

Powers of complex numbers

Revised ▮

▮ de Moivre's theorem

For $z = r\operatorname{cis}\theta$ and $n \in \mathbb{Z}$, $z^n = r^n\operatorname{cis}n\theta$.

> **IB SYLLABUS**
>
> You may be asked for the proof of de Moivre's theorem using mathematical induction in exams.

▮ The nth root of a complex number

- $\sqrt[n]{w}$ ($n \in \mathbb{Z}^+$) refers to all the n complex solutions of the equation $z^n = w$.
- For $w = 1$, the solutions of $z^n = 1$ are called n^{th} roots of unity.
  - ☐ These are $\operatorname{cis}0$, $\operatorname{cis}\dfrac{2\pi}{n}$, $\operatorname{cis}\dfrac{4\pi}{n}$, ..., $\operatorname{cis}\dfrac{2(n-1)\pi}{n}$.
  - ☐ Using the notation $\omega = \operatorname{cis}\dfrac{2\pi}{n}$, the nth roots of unity are ω, ω^2, ..., ω^{n-1}, $\omega^n = 1$.
    One of many interesting properties of these numbers is that $1 + \omega + \omega^2 + \ldots + \omega^{n-1} = 0$.

> **Example**
>
> The third roots of unity form an equilateral triangle in the unit circle of the Argand diagram. The fourth roots of unity form a square, the fifth roots of unity form a regular pentagon, and so on.

Complex roots of real polynomials

Revised ▮

▮ Claims

- For any complex number z, both $z + z^*$ and $z \cdot z^*$ are real.
- For any complex numbers z and w, $(z \pm w)^* = z^* \pm w^*$ and $(z \cdot w)^* = z^* \cdot w^*$
- If $P(x)$ is a polynomial with real coefficients, then $P(z^*) = (P(z))^*$ for any complex number z.
- **Complex roots of real polynomials.** If $P(x)$ is a polynomial with real coefficients, and z is a complex number such that $P(z) = 0$, then $P(z^*) = 0$.
- **Fundamental theorem of algebra.** If $P(x)$ is a non-constant polynomial, then there is a complex number z, such that $P(z) = 0$.

> **CROSS REFERENCE**
>
> For a more detailed discussion on real polynomials, see the sections on polynomials and polynomial functions on pages 4 and 14.

> **Note**
>
> The roots of polynomial equations with real coefficients come in conjugate pairs.

> **Note**
>
> Polynomials can be written as products of linear factors.

1.7 Systems of linear equations (HL 1.9)

■ Claims

Let us start with an equation system, naming the equations involved:

$$a_{11}x_1 + a_{12}x_2 + a_{13}x_3 = b_1 \quad (E_1)$$

$$a_{21}x_1 + a_{22}x_2 + a_{23}x_3 = b_2 \quad (E_2)$$

$$a_{31}x_1 + a_{32}x_2 + a_{33}x_3 = b_3 \quad (E_3)$$

> **IB SYLLABUS**
>
> Exam questions may include a maximum of three equations in three unknowns.

For given $a_{k,l}$ and b_k ($k, l \in \{1, 2, 3\}$) as parameters, we are looking for triples (x_1, x_2, x_3) such that all three equalities are true. These triples are the solution(s) of the equation system.

- There is a unique solution, no solution at all, or infinitely many solutions. A system is inconsistent if it has no solution, otherwise it is consistent.

- The solution set of the system does not change if we replace an equation by a linear combination of itself and another equation from the system. More precisely, for any $k \neq 0$ and l, the solution set of the system (E_1, E_2, E_3) is the same as the solution set of $(kE_1 + lE_2, E_2, E_3)$. Of course, any two equations can be used instead of and E_1 and E_2.

- If the system has a unique solution, then using the previous step repeatedly, we can get an equivalent system of the form:

$$x_1 + c_{12}x_2 + c_{13}x_3 = d_1 \quad (F_1)$$

$$x_2 + c_{23}x_3 = d_2 \quad (F_2)$$

$$x_3 = d_3 \quad (F_3)$$

- GDCs have built-in applications to perform these steps after inputting the coefficients of the equation system in a tabular form (called an augmented matrix):

$$\begin{pmatrix} a_{11} & a_{12} & a_{13} & b_1 \\ a_{21} & a_{22} & a_{23} & b_2 \\ a_{31} & a_{32} & a_{33} & b_3 \end{pmatrix}$$

- After applying row operations, in most cases we can get a matrix in the following form:

$$\begin{pmatrix} c_{11} & c_{12} & c_{13} & d_1 \\ 0 & c_{22} & c_{23} & d_2 \\ 0 & 0 & c_{33} & d_3 \end{pmatrix} \quad c_{11}, c_{22} \neq 0$$

- The number of solutions is determined by some entries of this matrix:

  □ If $c_{33} \neq 0$, the solution is unique.

  □ If $c_{33} = 0$, and

  – if $d_3 \neq 0$, then there are no solutions (the system is inconsistent)

  – if $d_3 = 0$, then there are infinitely many solutions.

> **Note**
>
> We discuss here a method of solving systems of linear equations with three equations in three unknowns. The method is general enough to use for any number of equations in any number of unknowns.

> **CROSS REFERENCE**
>
> See also: the relative position of planes or lines in Topic 4 Vectors (page 36).

> **Note**
>
> Applying this step, we can eliminate variables from the equations.

> **Note**
>
> Two systems of equations are called equivalent if the solution sets are the same.

> **USING A CALCULATOR**
>
> GDCs have built-in applications to find the reduced form of a matrix, but in exams these steps may be asked on the non-calculator paper.

> **Note**
>
> This tabular form is useful for solving an equation system with a GDC, but it can also be helpful for finding solutions algebraically.

> **CROSS REFERENCE**
>
> The number of solutions is determined by the last row of the reduced matrix. If there are infinitely many solutions, the general solution is expressed using a parameter. See, for example, the intersection of two planes on page 36.

Practice questions for Topic 1

To practice these skills, try these past paper questions. Start with the questions with lower numbers (1–7). In exams, the first questions tend to check your understanding of one specific concept (although this is not a rule, so don't assume this will always be the case). Questions 8–10 on the HL papers are still short questions, but usually you need an imaginative approach to find a solution. The long questions (HL 10–14 and SL 8–10) have multiple parts, often checking understanding of several concepts and connections between these concepts. For more detailed past paper references, see the charts on pages 97–113. (TZ1 and TZ2 refer to the papers for the two timezones in the May exams.)

Date	HL Paper 1	HL Paper 2	SL Paper 1	SL Paper 2
2014 November	8, 10	7	2, 4	6, 9
2014 May TZ1	3, 13	1, 3, 4, 7, 8a	2, 4, 10	2
2014 May TZ2	2, 3, 7, 9	1, 5, 13	2, 7	7
2013 November	6, 7, 9, 12abcd	2, 6	9	
2013 May TZ1	1, 8	2, 6, 8	7	1, 3
2013 May TZ2	3, 6, 7, 13	2b, 5, 8, 11ab	3	5, 6
2012 November	2, 6, 10	1, 5, 10		1, 4
2012 May TZ1	1, 3, 7, 8	3ab, 9		1, 6
2012 May TZ2	4, 6, 12, 13b	1, 4, 8, 11ab	7	3
2011 November	2, 6	2, 6, 7, 10, 12, 14		5, 8
2011 May TZ1	2, 3, 13	5, 9, 11		3, 10abci
2011 May TZ2	4, 10, 12ab	2, 13A	1	3
2010 November	3, 5, 6, 11, 12b	5, 6	1	3
2010 May TZ1	4, 13b	2, 4, 6, 7	3	2
2010 May TZ2	11, 13	1, 4, 7, 8, 9, 13	6	2, 4
2009 November	2, 11, 13	4, 7		1
2009 May TZ1	1, 3, 13A	2, 7		1, 6
2009 May TZ2	7, 8, 12abcd		3, 4	5
2008 November	2, 4, 13	2, 5, 11B	1	2
2008 May TZ1	1, 3, 7, 12e	1, 5, 10, 14	3	
2008 May TZ2	12, 14	9		1, 2, 10

Topic 2 Functions and equations

2.1 Functions in general (SL 2.1, 2.2, HL 2.1, 2.2)

A function $f: A \to \mathbb{R}$ is a mapping from a subset A of the real numbers into the set of real numbers. $f(x)$ is the value (image) of the function at x.

Note

A usual notation for a function is: $f: x \mapsto f(x)$, $x \in A$.

- A is called the domain of the function f. If the domain is not specifically given, then the usual assumption is that the domain is the largest set on which the value of the given function can be calculated.

- The range of the function $f: A \to \mathbb{R}$ is the set of possible values: $\{y : y = f(x) \text{ for some } x \in A\}$.
  Note that, in some books, authors use 'image' to refer to this set.

- The graph of the function f is the set of points of the form $(x, f(x))$ in the Cartesian plane.
  Note that the domain is the projection of the graph to the x-axis, the range is the projection of the graph to the y-axis.

- The function $I_A : x \mapsto x$ is called the identity function of A.

- The function defined by $(f \circ g)(x) = f(g(x))$ is the composition of the functions f and g. To be precise, we should specify domains in this definition, but for our purpose this informal definition is enough.

- A function f is a one-to-one mapping between its domain and range, if different x-values give different y-values: $x_1 \neq x_2$ implies $y_1 = f(x_1) \neq f(x_2) = y_2$.

  If f is not one-to-one, it is called many-to-one.

- For a one-to-one function f, there is another function, f^{-1}, called the inverse function with the property that if $f(a) = b$, then $f^{-1}(b) = a$.

  □ The graph of f^{-1} is the reflection in the line $y = x$ of the graph of f.

  □ Both $f \circ f^{-1}$ and $f^{-1} \circ f$ are identity functions:
  $(f \circ f^{-1})(x) = x$ and $(f^{-1} \circ f)(x) = x$
  (Note that the domains of these two compositions may be different.)

  □ The domain of f^{-1} is the same as the range of f.

  □ The range of f^{-1} is the same as the domain of f.

  □ If $f = f^{-1}$, then f is called self-inverse.

- (HL) A many-to-one function f does not have an inverse. However, in some cases the domain of f may be restricted, so that on this restricted domain the function is one-to-one, and an inverse exists.

Example

If the function is given by $f(x) = \sqrt{x - 3}$, then the domain is $x \geq 3$.

CROSS REFERENCE

In the Sets and Relations option (HL) there is also a related concept, the co-domain of a function.

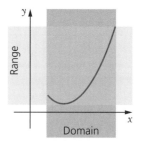

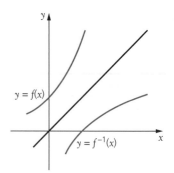

Example

The function defined by $y = \dfrac{1}{x}$ is self-inverse.

Example

$\ln(e^x) = x$, for $x \in \mathbb{R}$

$e^{\ln(x)} = x$, for $x > 0$

Example

$f(x) = x^2$, $x \geq 0$ is one-to-one, $f^{-1}(x) = \sqrt{x}$

$g(x) = x^2$, $x \leq 0$ is one-to-one, $g^{-1}(x) = -\sqrt{x}$

Graph sketching

Revised ☐

When drawing or sketching graphs of functions, we look for key features. The difference between 'drawing' and 'sketching' is the accuracy with which these key features are shown. In either case, the key features should be clearly visible on the graph.

IB SYLLABUS

The IB Mathematics guides for SL and HL define 'Draw' and 'Sketch' as follows:

Draw: Represent by means of a labelled, accurate diagram or graph, using a pencil. A ruler (straight edge) should be used for straight lines. Diagrams should be drawn to scale. Graphs should have points correctly plotted (if appropriate) and joined in a straight line or smooth curve.

Sketch: Represent by means of a diagram or graph (labelled as appropriate). The sketch should give a general idea of the required shape or relationship, and should include relevant features.

USING A CALCULATOR

Questions involving drawing and sketching simple graphs may be asked on a non-calculator paper.

The calculator paper may include questions on drawing and sketching more complicated graphs, including unfamiliar ones. GDCs have built-in applications to find the key features of graphs.

▣ Key features

- Domain

- x-intercepts: can be found by solving $f(x) = 0$ algebraically, or approximate solutions can be found using a GDC.

- y-intercept: $(0, f(0))$

- Values of the function at the endpoints of the domain

- Vertical asymptotes, typically at points where the function is not defined

- Horizontal asymptotes, the behaviour of the graph as $|x|$ gets large.
  (HL) Some functions may have oblique, instead of horizontal, asymptotes (or, of course, no asymptotes at all) as $|x|$ gets large.

- Local maximum/minimum points, points of inflexion. Approximate positions of maximum and minimum points can be found using GDCs.

- Symmetries of graphs:

  ☐ A function f is called even if $f(-x) = f(x)$ for all x in the domain. The graph of an even function is symmetric about the y-axis. Typical examples are $x \mapsto ax^n$ for even $n \in \mathbb{Z}$ (including the constant functions) and $x \mapsto \cos x$.

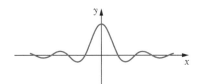

Graph of an even function

  ☐ A function f is called odd if $f(-x) = -f(x)$ for all x in the domain. The graph of an odd function is symmetric about the origin. Typical examples are $x \mapsto ax^n$ for odd $n \in \mathbb{Z}$ $a \neq 0$ and $x \mapsto \sin x$, $x \mapsto \tan x$.

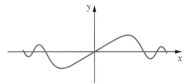

Graph of an odd function

CROSS REFERENCE

For vertical and horizontal asymptotes, see also the discussion on limits in Topic 6 Calculus (page 51).

For the definition of local maximum and minimum points and points of inflexion, and how to find them analytically, see the application of differentiation (pages 56–57).

2.2 Transformation of graphs (SL 2.3, HL 2.3)

Revised ☐

■ The graph of $y = f(x) + b$ is a vertical translation of the graph of $y = f(x)$ up by b units.

■ The graph of $y = f(x) - b$ is a vertical translation of the graph of $y = f(x)$ down by b units.

■ The graph of $y = f(x + a)$ is a horizontal translation of the graph of $y = f(x)$ by a units to the left.

■ The graph of $y = f(x - a)$ is a horizontal translation of the graph of $y = f(x)$ by a units to the right.

■ The graph of $y = -f(x)$ is a (vertical) reflection of the graph of $y = f(x)$ in the *x*-axis.

■ The graph of $y = f(-x)$ is a (horizontal) reflection of the graph of $y = f(x)$ in the *y*-axis.

■ For $p > 0$, the graph of $y = pf(x)$ is a vertical stretch of the graph of $y = f(x)$ with scale factor p.

■ For $q > 0$, the graph of $y = f(qx)$ is a horizontal stretch of the graph of $y = f(x)$ with scale factor $\dfrac{1}{q}$.

Note

These transformations can be applied after each other to get composite transformations. The order of the transformations is important, although the order of a horizontal and a vertical transformation can be changed.

■ **(HL)** Reflecting the part of the graph of $y = f(x)$ below the *x*-axis about the *x*-axis (and keeping the part above the *x*-axis), we get the graph of $y = |f(x)|$.

■ **(HL)** Replacing the part of the graph of $y = f(x)$ left of the *y*-axis with the reflection of the part to the right of the *y*-axis about the *y*-axis, we get the graph of $y = f(|x|)$.

■ **(HL)** When sketching the graph of $y = \dfrac{1}{f(x)}$ given the graph of $y = f(x)$, look for these key features:

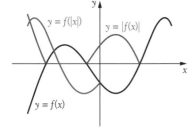

☐ Zeros of $y = f(x)$ usually correspond to vertical asymptotes of the graph of $y = \dfrac{1}{f(x)}$.

☐ Minimum/maximum points on the graph of $y = f(x)$ correspond to maximum/minimum points on the graph of $y = \dfrac{1}{f(x)}$.

☐ The graphs of $y = f(x)$ and $y = \dfrac{1}{f(x)}$ intersect where $f(x) = \pm 1$.

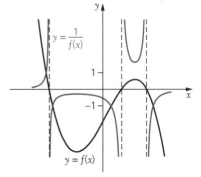

2.3 Basic functions (SL 2.4, 2.5, 2.6, HL 2.4, 2.5)

Revised ☐

Sketching the graphs of certain type of functions and recognising key features is expected, even without the help of a graphing calculator.

Linear functions

Revised ☐

> **Key definition**
>
> A function of the form $x \mapsto mx + c$ is called a **linear function**.

■ Key concepts and claims

- The graph of a linear function is a straight line. m is called the gradient (or slope) of the line. The y-intercept is $(0, c)$.

- Any non-vertical straight line has an equation of the form $y = mx + c$.

- A slightly more general form, $Ax + By = C$ (where not both A and B are 0), describes all possible lines, including the vertical ones.

- If (x_1, y_1) and (x_2, y_2) are two (different) points on the line, and $x_2 \neq x_1$, then:

  □ $m = \dfrac{y_2 - y_1}{x_2 - x_1}$

  □ a possible form of the equation of the line through these two points is

  $$y - y_1 = \frac{y_2 - y_1}{x_2 - x_1} (x - x_1).$$

- If m_1 is the slope of line l_1, and m_2 is the slope of line l_2, then:

  □ l_1 and l_2 are parallel if and only if $m_1 = m_2$

  □ l_1 and l_2 are perpendicular if and only if $m_1 m_2 = -1$.

> **CROSS REFERENCE**
>
> See also: the equations of tangents, normals, and vertical and horizontal asymptotes to a graph (page 53).

> **CROSS REFERENCE**
>
> Other forms of equations of a line (that can be generalised to 3D) are discussed in Topic 4 Vectors (page 34).

> **CROSS REFERENCE**
>
> (**HL**) See also: the equation of a plane in 3D on page 35.

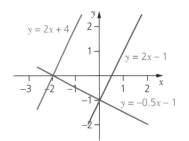

Quadratic functions

Revised ☐

> **Key definition**
>
> A function of the form $x \mapsto ax^2 + bx + c$, where $a \neq 0$ is called a **quadratic function**.

■ Key concepts and claims

- The graph of a quadratic function is a parabola. It is symmetric to the line $x = -\dfrac{b}{2a}$ (the axis of symmetry).

- The sign of a tells us if the parabola is facing upwards ($a > 0$) or downwards ($a < 0$).

- y-intercept: $(0, c)$

- x-intercepts are at the solutions of the quadratic equation $ax^2 + bx + c = 0$. The graph can have zero, one or two x-intercepts. In case of two x-intercepts, $(p, 0)$ and $(q, 0)$, the quadratic function can also be written in the form $x \mapsto a(x - p)(x - q)$. In case of one x-intercept, $(r, 0)$, the alternative form is $x \mapsto a(x - r)^2$. Conversely, these factor forms imply two or one x-intercepts respectively.

- The vertex is the turning point of the graph of a quadratic function. If its coordinates are (h, k), then an alternative form of the quadratic function is: $x \mapsto a(x - h)^2 + k$. Conversely, this completed square form implies the coordinates of the vertex. Since the vertex is on the axis of symmetry, $h = -\dfrac{b}{2a}$.

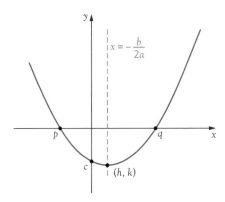

> **CROSS REFERENCE**
>
> See also: the quadratic formula and the discriminant (page 17) and (for **HL**) the factor theorem and the relationship between the roots and coefficients of a polynomial (pages 4 to 5).

IB SYLLABUS

In exams, you should be able to sketch a graph of a quadratic function without a calculator. Also, you should be able to find the defining equation from key features of a given parabola.

CROSS REFERENCE

See also: graph transformations on page 12.

Polynomial functions (HL)

Revised ☐

Key definition

For a polynomial $P(x)$, the function $x \mapsto P(x)$ is called a **polynomial function**.

CROSS REFERENCE

See also: the factor theorem on page 4.

 Key concepts and claims

- If $(x - a)$ is a factor of $P(x)$, then $(a, 0)$ is an x-intercept of the graph of $x \mapsto P(x)$.

- If $(x - a)$ is a repeated factor (i.e. $(x - a)^2$ is also a factor) of $P(x)$, then the tangent line to the graph of $x \mapsto P(x)$ at the x-intercept $(a, 0)$ is horizontal.

- If the degree of $P(x)$ is n, then there are no more than n x-intercepts of the graph of $x \mapsto P(x)$.

CROSS REFERENCE

See also: derivatives of polynomials on page 54.

USING A CALCULATOR

Approximate values of these x-intercepts can be found using a GDC.

The reciprocal function

Revised ☐

Key definition

The function $x \mapsto \dfrac{1}{x}$, $x \neq 0$ is called the **reciprocal function**.

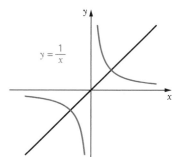

 Key concepts and claims

- The graph of the reciprocal function is a hyperbola. It has a vertical asymptote, $x = 0$, and a horizontal asymptote, $y = 0$.

- An interesting property is that the reciprocal function is self-inverse: for $f : x \mapsto \dfrac{1}{x}$, $f^{-1} = f$. (The graph of $f : x \mapsto \dfrac{1}{x}$ is symmetric to the line $y = x$.)

Rational functions

Revised ☐

Key definition

The function $x \mapsto \dfrac{ax + b}{cx + d}$, $x \neq -\dfrac{d}{c}$, where $c \neq 0$ is called a **rational function**.

 Key concepts and claims

- Applying graph transformations to the graph of the reciprocal function, we can get the graph of the rational function $x \mapsto \dfrac{ax + b}{cx + d}$, $x \neq -\dfrac{d}{c}$, where $c \neq 0$. This rational function has:

  □ vertical asymptote $x = -\dfrac{d}{c}$,

  □ horizontal asymptote $y = \dfrac{a}{c}$,

  □ x-intercept at $\left(-\dfrac{b}{a}, 0\right)$ if $a \neq 0$ and

  □ y-intercept at $\left(0, \dfrac{b}{d}\right)$ if $d \neq 0$.

- The asymptotes and one of the intercepts is enough to determine the defining equation of the graph.

IB SYLLABUS

In exams, graphs should include these asymptotes and possible intercepts with axes.

Example

If the vertical asymptote is $x = 1.5$, the horizontal asymptote is $y = -0.8$ and the x-intercept is $(2.125, 0)$, then:

- $\dfrac{d}{c} = -1.5, \dfrac{a}{c} = -0.8$ and $0 = 2.125a + b$

- this equation system has infinitely many solutions; any $c \neq 0$ determines d, a and b. These solutions all give the same graph.

- one possible solution (using $c = 10$) is $y = \dfrac{17 - 8x}{10x - 15}$, $x \neq 1.5$.

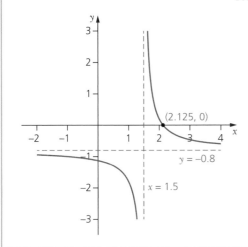

Exponential functions

Revised

Key definition

A function of the form $x \mapsto a^x$, when $a > 0$, $a \neq 1$ is called an **exponential function**.

CROSS REFERENCE

More detailed discussion on limits and limit notation can be found in Topic 6 Calculus (page 51–52).

■ Key concepts and claims

■ For $a > 1$, the exponential function is increasing ($x_1 > x_2$ implies $a^{x_1} > a^{x_2}$). It has a horizontal asymptote, $y = 0$, but the graph gets close to this asymptote only as x is negative and $|x|$ gets large (using the limit notation, $\lim\limits_{x \to -\infty} a^x = 0$ and $\lim\limits_{x \to \infty} a^x = \infty$).

■ For $0 < a < 1$, the exponential function is decreasing ($x_1 > x_2$ implies $a^{x_1} < a^{x_2}$). It has a horizontal asymptote, $y = 0$, but the graph gets close to this asymptote only as x is positive and x gets large (using the limit notation, $\lim\limits_{x \to -\infty} a^x = \infty$ and $\lim\limits_{x \to \infty} a^x = 0$).

■ The range of all exponential functions is $]0, \infty[$. It is particularly important to note that $a^x > 0$ for all $a > 0$, even if the exponent is negative.

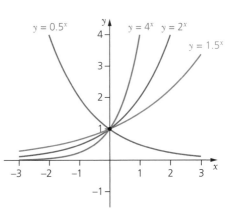

■ The y-intercept of all exponential functions is $(0, 1)$ (since $a^0 = 1$).

■ The slope of the tangent line at this y-intercept is changing as a changes. For a unique value of this base a, the slope is 1. This value is important in mathematics; it is called the Euler constant. The notation is e and its approximate value is e ≈ 2.718. The corresponding exponential function is $x \mapsto e^x$.

Logarithm functions

> **Key definition**
>
> For $a > 0$ and $a \neq 1$, the inverse of the exponential function $x \mapsto a^x$ is the **logarithm function**, $x \mapsto \log_a x$.

◼ Key concepts and claims

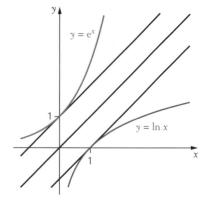

- ◼ The domain of the logarithm function is $x > 0$.

- ◼ The x-intercept of all logarithm functions is $(1, 0)$ (since $\log_a 1 = 0$).

- ◼ For $a > 1$ the logarithm function is increasing ($x_1 > x_2$ implies $\log_a x_1 > \log_a x_2$).

- ◼ For $0 < a < 1$ the logarithm function is decreasing ($x_1 > x_2$ implies $\log_a x_1 < \log_a x_2$).

- ◼ The line, $x = 0$, is a vertical asymptote of the graph of the logarithm function.

- ◼ The $x \mapsto \log_e x$ function, the inverse of $x \mapsto e^x$, is called the natural logarithm function. We use the notation $\ln x$ to denote the natural logarithm. It should be noted that other sources may use different notation for the natural logarithm function.

> **IB SYLLABUS**
>
> In this course, $\log_e x = \ln x$

- ◼ For $a > 0$, $a \neq 1$ and $x \in \mathbb{R}$, $a^x = e^{x \ln a}$

- ◼ Important relationships between the exponential and logarithm functions:

  - ☐ $\log_a a^x = x$ for all $x \in \mathbb{R}$, $a > 0$, $a \neq 1$

  - ☐ $a^{\log_a x} = x$ for all $x > 0$, $a > 0$, $a \neq 1$

> **USING A CALCULATOR**
>
> Use technology, for example Geogebra, to investigate the effect of changing the parameter a on the shape of the graph $y = a^x$ and $y = \log_a x$.

> **IB SYLLABUS**
>
> In the IB Mathematics formula booklets these two equalities are written as
>
> $\log_a a^x = x = a^{\log_a x}$
>
> This form does not emphasise that the second equality only holds for positive x, but the first is true for any real number .

Graph transformations applied to exponential and logarithm functions

- ◼ The graph of $y = Ae^{k(x - C)} + D$ has horizontal asymptote $y = D$.

- ◼ The graph of $y = A\ln k(x - C)$ has vertical asymptote $x = C$.

> **USING A CALCULATOR**
>
> Use technology, for example Geogebra, to investigate the effect of changing the parameters A, k, C and D on the shape of these curves.

2.4 Equation solving (SL 2.7, 2.8, HL 2.6, 2.7)

Revised ☐

Equation solving is part of most mathematical problems, including the ones related to real-life situations. GDCs can be used to find the approximate solutions of any equation, but technology is not always needed (or allowed). It is important to recognise when to use, and when not to use, a calculator. Sometimes it is enough to determine the number of solutions without solving the equation, especially with equations of the form $f(x) = k$. An analytic approach can also be used in certain type of equations, for example:

■ Quadratic equations, $ax^2 + bx + c = 0$ when $a \neq 0$

　☐ Quadratic formula: $x_{1,2} = \dfrac{-b \pm \sqrt{b^2 - 4ac}}{2a}$

　☐ The discriminant: $\Delta = b^2 - 4ac$

　　– If $\Delta > 0$, the equation has two distinct real roots.

　　– If $\Delta = 0$, the equation has one root (sometimes referred to as two equal real roots).

　　– If $\Delta < 0$, the equation has no real roots.

■ Linear equations and certain types of equations involving rational functions

　☐ **(HL)** The absolute value may also be involved.

■ Certain exponential and logarithmic equations.

　☐ Laws of exponents and/or laws of logarithms can be used.

　☐ For equations of the form $a^x = b$, rewrite using the logarithmic form, $x = \log_a b$.

IB SYLLABUS

The equivalence of these two forms is in the IB Mathematics formula booklet.

　　– For equations involving sums and differences of logarithmic expressions, laws of logarithms may help. Sometimes a change of base is also required. It should be noted that using the laws of logarithms may bring in new solutions, so the final results need to be checked back in the original equation.

　☐ Some equations involving sums of exponential expressions can be reduced to solving quadratic equations.

Example

To find the solution(s) of $4^x + 2^x = 6$ we rewrite it using $t = 2^x$ as $t^2 + t = 6$. So $2^x = t = 2$ or -3, hence $x = 1$.

■ **(HL)** Polynomial equations of the form $P(x) = 0$

　☐ For cubic and quartic polynomials there are general formulae to solve the equation, but they are beyond the syllabus.

　☐ For polynomials of degree greater than four, there are no general formulae.

　☐ For polynomials of degree greater than two, factorisation is helpful for finding solutions algebraically.

Inequalities of the form $f(x) \leq g(x)$ can also be solved in some cases:

■ Inspecting the graphs of f and g, finding intersection points and intervals where the graph of f is below the graph of g help finding the solution.

■ For simple f and g, the algebraic method is possible, otherwise technology should be used.

Note

Solutions of an equation of the form $f(x) = 0$ are sometimes referred to as roots of the equation or zeros of the function $x \mapsto f(x)$.

Example

The discriminant of the equation $kx^2 + 2x + k = 0$ is $\Delta = 4 - 4k^2$.

For $k = 0$, this is a linear equation with one solution, $x = 0$.

For $k = \pm 1$, $\Delta = 0$, so there are two equal real roots.

For $|k| > 1$, $\Delta < 0$, so there are no real solutions.

For $0 < |k| < 1$, $\Delta > 0$, so there are two distinct real solutions.

USING A CALCULATOR

When graphs on a GDC are used to solve an equation, it is important to set a wide enough window to contain all intersection points of the graphs.

Example

The solution(s) of $\log x + \log (x + 1) = \log 6$ can be found after rewriting the equation as $\log x(x + 1) = \log 6$, so $x(x + 1) = 6$. The solutions of this are $x = 2$ and $x = -3$, but only $x = 2$ is a solution of the original equation.

CROSS REFERENCE

See the factor theorem (page 4), the formulae about the sum and the product of the roots of polynomials (page 5), and also the claims about complex roots of real polynomials (page 7).

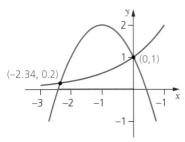

The solution set of $1 - 2x - x^2 > 2^x$ is $-2.34 < x < 0$.

Practice questions for Topic 2

To practice these skills, try these past paper questions. Start with the questions with lower numbers (1–7). In exams, the first questions tend to check your understanding of one specific concept (although this is not a rule, so don't assume this will always be the case). Questions 8–10 on the HL papers are still short questions, but usually you need an imaginative approach to find a solution. The long questions (HL 10–14 and SL 8–10) have multiple parts, often checking understanding of several concepts and connections between these concepts. For more detailed past paper references, see the charts on pages 97–113.

Date	HL Paper 1	HL Paper 2	SL Paper 1	SL Paper 2
2014 November	1, 2, 11ab	6	1, 5, 9	1, 4
2014 May TZ1	1, 4	5a, 6a, 10a, 12	1, 7	10
2014 May TZ2	4, 5, 8b, 14abd	3a, 7	3, 8	2, 8
2013 November	1, 3	3, 13bi	7, 8	2a, 5a
2013 May TZ1	11bii, 12abcd	9	2, 5	5a, 6, 9abc
2013 May TZ2	9, 12	7b	1, 4, 9bc	10ai
2012 November	3, 12acd	2	7	9abc
2012 May TZ1	2a, 4	1, 6	9	2, 10
2012 May TZ2	1, 7a, 10ab, 11abc	6a	2, 5, 6, 8ab	
2011 November	9	8	1, 7a	1, 6, 7a, 10a
2011 May TZ1	8, 10, 12d	4	1, 7	2, 10cde
2011 May TZ2	1, 5, 8	5	5, 9abc	1, 2
2010 November	1, 9	8	9abc	5, 8a
2010 May TZ1	1, 2, 5, 11ab	9	1, 7, 8b	
2010 May TZ2	2, 10	11, 14ab	1, 4	5
2009 November	1, 4, 5	1, 9	1, 4, 7	7
2009 May TZ1			5, 6	9abd
2009 May TZ2	1, 11abcd	4, 7, 13abc	1	2, 3, 7
2008 November	2	6, 12a	4	1, 4
2008 May TZ1	8	2	7, 9	4
2008 May TZ2	2, 4	8, 10	2, 5	3

Circular functions and trigonometry

3.1 Radian measure (SL 3.1, HL 3.1)

Revised ☐

> **Key definition**
>
> The **radian measure** θ of an angle is the length of the arc corresponding to the angle in the unit circle.

> **IB SYLLABUS**
>
> In exams, radian measures may be given as exact multiples of π (for example 2π or $\frac{5\pi}{12}$) or as decimals (for example 1.23).

■ Conversion between radian and degree measure

If the radian measure is given as an exact multiple of π, for example $\theta = k\pi$, then the corresponding degree measure is $k \times 180°$.

For example, $\frac{2\pi}{5}$ is the radian measure of 72°.

■ Claims

The use of radian measure sometimes simplifies formulae, for example in a circle with radius r, if the angle is measured in radians, then:

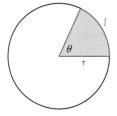

- the length of the arc l corresponding to an angle θ is given by the formula $l = r\theta$, and

- the area of the sector corresponding to an angle θ is given by the formula $A = \frac{r^2\theta}{2}$.

> **IB SYLLABUS**
>
> Note that in the IB Mathematics SL formula booklet, it is not emphasised that these formulae are valid only if the angle is measured in radians.

3.2 Circular functions (SL 3.2, 3.3, 3.4, HL 3.2, 3.3, 3.4, 3.5)

Revised ☐

Basic trigonometric ratios

Revised ☐

> **Key definitions**
>
> - $\cos\theta$ and $\sin\theta$ are defined as the two coordinates of the point on the unit circle that corresponds to the angle θ measured counterclockwise from the positive x-axis.
> - $\tan\theta = \frac{\sin\theta}{\cos\theta}$ if $\cos\theta \neq 0$

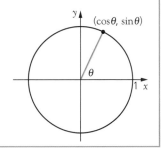

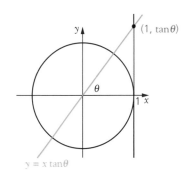

◾ (HL) Reciprocal trigonometric ratios

> ### Key definitions
>
> - $\sec\theta = \dfrac{1}{\cos\theta}$ if $\cos\theta \neq 0$
>
> - $\csc\theta = \dfrac{1}{\sin\theta}$ if $\sin\theta \neq 0$
>
> - $\cot\theta = \dfrac{\cos\theta}{\sin\theta}$ if $\sin\theta \neq 0$

◾ Values of the basic trigonometric ratios for some special angles

	0°	30°	45°	60°	90°
	0	$\frac{\pi}{6}$	$\frac{\pi}{4}$	$\frac{\pi}{3}$	$\frac{\pi}{2}$
$\sin x$	0	$\frac{1}{2}$	$\frac{1}{\sqrt{2}}$	$\frac{\sqrt{3}}{2}$	1
$\cos x$	1	$\frac{\sqrt{3}}{2}$	$\frac{1}{\sqrt{2}}$	$\frac{1}{2}$	0
$\tan x$	0	$\frac{1}{\sqrt{3}}$	1	$\sqrt{3}$	–

> **Note**
>
> Using the symmetries of the unit circle, we can find trigonometric ratios of other angles, for example $\cos 120° = -\frac{1}{2}$, $\sin\frac{11\pi}{3} = -\frac{\sqrt{3}}{2}$ or $\tan 240° = \sqrt{3}$

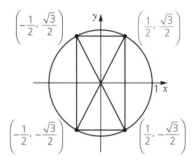

◾ Claims

- Pythagorean identities

    ☐ $\cos^2\theta + \sin^2\theta = 1$ for all $\theta \in \mathbb{R}$

    ☐ **(HL)** $1 + \tan^2\theta = \sec^2\theta$, $\qquad 1 + \cot^2\theta = \csc^2\theta$

- **(HL)** Compound angle identities

    ☐ $\sin(\alpha \pm \beta) = \sin\alpha\cos\beta \pm \cos\alpha\sin\beta$

    ☐ $\cos(\alpha \pm \beta) = \cos\alpha\cos\beta \mp \sin\alpha\sin\beta$

    ☐ $\tan(\alpha \pm \beta) = \dfrac{\tan\alpha \pm \tan\beta}{1 \mp \tan\alpha\tan\beta}$

- Double angle identities (for all $\theta \in \mathbb{R}$)

    ☐ $\sin(2\theta) = 2\sin\theta\cos\theta$

    ☐ $\cos(2\theta) = \cos^2\theta - \sin^2\theta = 2\cos^2\theta - 1 = 1 - 2\sin^2\theta$

    ☐ **(HL)** $\tan(2\theta) = \dfrac{2\tan\theta}{1 - \tan^2\theta}$

> **Example**
>
> If $\sin\theta = \dfrac{3}{5}$, then
> $$\cos^2\theta = 1 - \frac{9}{25} = \frac{16}{25}.$$
> If we also know that θ is obtuse, then (without finding θ) we can conclude that $\cos\theta = -\dfrac{4}{5}$ and $\tan\theta = -\dfrac{3}{4}$.

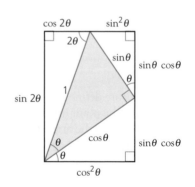

> **Note**
>
> The double angle identities are easy consequences of the compound angle identities using $\alpha = \beta = \theta$.

Basic circular functions

> **Key definitions**
> - $x \mapsto \sin x$, $x \mapsto \cos x$ (defined for all $x \in \mathbb{R}$) and
> - $x \mapsto \tan x$ (defined for $x \in \mathbb{R}$, $x \neq \pm\frac{\pi}{2}, \pm\frac{3\pi}{2}, \pm\frac{5\pi}{2} \dots$)
>
> are called **circular functions**.

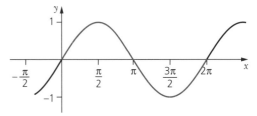

Part of the graph of $y = \sin x$

■ Properties

- $-1 \leq \sin x, \cos x \leq 1$, the range of $x \mapsto \sin x$ and $x \mapsto \cos x$ is [–1, 1].

- The range of $x \mapsto \tan x$ is $\mathbb{R}$.

- The graph of $x \mapsto \tan x$ has vertical asymptotes:
  $x = \frac{\pi}{2}, x = -\frac{\pi}{2}, x = \frac{3\pi}{2}, x = -\frac{3\pi}{2}, \cdots$

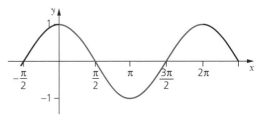

Part of the graph of $y = \cos x$

- Periodic nature:
  - $\sin(x + 2\pi) = \sin x$, $\cos(x + 2\pi) = \cos x$ for all $x \in \mathbb{R}$; both $x \mapsto \sin x$ and $x \mapsto \cos x$ are periodic with period 2π.

  - $\tan(x + \pi) = \tan x$ for all x in the domain; the function $x \mapsto \tan x$ is periodic with period π.

- Symmetries:
  - $\sin(-x) = -\sin x$ ($x \mapsto \sin(x)$ is an odd function)
  - $\cos(-x) = \cos x$ ($x \mapsto \cos(x)$ is an even function)
  - $\tan(-x) = -\tan(x)$ ($x \to \tan(x)$ is an odd function)
  - $\sin(\pi - x) = \sin x$
  - $\cos(\pi - x) = -\cos x$
  - $\tan(\pi - x) = -\tan(x)$

- Relationships between trigonometric ratios:
  - $\sin\left(x + \frac{\pi}{2}\right) = \cos x$
  - $\sin\left(x - \frac{\pi}{2}\right) = -\cos x$
  - $\sin\left(\frac{\pi}{2} - x\right) = \cos x$
  - $\cos\left(x + \frac{\pi}{2}\right) = -\sin x$
  - $\cos\left(x - \frac{\pi}{2}\right) = \sin x$
  - $\cos\left(\frac{\pi}{2} - x\right) = \sin x$

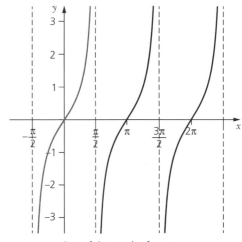

Part of the graph of $y = \tan x$

> **CROSS REFERENCE**
> See also: the definition of odd and even functions on page 11.

> **Examples**
>
> Similar relationships are of course true if angles are measured in degrees.
>
> $\sin 17° = \sin(180° - 163°) = \sin 163°$ $\sin 73° = \sin(90° - 17°) = \cos 17°$
>
> $\cos 17° = -\cos 163°$ $\cos 124° = \cos(90° + 34°) = -\sin 34°$
>
> $\tan 17° = -\tan 163°$ $\cos 34° = \cos(124° - 90°) = \sin 124°$
>
> $\sin 163° = \sin(90° + 73°) = \cos 73°$ $\cos 56° = \cos(90° - 34°) = \sin 34°$
>
> $\sin 73° = \sin(163° - 90°) = -\cos 163°$

Inverse circular functions (HL)

> ### Key definitions
> Although none of the basic circular functions are one-to-one, with appropriate domain restriction we can define their inverses:
> - On $\left[-\dfrac{\pi}{2}, \dfrac{\pi}{2}\right]$, $x \mapsto \sin x$ is a one-to-one function; it has an inverse, $x \mapsto \arcsin x$ (or with a different notation, $x \mapsto \sin^{-1} x$).
> - On $[0, \pi]$, $x \mapsto \cos x$ is a one-to-one function; it has an inverse, $x \mapsto \arccos x$ (or $x \mapsto \cos^{-1} x$).
> - On $\left]-\dfrac{\pi}{2}, \dfrac{\pi}{2}\right[$, $x \mapsto \tan x$ is a one-to-one function; it has an inverse, $x \mapsto \arctan x$ (or $x \mapsto \tan^{-1} x$).

■ Properties

■ The domain of the arcsin function is $[-1, 1]$, the range is $\left[-\dfrac{\pi}{2}, \dfrac{\pi}{2}\right]$.

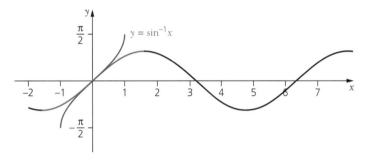

■ The domain of the arccos function is $[-1, 1]$, the range is $[0, \pi]$.

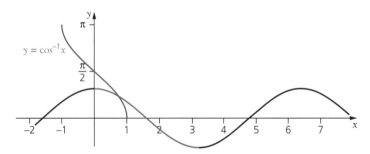

■ The domain of the arctan function is $\mathbb{R}$, the range is $\left]-\dfrac{\pi}{2}, \dfrac{\pi}{2}\right[$.

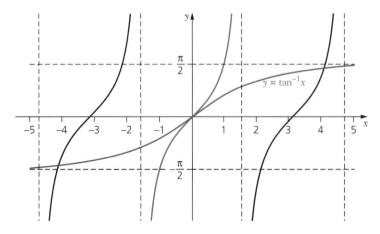

Transformation of graphs of circular functions

The diagram below shows the graph of the composite function

$$x \mapsto A \sin (B(x - C)) + D.$$

Different C-values give the same graph. The diagram shows the position of C if A and B are positive numbers and $0 < C < \frac{2\pi}{B}$.

Note

Applications of transformations of circular functions include modelling the tide and modelling the motion of a Ferris wheel.

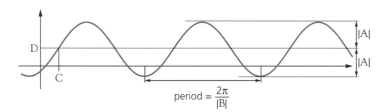

One possible transformation combination to convert the graph of $x \mapsto \sin x$ to this graph is:

- a vertical stretch by a factor of $|A|$
  (If $A < 0$, then a reflection in the x-axis is also involved.)

- followed by a horizontal stretch by a factor of $\frac{1}{|B|}$
  (If $B < 0$, then a reflection in the y-axis is also involved.)

- followed by a horizontal translation by C units to the right

- followed by a vertical translation by D units upwards.

It should be noted that the shape of the graph only determines D uniquely; there is some freedom to choose A, B and C.

- $|A|$ is unique; it is called the amplitude of the graph, but A can be positive or negative.

- $|B|$ is also unique, determined by the period of the graph, but B also can be positive or negative.

- For any combination of positive or negative A and B, there are infinitely many possible C-values, due to the periodic nature of the sine function.

Starting with the cosine function, we can get a composite function in the form $x \mapsto A \cos (B(x - C)) + D$ to give the same graph. The values of A, B and D are the same as for the sine function, only C should be chosen differently.

Example

If a sine curve has a minimum point at (5, −0.7) and the closest maximum point at (9, 2.3), then a possible equation can be found using the following steps:

Amplitude: $|A| = \frac{2.3 - (-0.7)}{2} = 1.5$

The period is $2 \times (9 - 5) = 8$

So $\frac{2\pi}{|B|} = 8$, hence $|B| = \frac{\pi}{4}$.

The point halfway between the minimum and maximum point is $\left(\frac{5+9}{2}, \frac{2.3 + (-0.7)}{2}\right) = (7, 0.8)$

Hence a possible choice is

$A = 1.5$, $B = \frac{\pi}{4}$, $C = 7$ and $D = 0.8$,

so a possible equation is

$$y = 1.5 \sin\left(\frac{\pi}{4}(x - 7)\right) + 0.8$$

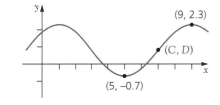

Linear combinations of trigonometric functions (HL)

For any $A, B \in \mathbb{R}$, $A, B \neq 0$, the function $x \mapsto A\cos x + B\sin x$ can be written in the form $x \mapsto C\sin(x + \theta)$ for some $C, \theta \in \mathbb{R}$. This C and θ are not unique, but:

- $C^2 = A^2 + B^2$
- $\dfrac{A}{C} = \sin\theta$, $\dfrac{B}{C} = \cos\theta$, $\dfrac{A}{B} = \tan\theta$.

Similarly, $A\cos x + B\sin x$ can also be written in the form $D\cos(x + \omega)$.

- $D^2 = A^2 + B^2$
- $\dfrac{A}{D} = \cos\omega$, $\dfrac{B}{D} = -\sin\omega$, $\dfrac{B}{A} = -\tan\omega$

> **Example**
>
> For $\cos x - \sqrt{3}\sin x$, $A = 1$, $B = -\sqrt{3}$.
>
> Let $C = \sqrt{1+3} = 2$. We need θ such that $\sin\theta = \dfrac{1}{2}$ and $\cos\theta = -\dfrac{\sqrt{3}}{2}$.
>
> One possible value is $\dfrac{5\pi}{6}$, so
>
> $\cos x - \sqrt{3}\sin x = 2\sin\left(x + \dfrac{5\pi}{6}\right)$
>
> Similarly, $\cos x - \sqrt{3}\sin x = 2\cos\left(x + \dfrac{\pi}{3}\right)$

3.3 Trigonometric equations (SL 3.5, HL 3.6)

Due to the periodic behaviour of circular functions, equations involving these functions often have infinitely many solutions. However, restricting the domain of the equation to a finite interval usually reduces the number of solutions to a finite number. In some cases these solutions can be found using analytic methods; in other cases it is necessary to use a calculator.

Understanding the nature of the solutions (the symmetries involved) in the following simple cases, is the basis of all analytic equation solving. For sine and cosine, either thinking about the definition of trigonometric ratios using the unit circle, or using the graph of the function, helps us realise that there is more than one solution. It is very important to keep in mind that using $\sin^{-1}$ or $\cos^{-1}$ on the calculator gives only one of the possible solutions.

- We are looking for the solutions of $\sin x = \dfrac{1}{2}$ on $0 \le x \le 2\pi$.

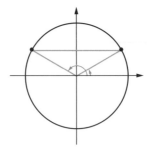
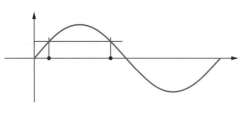

- ☐ There are two solutions, $x = \dfrac{\pi}{6}$ and $\dfrac{5\pi}{6}$.

> **USING A CALCULATOR**
>
> GDCs can give approximate solutions to any equation.

> **Example**
>
> The solutions of
> $2.1\sin^3 x - \cos 1.3x = \cos^2 x + 3\sin 0.7x$
> on the interval $]{-2}, 3\pi[$ are $x = -0.913$, 5.48 and 8.75.
>
>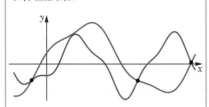

■ We are looking for the solutions of $\cos x = -\frac{1}{2}$ on $0 \le x \le 2\pi$.

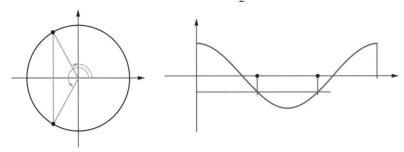

　□ There are two solutions, $x = \frac{2\pi}{3}$ and $\frac{4\pi}{3}$.

■ $\tan x = k$ has a unique solution in the interval $\left]-\frac{\pi}{2}, \frac{\pi}{2}\right[$ for any $k \in \mathbb{R}$. For $k = 0, \pm 1, \pm\sqrt{3}, \pm\frac{1}{\sqrt{3}}$ you should know how to find this solution without a calculator.

Strategies for solving trigonometric equations

■ Sometimes using the double angle formulae can help.

> ### Example
>
> To solve $\sqrt{3} \cos x = \sin 2x$ on $]-\pi, \pi[$, we can rewrite it as $\sqrt{3} \cos x = 2 \sin x \cos x$, or after a bit of rearrangement, $\cos x (\sqrt{3} - 2\sin x) = 0$. Note, that if you cancel $\cos x$ in the equation after using the double angle identity instead of the suggested rearrangement, you miss the solutions corresponding to $\cos x = 0$.
>
> The solutions are $x = \pm\frac{\pi}{2}, \frac{\pi}{3}$ and $\frac{2\pi}{3}$.
>
> The solutions $x = \pm\frac{\pi}{2}$ correspond to $\cos x = 0$.

■ Some trigonometric equations lead to quadratic equations.

> ### Example
>
> Using the Pythagorean identity, the equation $1 + \cos x = 2\sin^2 x$ is a quadratic equation in $t = \cos x$: $1 + t = 2(1 - t^2)$. This can be rearranged to $2t^2 + t - 1 = 0$.
>
> Hence, $\cos x = t = \frac{1}{2}$ or -1.
>
> The solutions satisfying, for example, $-180° < x < 360°$ are $x = -60°, 60°, 180°$ and $300°$.

■ Applying trigonometric identities can also lead to higher order polynomial equations. Since we don't learn about general solutions of higher order polynomials here, the solutions to these involve different approaches.

> ### Example
>
> **(HL)** Using the Pythagorean identity between $\tan$ and $\sec$, the equation $3\tan^3 x + 3\sec^2 x = \tan x + 4$ becomes the cubic equation $3t^3 + 3t^2 - t - 1 = 0$ in $t = \tan x$.
>
> Factorisation gives $\tan x = t = -1$ or $\pm\frac{1}{\sqrt{3}}$, which on $]-\pi, \pi[$ leads to the solutions
>
> $x = -\frac{\pi}{4}, \frac{3\pi}{4}, \pm\frac{\pi}{6}$ and $\pm\frac{5\pi}{6}$.

3.4 Triangle trigonometry (SL 3.6, HL 3.7)

> **Note**
>
> In the statements of the following theorems A, B, and C denote the vertices and also the angles at the vertices of triangle ABC, and a, b and c denote the lengths of the sides of the triangle opposite to the vertices A, B and C respectively.

Cosine rule

■ Claim

■ $c^2 = a^2 + b^2 - 2ab\cos C$ or $\cos C = \dfrac{a^2 + b^2 - c^2}{2ab}$

> **Note**
>
> Since $\cos 90° = 0$, the cosine rule is actually a generalisation of Pythagoras' theorem.

■ Applications

■ The first form of the rule can be used to find the length of a side of a triangle if the lengths of the other two sides and the angle between these two sides are given. In this case, any given data gives a unique solution.

■ The second form is usually used to find an angle in a triangle when the lengths of the sides are given.

   □ In this case, angles can only be found if the given lengths satisfy the triangle inequalities: $a + b > c$, $b + c > a$ and $c + a > b$.

   □ If the given lengths are not like this, the formula gives a $\cos C$ value outside of the $]{-}1, 1[$ interval.

   □ If the given data satisfies the triangle inequalities, then using $\cos^{-1}$ on the calculator gives the unique solution.

   □ The smallest angle is always opposite the shortest side of the triangle, and the largest angle is opposite the longest side.

Example
If $a = 1$, $b = 2$ and $c = 4$, then the second form of the cosine rule would give $\cos C = -2.75$.
There is no such angle, because $-1 \le \cos C \le 1$.
Also, trying to find $\cos^{-1}(-2.75)$ with a calculator would result in an error message.
These are indications that there is no triangle with the given side lengths.

Sine rule

■ Claim

■ $\dfrac{a}{\sin A} = \dfrac{b}{\sin B} = \dfrac{c}{\sin C}$ or $\dfrac{\sin A}{a} = \dfrac{\sin B}{b} = \dfrac{\sin C}{c}$

■ Applications

■ The first form of the rule is useful when at least two angles and the length of one side of the triangle are given. The third angle is easy to calculate, since the sum of the angles of a triangle is 180°. The sine rule can be used to find the lengths of the other sides. In this case the solution is always unique.

> **USING A CALCULATOR**
>
> Geogebra is an ideal tool to illustrate the way a triangle might be constructed from a given set of data.

- The second form is useful when the lengths of two sides of a triangle are given, along with an angle opposite to one of these sides. Assume now that a, b and the acute angle at A are given. In this case the rule can be used to calculate $\sin B$. Unfortunately, depending on the data, this is not always enough to uniquely find the angle at B:

  □ If $a \geq b$, then applying $\sin^{-1}$ to the value the rule gives for $\sin B$, we get the unique solution for the angle at B.

  □ If $a < b$, then:

    – it can happen that we get $\sin B > 1$, in which case there is no solution for the angle at B (there is no triangle with the given data, a is 'too small')

    – if we get $\sin B = 1$, the solution is unique; there is a unique right-angled triangle with the given data

    – if $\sin B < 1$, applying $\sin^{-1}$ to this value gives θ, a possible angle at B. In this case $180° - \theta$ is also a possible solution. So there are two different triangles with the given a, b and the angle at A.

Example

Try to construct a triangle with $b = 4$, the angle at A of $30°$ and with different values for a.

For $a < 2$, there is no such triangle.

For $a = 2$, there is a unique right-angled triangle.

For $2 < a < 4$, there are two possible triangles.

For $a \geq 4$, there is, again, a unique solution.

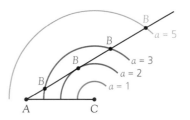

Area of a triangle

Revised ☐

▨ Claim

- Area $= \frac{1}{2}ab\sin C$

▨ Application

This formula is usually used to find the area of a triangle, but it can also be used to find, for example, the angle at C if the area and the lengths of two sides, a and b are given. It should be noted, that in this case only $\sin C$ can be found uniquely.

- If $\sin C > 1$, then there is no triangle with the given data.

- If $\sin C = 1$, then there is a unique right-angled triangle.

- If $\sin C < 1$, then there are two possibilities for the angle at C, and there are two triangles with the given area and a and b values.

Real life application of triangle trigonometry

Revised ☐

Triangle trigonometry is a useful tool in land surveying and navigation. It is important to know the meaning of terms such as:

- bearing (usually means the direction compared to the north, measured clockwise from North)

- angle of elevation and angle of depression (the angle formed with the horizontal).

CROSS REFERENCE

See also: the cross product of two vectors in Topic 4 Vectors on page 32. **(HL)**

Note

It is beyond the syllabus, but there is another formula for the area of the triangle that uses only the length of the sides. Using

$$s = \frac{a + b + c}{2},$$ the area is

$$\sqrt{s(s - a)(s - b)(s - c)}.$$

This is called Heron's formula.

Practice questions for Topic 3

To practice these skills, try these past paper questions. Start with the questions with lower numbers (1–7). In exams, the first questions tend to check your understanding of one specific concept (although this is not a rule, so don't assume this will always be the case). Questions 8–10 on the HL papers are still short questions, but usually you need an imaginative approach to find a solution. The long questions (HL 10–14 and SL 8–10) have multiple parts, often checking understanding of several concepts and connections between these concepts. For more detailed past paper references, see the charts on pages 97–113.

Date	HL Paper 1	HL Paper 2	SL Paper 1	SL Paper 2
2014 November		9, 10a, 14		3, 5
2014 May TZ1	5ab, 7, 10			1, 9
2014 May TZ2	5, 9	4	1	1, 5, 6
2013 November	8	8	5	8
2013 May TZ1	10a, 11	5, 7		8, 10
2013 May TZ2	10	1, 6	5	3, 7
2012 November	1, 7		5	8
2012 May TZ1	5, 10		5, 7	9
2012 May TZ2	9	3, 9	3a	1
2011 November	1, 4ab, 8a	4	6, 9ab	3, 4
2011 May TZ1	5	3, 6	6	1, 8ab
2011 May TZ2	7	1, 8	10	5, 10
2010 November		1	3, 5	6, 10
2010 May TZ1	13ac	1, 3, 13ab	4	5, 8
2010 May TZ2	6	5, 13		8
2009 November		3, 12	6	8
2009 May TZ1	2, 5, 6			2, 3
2009 May TZ2	9	12	7	4, 10abc
2008 November	11	1	7, 10	6
2008 May TZ1	4	7, 12	2, 4	2, 3
2008 May TZ2	3, 9	2, 5	4, 10abc	8

Topic 4 Vectors

4.1 Vector algebra (SL 4.1, 4.2, HL 4.1, 4.2, 4.5)

Vectors

> **Key definition (informal)**
>
> A **vector** in two or three dimensions is an object with direction and magnitude. One can view vectors as displacements in the plane (two dimensions) or space (three dimensions).

▓ Illustration

We can illustrate vectors using directed line segments. The line segment with the same length and same direction represents the same vector. (The five line segments in this diagram represent four different vectors; $\boldsymbol{u}$, $\boldsymbol{v}$, $\boldsymbol{w}$ and $-\boldsymbol{v}$.)

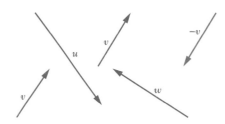

> **Note**
>
> Vectors are important objects in mathematics. Usually they are defined axiomatically through algebraic properties, but this approach is beyond the scope of this course. Our aim is to illustrate these algebraic properties using two- and three-dimensional vectors.

▓ Notation

- We can use the labels of the start and end points of directed line segment to denote vectors: $\overrightarrow{AB}$. Note that for the parallelogram in the diagram (right), $\overrightarrow{AB} = \overrightarrow{DC}$.

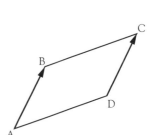

- In print, usually boldface typesetting represents vectors: $\boldsymbol{v}$.

- In handwritten notes, and sometimes in print, underlined letters, or an arrow above a letter is also common notation: $\underline{v}$ or $\vec{v}$.

- The magnitude of the vector $\boldsymbol{v}$ is $|\boldsymbol{v}|$.

- For a vector $\boldsymbol{v}$, there is another vector with the same magnitude such that the corresponding directed line segments point in the opposite direction. This vector is $-\boldsymbol{v}$.

- There is a unique vector with magnitude 0, the zero vector: $\boldsymbol{0}$.

- In a two- or three-dimensional coordinate system, the directed line segment $\overrightarrow{OA}$ from the origin O to a point A is called the position vector of A.

- In two dimensions, for A = (a_1, a_2), the usual notation for the position vector is
$$\overrightarrow{OA} = \begin{pmatrix} a_1 \\ a_2 \end{pmatrix}.$$
In 3D space, for A = (a_1, a_2, a_3), the notation is $\overrightarrow{OA} = \begin{pmatrix} a_1 \\ a_2 \\ a_3 \end{pmatrix}$.

a_1, a_2, (and in three dimensions, a_3) are the components of $\overrightarrow{OA}$.

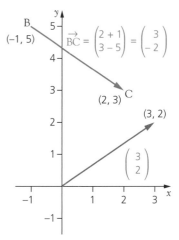

Operations on vectors

- **Addition**

  If the two line segments representing vectors a and b have a common starting point, then the sum $a + b$ is represented by the diagonal of the parallelogram spanned by the two vectors as shown on the diagram.

  Alternatively, if the starting point of the line segment representing the second vector is the same as the end point of the line segment representing the first vector, then the sum is $\overrightarrow{AB} + \overrightarrow{BC} = \overrightarrow{AC}$.

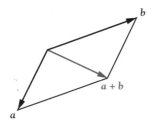
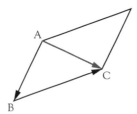

- **Subtraction**

  The difference of two vectors v and w is defined by $v - w = v + (- w)$. If the starting points of the representing line segments are the same, then the difference of the two vectors is again represented by a diagonal of the parallelogram spanned by the vectors: $\overrightarrow{AD} - \overrightarrow{AB} = \overrightarrow{BD}$.

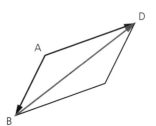

- **Multiplication by a scalar**

  For a vector v and a real number $k \in \mathbb{R}$, the magnitude of the vector v is multiplied by $|k|$ to get the magnitude of the vector kv : $|kv| = |k||v|$. The vectors v and kv are parallel.

  ☐ If $k > 0$, then the direction of kv and v is the same.

  ☐ If $k < 0$, then these vectors point in opposite directions.

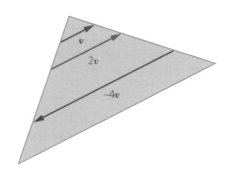

- ## Properties of vector operations

- $v + w = w + v$

- $(v + w) + u = v + (w + u)$

- $(-1) v = -v$

- $0v = 0$

- $(k \pm l)v = kv \pm lv$

- $k(v \pm w) = kv \pm kw$

- $\begin{pmatrix} v_1 \\ v_2 \\ v_3 \end{pmatrix} \pm \begin{pmatrix} w_1 \\ w_2 \\ w_3 \end{pmatrix} = \begin{pmatrix} v_1 \pm w_1 \\ v_2 \pm w_2 \\ v_3 \pm w_3 \end{pmatrix}$

- $k \begin{pmatrix} v_1 \\ v_2 \\ v_3 \end{pmatrix} = \begin{pmatrix} kv_1 \\ kv_2 \\ kv_3 \end{pmatrix}$

- There are three special unit vectors in 3D space:

$$i = \begin{pmatrix} 1 \\ 0 \\ 0 \end{pmatrix}, j = \begin{pmatrix} 0 \\ 1 \\ 0 \end{pmatrix} \text{ and } k = \begin{pmatrix} 0 \\ 0 \\ 1 \end{pmatrix}.$$

Using these vectors we can express any three-dimensional vector using its components: $\begin{pmatrix} v_1 \\ v_2 \\ v_3 \end{pmatrix} = v_1 i + v_2 j + v_3 k.$

Example

In 2D, if $a = \begin{pmatrix} 2 \\ 1 \end{pmatrix}$, $b = \begin{pmatrix} -1 \\ 3 \end{pmatrix}$ and $c = \begin{pmatrix} 5 \\ -4 \end{pmatrix}$,

then

$7a + 6b - c = \begin{pmatrix} 14 - 6 - 5 \\ 7 + 18 + 4 \end{pmatrix} = \begin{pmatrix} 3 \\ 29 \end{pmatrix}.$

IB SYLLABUS

Both of these notations are used in exams.

Of course, similar unit vectors can be used in two dimensions:

$$\begin{pmatrix} v_1 \\ v_2 \end{pmatrix} = v_1 \begin{pmatrix} 1 \\ 0 \end{pmatrix} + v_2 \begin{pmatrix} 0 \\ 1 \end{pmatrix} = v_1 \boldsymbol{i} + v_2 \boldsymbol{j}.$$

- The magnitude of a vector in component form is:

$$|\boldsymbol{v}| = \sqrt{v_1^2 + v_2^2}, \text{ and in 3D space } |\boldsymbol{v}| = \sqrt{v_1^2 + v_2^2 + v_3^2}.$$

- A vector $\boldsymbol{u}$ is called a unit vector, if $|\boldsymbol{u}| = 1$. For any non-zero vector $\boldsymbol{v}$, the unit vector in the direction of $\boldsymbol{v}$ is $\dfrac{1}{|\boldsymbol{v}|} \boldsymbol{v}$.

Scalar (or dot) product

Revised

Key definition

For two vectors $\boldsymbol{v}$ and $\boldsymbol{w}$, the **scalar (or dot) product** is defined as:

$\boldsymbol{v} \cdot \boldsymbol{w} = |\boldsymbol{v}||\boldsymbol{w}| \cos \theta$, where θ is the angle between the directions of $\boldsymbol{v}$ and $\boldsymbol{w}$.

■ Claims

- $\boldsymbol{v} \cdot \boldsymbol{w} = \boldsymbol{w} \cdot \boldsymbol{v}$

- $k(\boldsymbol{v} \cdot \boldsymbol{w}) = (k\boldsymbol{v}) \cdot \boldsymbol{w} = \boldsymbol{v} \cdot (k\boldsymbol{w})$

- $\boldsymbol{v} \cdot (\boldsymbol{w} + \boldsymbol{u}) = \boldsymbol{v} \cdot \boldsymbol{w} + \boldsymbol{v} \cdot \boldsymbol{u}$

- In two dimensions for $\boldsymbol{v} = \begin{pmatrix} v_1 \\ v_2 \end{pmatrix}$ and $\boldsymbol{w} = \begin{pmatrix} w_1 \\ w_2 \end{pmatrix}$:

  □ $\boldsymbol{v} \cdot \boldsymbol{w} = v_1 w_1 + v_2 w_2$

  □ $\cos \theta = \dfrac{v_1 w_1 + v_2 w_2}{|\boldsymbol{v}| \, |\boldsymbol{w}|}$, where θ is the angle between these two vectors.

- In three dimensions for $\boldsymbol{v} = \begin{pmatrix} v_1 \\ v_2 \\ v_3 \end{pmatrix}$ and $\boldsymbol{w} = \begin{pmatrix} w_1 \\ w_2 \\ w_3 \end{pmatrix}$:

  □ $\boldsymbol{v} \cdot \boldsymbol{w} = v_1 w_1 + v_2 w_2 + v_3 w_3$

  □ $\cos \theta = \dfrac{v_1 w_1 + v_2 w_2 + v_3 w_3}{|\boldsymbol{v}| \, |\boldsymbol{w}|}$, where θ is the angle between these two vectors.

- If two vectors, $\boldsymbol{v}$ and $\boldsymbol{w}$, are perpendicular, then $\boldsymbol{v} \cdot \boldsymbol{w} = 0$. Conversely, if $\boldsymbol{v} \cdot \boldsymbol{w} = 0$, then either $\boldsymbol{v}$ and $\boldsymbol{w}$ are perpendicular, or one of the vectors is 0. This is a very useful and important characterisation of perpendicularity.

- $\boldsymbol{v}^2 = \boldsymbol{v} \cdot \boldsymbol{v} = |\boldsymbol{v} \cdot \boldsymbol{v}| = |\boldsymbol{v}||\boldsymbol{v}| = |\boldsymbol{v}|^2$

- More generally, if two vectors are parallel, then $|\boldsymbol{v} \cdot \boldsymbol{w}| = |\boldsymbol{v}||\boldsymbol{w}|$. This is a consequence of the fact that if $\boldsymbol{v}$ and $\boldsymbol{w}$ are parallel, then $\boldsymbol{v} = k\boldsymbol{w}$. Conversely, if $|\boldsymbol{v} \cdot \boldsymbol{w}| = |\boldsymbol{v}||\boldsymbol{w}|$, then either $\boldsymbol{v}$ and $\boldsymbol{w}$ are parallel, or one of the vectors is 0.

IB SYLLABUS

Note that in the IB Mathematics formula booklets the angle formula is given only in 3D form. Also, in the IB Mathematics SL formula booklet, it is given in

the form $\cos \theta = \dfrac{\boldsymbol{v} \cdot \boldsymbol{w}}{|\boldsymbol{v}||\boldsymbol{w}|}$.

Vector (or cross) product (HL)

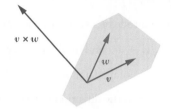

Key definition

For two vectors, v and w in 3D space, the **vector product** $v \times w$ is defined as follows:

- $v \times w$ is also a vector in 3D space.
- $|v \times w| = |v||w|\sin\theta$, where θ is the angle between these two vectors.
- If v and w are not parallel, then $v \times w$ is perpendicular to both v and w, and the direction is specified by the right-hand screw rule.
- If v and w are parallel (or one of these vectors is 0), then $v \times w = 0$.

CROSS REFERENCE

See also: the area of a triangle in the section on trigonometry on page 27.

■ Alternative definition

For two vectors, $v = v_1 i + v_2 j + v_3 k$ and $w = w_1 i + w_2 j + w_3 k$,

$$v \times w = (v_2 w_3 - v_3 w_2)\, i + (v_3 w_1 - v_1 w_3)\, j + (v_1 w_2 - v_2 w_1) k$$

Note

We do not prove the equivalence of these two definitions, but we use both of them.

The first definition is used to interpret the vector product; the alternative definition is used in calculating the vector product.

■ Claims

- $v \times w = -w \times v$

- $k(v \times w) = (kv) \times w = v \times (kw)$

- $v \times (w + u) = v \times w + v \times u$

- $|v \times w|$ is the area of the parallelogram spanned by v and w.

- If v and w are parallel, then $v \times w = 0$. In particular, $v \times v = 0$.

Example

For $v = i + 2j - 5k$ and $w = 3i - j + 4k$,

$$v \times w = \begin{pmatrix} 2 \cdot 4 - (-5)(-1) \\ (-5)3 - 1 \cdot 4 \\ 1(-1) - 2 \cdot 3 \end{pmatrix}$$

$v \times w = 3i - 19j - 7k$

It is an easy check that $v \cdot (v \times w) = 0$, and $w \cdot (v \times w) = 0$, so $v \times w$ is indeed perpendicular to both v and w in this case.

Mixed (or triple) product of three vectors (HL)

In 3D space, $|u \cdot (v \times w)|$ is the volume of the parallelepiped spanned by the three vectors, u, v and w.

Note

The three vectors, u, v and w are coplanar, if and only if $u \cdot (v \times w) = 0$.

4.2 Equations of lines and planes
(SL 4.3, 4.4, HL 4.3, 4.4, 4.6, 4.7)

Revised ☐

Lines in the Cartesian plane (except vertical lines) can be described by a point and the gradient of the line. Unfortunately, the gradient is only used for two dimensions, it is not easy to generalise this concept to three dimensions.

Equations of lines

Revised ☐

We can use vectors to specify the position of a line in the space (or similarly in the plane). A position vector $p = \overrightarrow{OP}$ points to a point P on the line. A vector v specifies the direction of the line.

- The vector equation of the line is $r = p + tv$ (where t is any real number), or in component form:

$$\begin{pmatrix} x \\ y \\ z \end{pmatrix} = \begin{pmatrix} p_1 \\ p_2 \\ p_3 \end{pmatrix} + t \begin{pmatrix} v_1 \\ v_2 \\ v_3 \end{pmatrix}.$$

- **(HL)** Parametric form: $x = p_1 + tv_1$, $y = p_2 + tv_2$, $z = p_3 + tv_3$.

- **(HL)** Cartesian form: $\dfrac{x - p_1}{v_1} = \dfrac{y - p_2}{v_2} = \dfrac{z - p_3}{v_3}$.

It is necessary to be able to find the vector equation of a line if the line is specified in a variety of ways, for example by two points. It is also important to know how to read off the direction vector and a point on a line if the equation is given.

(HL) Conversion between forms of equations is also important.

Example
In 2D we can convert the equation $y = 2x - 3$ to these new forms by finding a point, e.g. $(0, -3)$ on the line and a direction vector, e.g. $\begin{pmatrix} 1 \\ 2 \end{pmatrix}$.
Vector form: $\begin{pmatrix} x \\ y \end{pmatrix} = \begin{pmatrix} 0 \\ -3 \end{pmatrix} + t \begin{pmatrix} 1 \\ 2 \end{pmatrix}$.
Parametric form: $x = t$, $y = -3 + 2t$
Cartesian form: $\dfrac{x}{1} = \dfrac{y + 3}{2}$

Lines in the plane

Revised ☐

The possible positions of two lines in the plane are not too complicated. If the two direction vectors are v_1 and v_2, then:

- If v_1 is parallel to v_2, the lines are either parallel, or they are coincident (all points are common).

- If v_1 is not parallel to v_2, the lines intersect. Note that this is only true in two dimensions. In 3D space there are other possibilities.

It is important to know how to find the intersection point of intersecting lines, and how to find the angle between two lines.

Lines in 3D space

Let $\begin{pmatrix} x \\ y \\ z \end{pmatrix} = \begin{pmatrix} a_1 \\ a_2 \\ a_3 \end{pmatrix} + t \begin{pmatrix} v_1 \\ v_2 \\ v_3 \end{pmatrix}$ and $\begin{pmatrix} x \\ y \\ z \end{pmatrix} = \begin{pmatrix} b_1 \\ b_2 \\ b_3 \end{pmatrix} + s \begin{pmatrix} w_1 \\ w_2 \\ w_3 \end{pmatrix}$ be the vector equation of two

lines in 3D space.

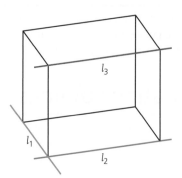

- If the direction vectors v and w are parallel, then the lines are either parallel (they have no common point, but there is a plane that contains both lines), or they are coincident (all points are common, they are on top of each other).

- If the direction vectors are not parallel, then the lines either intersect (there is a unique common point and there is a unique plane containing both lines), or they are skew (they have no common point and there is no plane containing both lines).

To decide, we need to also consider the position vectors a and b of the points on the lines. A possible intersection point with coordinates (x, y, z) has to be on both lines, which leads to the following equation system to solve:

l_1 and l_2 intersect
l_2 and l_3 are parallel lines
l_1 and l_3 are skew lines

$$a_1 + v_1 t = b_1 + w_1 s$$
$$a_2 + v_2 t = b_2 + w_2 s$$
$$a_3 + v_3 t = b_3 + w_3 s$$

This is a linear equation system, using three equations to solve for two unknowns, t and s. If there is a solution, the lines intersect. If there is a contradiction in the system, then the lines do not have a common point.

- The angle between two lines (even when they do not intersect) is defined as the angle between any two intersecting lines that are parallel to the original two lines. This angle can be calculated using the formula $\cos \theta = \dfrac{|v \cdot w|}{|v||w|}$ (where v and w are the direction vectors).

CROSS REFERENCE

See also: the dot product on page 31.

Note the modulus sign in the numerator. The angle between two lines is never more than 90°.

Kinematics

An important application of the vector equation of lines is the description of constant speed movements of an object along a straight line. In the equation $r = p + tv$, t represents time, p is the position vector of the starting point (the position of the object at $t = 0$), v is the velocity vector, specifying the speed $|v|$ and the direction of the movement, and r is the position of the object at time t. Examples include moving cars or boats (in two dimensions) or moving aeroplanes (in three dimensions).

- It is important to know how to find the position of the object at any given time. For two objects, it is important to know how to find the distance between them at any given time.

- For two objects, there is an important difference between questions such as: 'Do the paths intersect?' or 'Do the objects meet?' We have discussed already how to find intersection points of lines by solving an equation system in two variables, t and s. To answer questions about a meeting point, we have to find the intersection point of the paths, and also the objects have to be at the intersection at the same time.

Example

If two cars are moving on straight roads according to the equations

$r = \begin{pmatrix} 3 \\ 2 \end{pmatrix} + t \begin{pmatrix} 1 \\ 4 \end{pmatrix}$ and $r = \begin{pmatrix} 1 \\ 13 \end{pmatrix} + t \begin{pmatrix} 4 \\ -3 \end{pmatrix}$, then the crossing of the roads is at

$(5, 10)$ (so the paths intersect), but since the cars are at the crossing at different times ($t = 2$ and $t = 1$ respectively), they do not collide.

The minimum distance between these two cars can be found by minimising the distance function, $\sqrt{(2 - 3t)^2 + (7t - 11)^2}$ or the square of this distance function, $58t^2 - 166t + 125$.

Equation of planes in 3D space (HL)

We can use vectors to specify the position of a plane in 3D space. A position vector $p = \overrightarrow{OP}$ points to a point P on the plane. Two non-parallel vectors v and w are needed to specify the 'direction' of the plane.

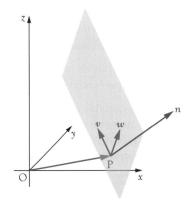

- The vector equation of the plane is $r = p + tv + sw$ (where t and s range over all real numbers), or in component form,

$$\begin{pmatrix} x \\ y \\ z \end{pmatrix} = \begin{pmatrix} p_1 \\ p_2 \\ p_3 \end{pmatrix} + t \begin{pmatrix} v_1 \\ v_2 \\ v_3 \end{pmatrix} + s \begin{pmatrix} w_1 \\ w_2 \\ w_3 \end{pmatrix}$$

Instead of the two vectors v and w parallel to the plane, we can specify the 'direction' of the plane using a vector n perpendicular to the plane. We call such a vector normal to the plane. Using the normal vector and scalar product, the equation of the plane is $r \cdot n = p \cdot n$, or in component form,

$$\begin{pmatrix} x \\ y \\ z \end{pmatrix} \cdot \begin{pmatrix} a \\ b \\ c \end{pmatrix} = \begin{pmatrix} p_1 \\ p_2 \\ p_3 \end{pmatrix} \cdot \begin{pmatrix} a \\ b \\ c \end{pmatrix}$$

- This leads to the Cartesian equation of the plane,

$$ax + by + cz = d$$

It is necessary to be able to find the equation of a plane if it is specified in a variety of ways, for example by three points. It is also important to know how to read off a normal vector and a point on the plane if an equation is given.

Example
A vector equation of the plane through the point (3, 4, −1) and parallel to the vectors $a = \begin{pmatrix} -2 \\ 1 \\ 1 \end{pmatrix}$ and $b = \begin{pmatrix} -1 \\ 2 \\ 0 \end{pmatrix}$ is $r = \begin{pmatrix} 3 \\ 4 \\ -1 \end{pmatrix} + t \begin{pmatrix} -2 \\ 1 \\ 1 \end{pmatrix} + s \begin{pmatrix} -1 \\ 2 \\ 0 \end{pmatrix}$.
Using $b \times a = \begin{pmatrix} 2 \\ 1 \\ 3 \end{pmatrix}$ as normal, we get a Cartesian equation
$2x + y + 3z = 7$.

Angle between lines and planes (HL)

- The angle between two planes is the angle between any two lines parallel to the normal vectors.

  If n_1 and n_2 are the two normal vectors, then this angle can be calculated using the formula $\cos \theta = \dfrac{|n_1 \cdot n_2|}{|n_1||n_2|}$

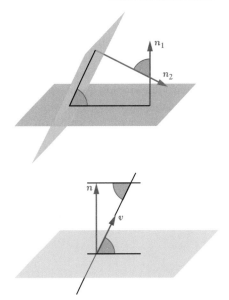

- The angle between a plane with normal vector n and a line with direction vector v can be calculated using the formula $\sin \theta = \dfrac{|n \cdot v|}{|n||v|}$.

Relative position of lines and planes (HL)

- A line with direction vector $\boldsymbol{v}$ and a plane with normal vector $\boldsymbol{n}$ can have zero, one or infinitely many common points.

  ☐ There are no common points if the line is parallel to the plane. In this case, $\boldsymbol{v}$ is perpendicular to $\boldsymbol{n}$.

  ☐ There are infinitely many common points if the line is completely in the plane. $\boldsymbol{v}$ is perpendicular to $\boldsymbol{n}$ in this case too.

  ☐ The line can also intersect the plane at a unique point. To find the intersection point, the parametric equation of the line and the Cartesian equation of the plane are useful. An important special case is when the line is perpendicular to the plane, in which case $\boldsymbol{v}$ is parallel to $\boldsymbol{n}$.

> ### Example
>
> The intersection of the line $x = 1 + t$, $y = 2t - 1$, $z = 2 - 3t$ with the plane $2x + y - z = 6$ can be found by solving the equation $2(1 + t) + (2t - 1) - (2 - 3t) = 6$.
>
> The intersection point $(2, 1, -1)$ corresponds to the solution $t = 1$.

- Two planes with normal vectors $\boldsymbol{n}_1$ and $\boldsymbol{n}_2$ can have zero or infinitely many common points.

  ☐ There are no common points if the planes are parallel. In this case $\boldsymbol{n}_1$ is parallel to $\boldsymbol{n}_2$.

  ☐ $\boldsymbol{n}_1$ is also parallel to $\boldsymbol{n}_2$ if the two planes are the same (and hence all points are common).

  ☐ The two planes can intersect in a line. The direction vector of the intersection line is perpendicular to both normal vectors. The vector product $\boldsymbol{n}_1 \times \boldsymbol{n}_2$ is useful in finding this direction vector and hence the equation of the intersection line. An important special case is when the planes are perpendicular, in which case $\boldsymbol{n}_1$ is perpendicular to $\boldsymbol{n}_2$.

> ### Example
>
> To find the equation of the intersection line of the planes $3x - y + z = 0$ and $x + y - 2z = 5$, it is useful to find a common point of the two planes (for example, $(1, 2, -1)$), and a possible direction vector as the cross product of the normals of
>
> the planes: $\begin{pmatrix} 3 \\ -1 \\ 1 \end{pmatrix} \times \begin{pmatrix} 1 \\ 1 \\ -2 \end{pmatrix} = \begin{pmatrix} 1 \\ 7 \\ 4 \end{pmatrix}$

USING A CALCULATOR

GDCs have built-in applications to find solutions of equation systems, even if the solution is not unique. For the intersection of the two planes in the example, the output is

$x_1 = 1.25 + 0.25x_3$

$x_2 = 3.75 + 1.75x_3$

$x_3 = x_3$

CROSS REFERENCE

See also: how to solve linear equation systems on page 8.

- Depending on their relative position, three planes can have zero, one, or infinitely many common points. Where there are infinitely many common points and the three planes are not all the same, then the common points form a line. To find the possible common points, the Cartesian equations of the planes are useful. They will give a linear equation system (three equations, three unknowns) to solve for the coordinates of the possible common points.

- Given two intersecting lines with direction vectors $\boldsymbol{v}_1$ and $\boldsymbol{v}_2$, there is a unique plane containing both lines. The normal vector of this plane is perpendicular to both direction vectors. The vector product $\boldsymbol{v}_1 \times \boldsymbol{v}_2$ is useful in finding this normal vector and hence the equation of the plane.

Typical questions involving lines and planes

> **Note**
>
> Thinking about the direction vectors of the lines involved and the normal vectors of the planes involved helps solve these kinds of problems. It is especially important to recognise when vectors are perpendicular, and use the scalar or vector product as appropriate.

- Equation of a line through
    - ☐ two given points
    - ☐ a given point and
        - − parallel to a given line
        - − perpendicular to a given line in 2D
        - − perpendicular to two given lines in 3D
        - − **(HL)** perpendicular to a given plane
        - − **(HL)** parallel to two given planes
- **(HL)** Equation of a plane containing
    - ☐ three given points
    - ☐ a given point and a given line
    - ☐ two intersecting lines
    - ☐ a given point and
        - − parallel to a given plane
        - − perpendicular to a given line
    - ☐ two given points and parallel to a given line
    - ☐ a given line and perpendicular to a given plane
- Intersection of
    - ☐ two lines
    - ☐ **(HL)** a line and a plane
    - ☐ **(HL)** two planes
    - ☐ **(HL)** three planes

> **Note**
>
> Intersection questions usually involve solving linear equation systems.
> In 3D the parametric equation of the line is the most helpful.

Practice questions for Topic 4

To practice these skills, try these past paper questions. Start with the questions with lower numbers (1–7). In exams, the first questions tend to check your understanding of one specific concept (although this is not a rule, so don't assume this will always be the case). Questions 8–10 on the HL papers are still short questions, but usually you need an imaginative approach to find a solution. The long questions (HL 10–14 and SL 8–10) have multiple parts, often checking understanding of several concepts and connections between these concepts. For more detailed past paper references, see the charts on pages 97–113.

Date	HL Paper 1	HL Paper 2	SL Paper 1	SL Paper 2
2014 November	3, 12	1, 5	7, 10	
2014 May TZ1	12		8	4
2014 May TZ2	3b, 6, 12		4, 9	
2013 November	11	7, 9	1	9
2013 May TZ1	2	11	1, 8	
2013 May TZ2	11			4, 8
2012 November	6, 9, 11c	13	6, 9	
2012 May TZ1		4, 13	8	
2012 May TZ2	2	11		8
2011 November	12	13	8	
2011 May TZ1	4, 11	10, 11	2, 9	
2011 May TZ2	6	11	3	8
2010 November	7, 10	9, 12	8	4
2010 May TZ1	3, 6	11	10	
2010 May TZ2	3, 12	7	2	9
2009 November		2, 11	2	
2009 May TZ1	8	5, 7, 11	9	5
2009 May TZ2	10	2	2, 10	
2008 November	10	4, 5, 10	2	8
2008 May TZ1	11	3, 5		7, 9
2008 May TZ2	10, 11		8	7

Topic 5 Statistics and probability

5.1 One variable statistics (SL 5.1, 5.2, 5.3, HL 5.1)

Revised ☐

In statistical applications, we would often like to investigate properties of a large population, where collecting data from all the individuals is not practical or is impossible. The method often used is:

- to collect data from a randomly chosen sample (a subset of the population)

- to evaluate the data from the sample (find the mean, variance, etc) using the concepts we have learnt

- to draw some conclusion to estimate the characteristics of the population (mean, variance, etc).

In this case, statisticians distinguish between population mean, variance, etc (which we don't know due to lack of data) and sample mean, variance, etc (which we can calculate and use to estimate the characteristics of the population).

However, these finer points of statistics are beyond the scope of this course. In this course we only work with data sets where all the data is known. We are not learning how to estimate population parameters from sample statistics.

> **Note**
>
> Statistics are used to collect and evaluate data. They are also used to draw conclusions and make predictions from the information gathered.

> **IB SYLLABUS**
>
> In exams, data will be treated as the population.

Key concepts

- The data is a list of numbers: $x_1, x_2, \ldots, x_n$.

  - ☐ We talk about discrete data if the unit of measurement cannot be split infinitely (for example 'number of …').

  - ☐ We talk about continuous data if any real number (from an interval) is meaningful (for example 'height of …').

- If numbers appear several times in this list, then instead of writing them down repeatedly, we can introduce frequencies and present the data by saying: x_1 appears f_1 times, x_2 appears f_2 times, …. .

- If the data is given using frequencies, then the mean of the data is the average: $\bar{x} = \dfrac{f_1 x_1 + f_2 x_2 + \cdots + f_k x_k}{f_1 + f_2 + \cdots + f_k}$. In the IB Mathematics HL formula booklet, in the core section, the mean is denoted by μ. The reason for this is that in statistics μ is usually reserved to denote the mean of the large population and $\bar{x}$ is used to denote the mean of the sample we take from the population.

- The mode of a set of data is the number that appears the most in the list. A dataset may have more than one mode (or be considered to have no mode).

- The median of a set of data is the number such that half of the data is below that number and half of the data is above that number. More precisely, if $x_1 \leq x_2 \leq \cdots \leq x_n$, and:

  - ☐ if $n = 2l + 1$, then the median is x_{l+1}

  - ☐ if $n = 2l$, then the median is $\dfrac{x_l + x_{l+1}}{2}$.

- The range of the data is the difference between the largest and smallest element of the list.

> **Example**
>
> The discrete data
>
> 1, 1, 1, 1, 1, 1, 1, 1, 1, 1, 2, 2, 2, 2, 2, 3, 3, 3, 3, 3, 5, 5, 6, 6, 6, 6, 6, 6, 6, 6, 6, 6, 6, 7, 7, 7, 9, 13, 13
>
> can be represented using frequencies in a table:
>
> | x_i | f_i |
> |-------|-------|
> | 1 | 10 |
> | 2 | 5 |
> | 3 | 5 |
> | 5 | 2 |
> | 6 | 11 |
> | 7 | 3 |
> | 9 | 1 |
> | 13 | 2 |

> **USING A CALCULATOR**
>
> GDCs have built-in applications to find mean, median, quartiles, etc. However, in exams, you may be asked to find these statistics without using a calculator.

- The *P*th ($0 \leq P \leq 100$) percentile of a dataset is the number such that *P* percent of the data is below that number.

- The 25th percentile is the first (lower) quartile, Q_1. The 75th percentile is the third (upper) quartile, Q_3.

- The interquartile range of the dataset is $Q_3 - Q_1$.

- A particular piece of data is an outlier if it is 'too far from the mean'.

> **IB SYLLABUS**
>
> In this course we will consider a piece of data to be an outlier if the distance of the data from the nearest quartile is more than one and a half times the interquartile range.

- If the data is given using frequencies, and the mean is denoted by μ, then the variance of the data is $\sigma^2 = \dfrac{f_1(x_1 - \mu)^2 + f_2(x_2 - \mu)^2 + \cdots + f_k(x_k - \mu)^2}{f_1 + f_2 + \cdots + f_k}$.

- The square-root of the variance, σ, is called the standard deviation of the dataset.

> **Note**
>
> This formula is not in the IB Mathematics SL formula booklet. The calculation of standard deviation is only expected using a GDC. However, calculators may give two very close values related to standard deviation and it is important to know which one is needed. The smaller one is the σ-value defined here, which is the standard deviation when the data is treated as the population. In some books this is denoted by s_n. The other value is used when the data is treated as a sample from the population, and we calculate an estimate for the variance of the population. In some books, and in the option part of the IB Mathematics HL formula booklet, this is denoted by s_{n-1}. This estimate is not required in SL and the core HL.

Ways of presenting data

- Understanding data presented using tables, charts, histograms, stem and leaf plots, etc is important.

- For a large dataset, especially if the data is continuous, grouping is customary. Instead of giving all the specific values of the dataset, we give intervals, $[v_1, v_2[$, $[v_2, v_3[$, … and frequencies f_1, f_2 … that give the number of elements of the data in the corresponding interval. With this we lose information, but the result is easier to present and still useful for evaluation purposes. For grouped data we use the mid-interval values $x_1 = \dfrac{v_1 + v_2}{2}$, $x_2 = \dfrac{v_2 + v_3}{2}$, … (and frequencies) to estimate the mean, etc of the data (unless a question asks us to use upper or lower interval boundary values).

- Modal class of a grouped data
  - □ If all the class intervals have the same lengths, then the modal class is the one with the most elements.
  - □ **(HL)** If the class intervals do not all have the same lengths, then the modal class is the one with the largest frequency density, i.e. the class with the largest $\dfrac{f_i}{v_{i+1} - v_i}$ value. In this case, a frequency density histogram is a more useful presentation of the data than a frequency histogram.

- The number of elements of a dataset below a specific number are called cumulative frequencies. (For a grouped data, for example, the cumulative frequencies corresponding to v_2, v_3, v_4, … respectively are $f_1, f_1 + f_2, f_1 + f_2 + f_3$, …).

- The cumulative frequency table and graph are useful tools for presenting information about a dataset. It is relatively easy to read off the median and percentiles.

- A box-and-whisker plot is a compact way of presenting information about a dataset. It needs to be scaled.

Example

For the data on the previous page, a GDC gives

mean: 4.28

standard deviation: 3.09

lower quartile: 1

median: 3

upper quartile: 6

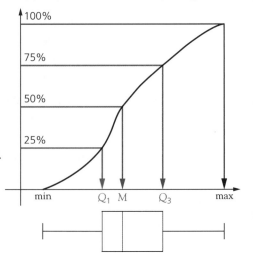

■ Claims

■ Another formula for the variance (still assuming that the data is given using frequencies) is: $\sigma^2 = \dfrac{f_1 x_1^2 + f_2 x_2^2 + \cdots + f_k x_k^2}{f_1 + f_2 + \cdots + f_k} - \mu^2$.

Although GDCs are usually used to calculate variance, when manual calculation is required this form is easier to use.

IB SYLLABUS

The IB Mathematics HL formula booklet presents this formula using the compact sigma notation.

■ Let μ be the mean, σ^2 the variance, m the mode and M the median of a dataset. If all the data items x are modified linearly using the formula $ax + b$, then:

☐ the mean of the new dataset is $a\mu + b$

☐ the variance of the new dataset is $a^2\sigma^2$

☐ the standard deviation of the new dataset is $|a|\sigma$

☐ the mode of the new data set is $am + b$

☐ the median of the new data set is $aM + b$

☐ the minimum, maximum, lower and upper quartiles and any percentiles also change according to this linear transformation. If $a < 0$, then some caution is needed because the maximum becomes the minimum and the lower quartile becomes the upper quartile after the linear transformation. The new box-and-whisker plot is a scaled (by a factor of a) and shifted (by b) version of the old one.

Example

If μ, σ, m, M, min, max are the mean, standard deviation, mode, median, minimum and maximum, respectively, of a dataset, and all data values are multiplied by −3 and 5 is added, then:

The new mean is $-3\mu + 5$.

The new variance is $9\sigma^2$.

The new standard deviation is 3σ.

The new mode is $-3m + 5$.

The new median is $-3M + 5$.

The new minimum is -3max $+ 5$.

The new maximum is -3min $+ 5$.

5.2 Two variable statistics (SL 5.4)

Revised ☐

Sometimes there is more than one characteristic associated with the members of the population and we would like to investigate possible relationships between these characteristics. An example is the age and wing length of a particular bird species. This data will be used to illustrate the key concept.

Wing length (cm)	Age (days)
1.5	4
2.2	5
3.1	8
3.2	9
3.2	10
3.9	11
4.1	12
4.7	14
5.2	16

■ Key concepts

- If data has two variables, we talk about **bivariate** data.

- Sometimes one of the variables influences the other; in this case we talk about independent variable (x) and dependent variable (y).

- A **scatter diagram** is a tool to visually display bivariate data in a coordinate system. The data is represented by points; the two coordinates are the two variables associated with a member of the population. The scatter diagram for our data is:

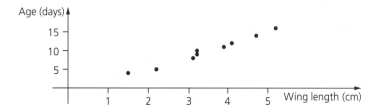

- Usually the independent variable is on the horizontal x-axis and the dependent variable is on the vertical y-axis. In our case the role of dependent and independent variable depends on our aim. If we want to use the information in the table to predict the age of a bird we catch and we can measure the wing length, we use the wing length as the independent variable and the bird's age as the dependent variable. In the case where we know the age and would like to predict the wing length (without picking the bird out from the nest), we change the roles.

- **Regression**

  □ We will only discuss possible linear relationships. A regression line is a linear function $y = ax + b$ which is in some sense 'close' to the points on the scatter plot. There are different ways of finding a line of best fit; one of the most common is to use the method of least squares.

  □ The regression line can be used to make predictions. In our example, the equation of the best fit line is $y = 3.33x - 1.61$ (where x represents the length of the wing of the bird in cm, and y represents the bird's age in days). We can use this line to predict that a bird with a 4 cm wing length is around $3.33 \times 4 - 1.61 = 11.71$ days old. This type of prediction is called interpolation: the value 4 cm is within the range of data values.

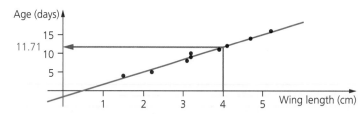

> **Note**
>
> Regression analysis is used to investigate possible relationships between the variables of the data. The relationship may be described using different types of functions.

> **USING A CALCULATOR**
>
> GDCs have built-in applications to draw scatter plots and find and draw regression lines.

> **Note**
>
> Prediction is only valid from the independent variable to the dependent variable.

  □ The other type of prediction would be to try to estimate the age of the bird when the wing length is 1 cm or 6 cm or 10 cm, etc. These numbers are outside of the measurements of our data points: this type of prediction is called extrapolation.

  It should be noted that extrapolation for values well outside the original data is probably not very reliable.

- **Correlation**

  □ Pearson's product–moment correlation coefficient, r, is a measure of linear dependence between two variables.

> **USING A CALCULATOR**
>
> GDCs have built-in applications to find the correlation coefficient, r, and also the coefficient of determination, r^2, which is not needed for this course.

Formulae and claims

Let $x_1, x_2, \ldots, x_n$ and $y_1, y_2, \ldots, y_n$ be the list of values of two variables associated with the data. Let $\bar{x}$ and $\bar{y}$ be the means of these data sets.

■ If the line of best fit is $y = ax + b$, then:

    ☐ it passes through the point $(\bar{x}, \bar{y})$

    ☐ $a = \dfrac{(x_1 y_1 + \cdots + x_n y_n) - \dfrac{(x_1 + \cdots + x_n)(y_1 + \cdots + y_n)}{n}}{(x_1^2 + \cdots + x_n^2) - \dfrac{(x_1 + \cdots + x_n)^2}{n}}$

    ☐ $b = \bar{y} - a\bar{x}$.

> **IB SYLLABUS**
>
> When a sketch of the scatter plot and the line of best fit are required, it is important to indicate the fact that the line of best fit passes through the mean point.

■ Pearson's correlation coefficient:

$$r = \frac{(x_1 - \bar{x})(y_1 - \bar{y}) + \cdots + (x_n - \bar{x})(y_n - \bar{y})}{\sqrt{(x_1 - \bar{x})^2 + \cdots + (x_n - \bar{x})^2}\ \sqrt{(y_1 - \bar{y})^2 + \cdots + (y_n - \bar{y})^2}}$$

or a different formula, giving the same value:

$$r = \frac{n\sum_{i=1}^{n} x_i y_i - \sum_{i=1}^{n} x_i \sum_{i=1}^{n} y_i}{\sqrt{n\sum_{i=1}^{n} x_i^2 - \left(\sum_{i=1}^{n} x_i\right)^2}\ \sqrt{n\sum_{i=1}^{n} y_i^2 - \left(\sum_{i=1}^{n} y_i\right)^2}}$$

> **IB SYLLABUS**
>
> In exams, you will not be expected to use these formulae. Both the equation of the line of best fit and the correlation coefficient need to be found using a GDC. The formulae are included here to enhance understanding.

■ The value of r is between -1 and 1.

    ☐ $r = 1$ implies that the points on the scatter diagram are on a line with positive slope.

    ☐ $r = -1$ again implies a perfect linear relationship between the variables, but with negative slope.

    ☐ $|r|$-values close to 1 suggest strong correlation; the scatter diagram is 'close' to a straight line.

    ☐ Positive r means positive correlation; a larger x-value tends to correspond to a larger y-value.

    ☐ Negative r means negative correlation; a larger x-value tends to correspond to a smaller y-value.

    ☐ $|r|$-values close to 0 suggest weak correlation; the scatter diagram is quite spread out, showing no linear pattern.

    ☐ $r = 0$ means complete lack of linear correlation.

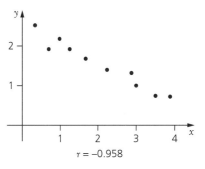

$r = -0.958$

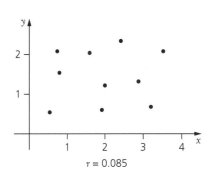

$r = 0.085$

5.3 Elementary probability (SL 5.5, 5.6, HL 5.2, 5.3, 5.4)

Revised ▢

■ Key concepts

- An experiment is a procedure that can be repeated any number of times. One repetition of the experiment is called a trial.

- The set of possible outcomes of an experiment is called the sample space. If an experiment has more than one possible outcome, then it is called a random experiment. (A deterministic experiment with only one possible outcome is not interesting to investigate using probability.)

- We will mostly investigate sample spaces with finitely many possible outcomes. We use the notation U for the set of possible outcomes and $n(U)$ for the number of possible outcomes.

- Outcomes of a finite sample space are equally likely if they have the same chance of occurrence. In several experiments (like tossing a coin or throwing a dice), it is reasonable to assume that the outcomes are equally likely. This assumption simplifies the calculation of probabilities.

- Certain sets of outcomes of an experiment are called events. In a finite sample space any subset of the sample space is an event. Events containing only one outcome are sometimes called elementary events. The number of outcomes in an event A is denoted by $n(A)$.

- A' denotes the event containing the outcomes of the sample space that are not in A.

  In this case A' is called the complement of A.

- Events A and B are mutually exclusive if $A \cap B = \varnothing$ (if A and B cannot occur at the same time).

> **Key definition (informal)**
>
> Let U be a finite sample space and for the moment let us assume that all outcomes are equally likely. Let A be an event in this sample space.
>
> We define the **probability** of A as $P(A) = \dfrac{n(A)}{n(U)}$.

■ Claims

- Let us try an experiment with possible outcomes from the finite sample space U such that these outcomes are equally likely and let A be an event in this sample space. Let us try this experiment N times. Let K be the number of times we have the outcome from A. Informally, the law of large numbers states that the probability $P(A)$ is a 'good prediction' of the relative frequency $\dfrac{K}{N}$ of A happening.

- $P(\varnothing) = 0$ and $P(U) = 1$

- If A and A' are complementary events, then $P(A) + P(A') = 1$.

- For any two events, $P(A \cup B) = P(A) + P(B) - P(A \cap B)$.

- For mutually exclusive events (since in this case $P(A \cap B) = 0$), the previous formula becomes: $P(A \cup B) = P(A) + P(B)$.

> **IB SYLLABUS**
>
> These formulae are in the IB Mathematics formula booklets.

> **Note**
>
> The formal, axiomatic introduction to probability is beyond the scope of this course. Instead of formal justifications, we introduce the concepts informally and use intuition.

> **Note**
>
> Experimenting with dice, coins or cards and using technology to simulate experiments can enhance understanding.

> **Example**
>
> The equally likely outcomes of flipping three coins are HHH, HHT, HTH, HTT, THH, THT, TTH and TTT (H = head, T = tail).
>
> The event 'obtaining two heads' consists of outcomes HHT, HTH and THH. The elementary event 'obtaining three heads' consists of only one outcome, HHH.
>
> Obtaining exactly two heads is more likely than obtaining three heads.

> **CROSS REFERENCE**
>
> This definition is not enough to study, for example, infinite sample spaces or sample spaces where it is not reasonable to assume that the outcomes are equally likely. We will discuss these situations later in the probability distributions section on pages 46 to 49.

> **Example**
>
> When a regular dice is rolled and the obtained number is recorded, the equally likely outcomes are the numbers 1, 2, 3, 4, 5 and 6. The probability of the event 'obtaining a prime number' is $\dfrac{3}{6} = 0.5$. If this experiment is carried out 100 times, then it is likely that we will get a prime number result around $100 \times 0.5 = 50$ times.

Conditional probability and independence

> ## Key definitions
>
> - **Conditional probability.** The probability of event A happening under the condition that event B has happened (assuming that $P(B) \neq 0$) is
>
> $$P(A|B) = \frac{P(A \cap B)}{P(B)}.$$
>
> - **Independence.** Two events A and B are called independent if $P(A)P(B) = P(A \cap B)$. We will only use this definition with the added assumption that $P(A) \neq 0, 1$ and $P(B) \neq 0, 1$.

> **IB SYLLABUS**
>
> In the IB Mathematics SL formula booklet, the conditional probability formula is presented in the form $P(A \cap B) = P(A)P(B|A)$. This is an equation for the conditional probability of event B happening under the condition that event A has happened.

Claims

- If we perform an experiment several times and event B happened M times, and in K of these M outcomes A also happened, then $P(A|B)$ is a 'good prediction' of the relative frequency $\frac{K}{M}$.

- For independent events, $P(A|B) = P(A)$ and $P(B|A) = P(B)$.

- If A and B are independent events, then A' and B' are also independent.

- Informally, events are independent if information about one of them does not change the likelihood of the other happening (or not happening).

- **(HL) Bayes' theorem**

  □ If $P(A) \neq 0$, $P(B) \neq 0, 1$, then

  $$P(B|A) = \frac{P(B)P(A|B)}{P(B)P(A|B) + P(B')P(A|B')}$$

  □ If B_1, B_2, B_3 are (pairwise) mutually exclusive events such that $B_1 \cup B_2 \cup B_3 = U$, $P(A)$, $P(B_1)$, $P(B_2)$, $P(B_3) \neq 0$, then for $i = 1, 2, 3$

  $$P(B_i|A) = \frac{P(B_i)\,P(A|B_i)}{P(B_1)\,P(A|B_1) + P(B_2)\,P(A|B_2) + P(B_3)\,P(A|B_3)}$$

> **Note**
>
> $P(A|B)$ and $P(B|A)$ are different conditional probabilities.

> **Example**
>
> In the dice rolling experiment, let A be the event 'even' and B be the event 'prime'. Then
>
> $$P(A|B) = \frac{P(\text{even prime})}{P(\text{prime})} = \frac{1}{3}.$$
>
> This means that after rolling the dice several times, it is likely that around one-third of the prime number outcomes will be the number 2 (the only even prime number).

> **Example**
>
> Three white bags each contain one yellow and one purple marble. A black bag contains one yellow and seven purple marbles. A bag is chosen at random then a marble is picked from the chosen bag. The marble turns out to be purple. The probability that it came from the black bag is
>
> $$\frac{0.25 \cdot 0.875}{0.25 \cdot 0.875 + 0.75 \cdot 0.5} = \frac{7}{19}$$
>
> The tree diagram on the next page illustrates this experiment.

Methods of calculating probabilities

- Using counting principles

  □ The number of possible ways to choose k items out of n possible objects (without replacement):

  $$^nC_k = \binom{n}{k} = \frac{n!}{k!(n-k)!}.$$

  □ Arranging n different objects in a row: $n! = n(n-1) \ldots 2 \cdot 1$.

  □ **(HL)** The number of possible ways to form a sequence of length k using n different elements (without replacement):

  $$^nP_k = n(n-1) \ldots (n-k+1) = \frac{n!}{(n-k)!}$$

  □ It is sometimes necessary to consider several cases, and add the number of possibilities found in the different cases. The key word here is 'or'. If something can happen either this **or** that way but **not both**, then the total number of possible outcomes is the sum of the possibilities in the different cases.

> **CROSS REFERENCE**
>
> See also: Pascal's triangle and the binomial theorem (page 3).

> **Example**
>
> There are five cats and four dogs in a pet shop. We would like to choose three animals, and have more dogs than cats. The number of ways this can be done is:
>
> $$\binom{4}{3}\binom{5}{0} + \binom{4}{2}\binom{5}{1} = 4 \cdot 1 + 6 \cdot 5 = 34$$

□ If something can have N outcomes, **and** whatever happens something else can have M outcomes, then the total number of possible pairs of outcomes is NM, the product of N and M.

■ Using visualisation

□ Venn diagrams

□ tree diagrams

□ tables of outcomes.

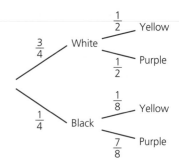

5.4 Probability distributions (SL 5.7, 5.8, 5.9, HL 5.5, 5.6, 5.7)

Revised ☐

In this section we discuss situations when the possible outcomes are not necessarily assumed to be equally likely in the sample space. We will talk about random variables, where a numerical value is assigned to the elements of the sample space. We will assign probabilities to subsets of the sample space differently to the classical case discussed earlier. Our approach will be different in the case of finite and infinite sample spaces.

Discrete random variables

Revised ☐

Key definitions

- A random variable is called **discrete** if the set of possible values is finite.
- (**HL**) Actually, it is also called **discrete**, if the set of possible values can be arranged in an infinite sequence.
- For a discrete random variable X with possible values $x_1, x_2, \ldots, x_n$, a sequence of numbers $p_1, p_2, \ldots, p_n$ is called a **probability distribution**, if:
  - $0 \leq p_i \leq 1$ for all $1 \leq i \leq n$

  - $\sum_{i=1}^{n} p_i = p_1 + p_2 + \cdots + p_n = 1$

  (**HL**) The definition is similar even if the set of possible values is infinite, $(x_1, x_2, \cdots)$. The only difference is that an infinite sum needs to be considered: $\sum_{i=1}^{\infty} p_i = p_1 + p_2 + \cdots = 1$

- The **probability** of an event A is $P(A) = \sum_{x_i \in A} p_i$
- The **expected value** (or mean) of the discrete random variable X is

  $E(X) = \sum_{i=1}^{n} x_i p_i = x_1 p_1 + x_2 p_2 + \cdots + x_n p_n.$

  (**HL**) The summation may go up to infinity.

- (**HL**) The **variance** of the discrete random variable X is defined by $\text{Var}(X) = \sum_{i=1}^{n} (x_i - E(X))^2 p_i.$ (The summation may go up to infinity.) The standard deviation of the discrete random variable is the square root of the variance.

- (**HL**) The **mode** of the discrete random variable is the value with the highest probability. There may be more than one mode if there are values with equal probability.

- (**HL**) m is the **median** of the discrete random variable X, if m is such that $P(X \leq m) \geq \frac{1}{2}$ and also $P(X \geq m) \geq \frac{1}{2}.$ (The median of a probability distribution may not be unique.)

Note

We think of p_i as the probability value corresponding to x_i, a usual notation is $P(X = x_i) = p_i$.

Note

The usual summary of the information about the probability distribution of a discrete random variable is a distribution table:

X	x_1	x_2	$\ldots$	x_n
$P(X = x_i)$	p_1	p_2	$\ldots$	p_n

(**HL**) The table may be infinite.

Note

The claims about probabilities mentioned earlier are still true with this definition.

Example

For the probability distribution

X	−5	0	5	20
$P(X = x_i)$	0.4	0.3	0.2	k

the value of k is

$1 - 0.4 - 0.3 - 0.2 = 0.1,$

the expected value is

$E(X) = -2 + 0 + 1 + 2 = 1,$

the mode is −5

and the median is 0.

◼ Interpretation

If the random variable X represents the winning of a player in a two-player game, and the p_i values represent the chance of winning the corresponding x_i amount, then E(X), the expected value, is a good prediction of the average winnings of the player per game in the long run. The interpretation of E(X) = 0 is that the game is fair; neither player has an advantage.

Detailed investigation of properties of discrete random variables is beyond this course, although the HL statistics and probability option includes more details. One can define, for example, sums, linear combinations of random variables along with other operations, and also the notion of independence of random variables, etc. We are not discussing any of these points. We concentrate only on one (and in **HL** two) of the several important discrete probability distributions, the binomial distribution (and in **HL** also the Poisson distribution).

◼ Binomial distribution

Key definition

Let us look at an experiment with two possible outcomes, success and failure. (These are the so-called Bernoulli trials.) Let p be the probability of a success in one trial. Let us perform this experiment n times. Let the random variable X represent the number of successes in these n trials. The probability distribution of this random variable is called the **binomial distribution**. The number of trials, n, and the probability of success, p, are the parameters of the distribution.

Notation: $X \sim B(n, p)$

◼ Claims

If $X \sim B(n, p)$, then

- the possible values of the variable are 0, 1, 2, …, n

- the corresponding probabilities are $P(X = k) = \binom{n}{k} p^k (1 - p)^{n-k}$

- If $X \sim B(n, p)$, then $E(X) = np$

- If $X \sim B(n, p)$, then $Var(X) = np(1 - p)$

◼ Poisson distribution (HL)

Key definition

A random variable X follows a **Poisson distribution** with parameter $\lambda > 0$, if the probability distribution is given by
$P(X = k) = e^{-\lambda} \dfrac{\lambda^k}{k!}$ for $k = 0, 1, 2 \dots$
Notation: $X \sim Po(\lambda)$.

◼ Claims

- If $X \sim Po(\lambda)$, then $E(X) = \lambda$.

- If $X \sim Po(\lambda)$, then $Var(X) = \lambda$.

- If the occurrence of an event satisfies the following:

  □ the average rate of occurrence is constant, and

  □ the event occurs independently in disjoint time (or space) intervals,

  then the number of events occurring in an interval of fixed length can be modelled by a random variable that follows a Poisson distribution with parameter λ, where λ is the average number of occurrences in the interval of the given length.

Example

A player has to put in 10 points to play a game. The probability of winning 15 points is 0.2 and the probability of winning W points is 0.001. In any other case, the player does not win any points. The expected winning of the player is $15 \cdot 0.2 + W \cdot 0.001$. To be a fair game, this expected winning should compensate the 10 points entry, so $15 \cdot 0.2 + W \cdot 0.001 = 10$. Hence, to be a fair game, W must be 7000.

From the player's point of view, the probability distribution table for this game (considering the loss of the entry fee as negative winnings) is:

winning	−10	5	6990
probability	0.799	0.2	0.001

USING A CALCULATOR

GDCs have built-in applications to find binomial probabilities, $P(X = k)$, and also cumulative binomial probabilities, $P(X \le k)$.

CROSS REFERENCE

Using the binomial theorem (see page 3), we can show that the binomial probabilities add up to 1:

$1 = (p + (1 - p))^n = \sum_{k=0}^{n} \binom{n}{k} p^k (1 - p)^{n-k}$

USING A CALCULATOR

GDCs have built-in applications to find Poisson probabilities, $P(X = k)$, and also cumulative Poisson probabilities, $P(X \le k)$.

Note

The mode of the Poisson distribution is close to the mean.

Example

The number of cars passing a control point in a minute follows a Poisson distribution with parameter $\lambda = 15$. This means that on average 15 cars are passing in a minute. It is also true that on average $15 \cdot 60 = 900$ cars are passing in an hour, so if X denotes the number of cars passing this control point in an hour, then $X \sim Po(900)$.

Continuous random variables

■ Probability density function

> **Key definition**
>
> When the sample space X is a finite or infinite interval $]a, b[$, we will use an integrable function $f :]a, b[\to \mathbb{R}$ with properties:
>
> • $f(x) \geq 0$ for all $x \in]a, b[$
> • $\int_a^b f(x)\,\mathrm{d}x = 1$
>
> to assign probabilities to some subsets of the sample space as follows:
>
> $$P(c \leq X \leq d) = \int_c^d f(x)\,\mathrm{d}x$$
>
> Such a function is called the **probability density function** of the continuous distribution.

For continuous random variables the probability $P(c < X < d)$ is the same integral, so $P(c < X < d) = P(c \leq X \leq d)$. This is of course not true for discrete random variables.

> **Note**
>
> In fact the sample space (and hence the domain of a probability density function) can be a more general infinite set. Our definition and claims can be modified for these cases.

> **Note**
>
> If $]a, b[$ is an infinite interval, then we don't learn how to define the integral (except in the calculus option of HL). This second condition means that the area below the graph of a non-negative function f and above the x-axis is 1.

■ Continuous random variables in general (HL)

> **Key definitions**
>
> Let $f :]a, b[\to \mathbb{R}$ be a probability density function describing the probability distribution of the continuous random variable X. Then:
>
> • The **mean** of the continuous random variable is $E(X) = \int_a^b x f(x)\,\mathrm{d}x$.
> • The **variance** of the continuous random variable is
>
> $$\mathrm{Var}(X) = \int_a^b (x - E(X))^2 f(x)\,\mathrm{d}x.$$
>
> Although this integral defines the variance, in practice a rearrangement (using properties of integration) is more convenient to use:
>
> $$\mathrm{Var}(X) = \int_a^b x^2 f(x)\,\mathrm{d}x - (E(X))^2$$
>
> • The **mode** of the continuous random variable is the value where the probability density function has a maximum. There may be more than one mode of a distribution. We consider only the global maximum(s) as mode(s).
> • The **median** of the continuous random variable is the number m, for which
>
> $$\int_a^m f(x)\,\mathrm{d}x = \frac{1}{2}$$

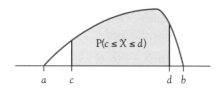

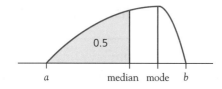

> **IB SYLLABUS**
>
> The formulae for the mean and the variance are in the IB Mathematics HL formula booklet, but with integration bounds $-\infty$ and ∞.

■ Calculation of mode and median of a continuous random variable (HL)

- We can use a GDC or differentiation to find the mode.

- For simple probability density functions, the median can be found by integration and then solving the resulting equation for m. In most cases, however, it is quicker to use a GDC to get an approximate answer.

> **USING A CALCULATOR**
>
> The equation solver application of a GDC can be helpful to find the median.

◼ Normal distribution

> ### Key definition
> The graph of the probability density function of a random variable that follows a **normal distribution** is a bell-shaped curve like the one in the following diagram:
>
>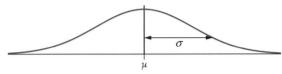
>
> - The graph is a scaled and shifted version of the graph of $x \mapsto e^{-x^2}$.
> - The graph is symmetric about the line $x = \mu$ (where μ is the mean).
> - The horizontal distance of the points of inflexion from the axis of symmetry is the standard deviation, σ.
> - The area of the region below the graph and above the x-axis is 1.
>
> The normal distribution has two parameters, the mean (expected value) μ, and the variance σ^2. If the random variable X follows a normal distribution with these parameters, we use the notation $X \sim N(\mu, \sigma^2)$.

◼ Claims

- **Standardisation:** If $X \sim N(\mu, \sigma^2)$, then for any μ and σ, the new random variable Z, defined by $Z = \dfrac{X - \mu}{\sigma}$, also follows a normal distribution. Moreover, $Z \sim N(0, 1^2)$. For any x-value, the corresponding z-value, $z = \dfrac{x - \mu}{\sigma}$, is called the standardised value of x.

- The standardised value (z-value) of μ is 0.

- If x is such that $x - \mu = \sigma$, then the standardised value of x is 1.

- Or in general, if x is such that $x - \mu = k\sigma$, then the standardised value of x is k.

- If $X \sim N(\mu, \sigma^2)$, then for any $c < d$,

$$P(c \le X \le d) = P\left(\frac{c - \mu}{\sigma} \le Z \le \frac{d - \mu}{\sigma}\right).$$

The following two diagrams illustrate this claim.

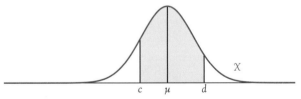

After standardisation:

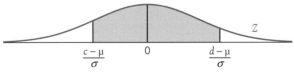

The area of the shaded regions on the two diagrams are the same. These areas represent the probabilities on the left- and right-hand side of the equality.

> ### Note
> The reason the actual formula for the probability density function $x \mapsto f(x)$ is not given here is the fact that $\int e^{-x^2} \, dx$ cannot be expressed using basic functions. This means that the probability values
>
> $$P(c \le X \le d) = \int_c^d f(x) \, dx$$
>
> cannot be found analytically.

> ### USING A CALCULATOR
> We need to use technology to find these probabilities. GDCs have built-in applications for this task.
>
> A GDC can also find the value of k, if $P(X < k)$ is given.

> ### Example
> Standardisation is needed when both the mean and the standard deviation are to be found in a question.
>
> For example, if $X \sim N(\mu, \sigma^2)$,
>
> $P(X < 3) = 0.2$ and $P(X > 8) = 0.6$,
>
> then $P\left(Z < \dfrac{3 - \mu}{\sigma}\right) = 0.2$,
>
> so $\dfrac{3 - \mu}{\sigma} = -0.84162$.
>
> Also, $P\left(Z < \dfrac{8 - \mu}{\sigma}\right) = 0.4$,
>
> so $\dfrac{8 - \mu}{\sigma} = -0.25335$.
>
> The solution of this equation system is $\mu = 10.2$, $\sigma = 8.50$.

> ### USING A CALCULATOR
> If either the standard deviation or the mean is given and the other is to be determined, then standardisation can help, but the answer can also be found using the equation solver on a GDC.

Practice questions for Topic 5

To practice these skills, try these past paper questions. Start with the questions with lower numbers (1–7). In exams, the first questions tend to check your understanding of one specific concept (although this is not a rule, so don't assume this will always be the case). Questions 8–10 on the HL papers are still short questions, but usually you need an imaginative approach to find a solution. The long questions (HL 10–14 and SL 8–10) have multiple parts, often checking understanding of several concepts and connections between these concepts. For more detailed past paper references, see the charts on pages 97–113.

Date	HL Paper 1	HL Paper 2	SL Paper 1	SL Paper 2
2014 November	4, 9	2, 3, 11, 12	3, 8	2, 8, 10
2014 May TZ1	2	2, 8b, 9, 11	5, 9	3, 8
2014 May TZ2	1, 11	2, 6, 8, 11		3, 4, 10
2013 November	2	4, 5, 11	3	4, 6, 10
2013 May TZ1	4, 9	1, 3, 10	9	2, 7
2013 May TZ2	4	3, 7, 9, 11c	8	2, 9
2012 November	5	4, 7, 11	2, 8	6, 10
2012 May TZ1		2, 3, 5, 7, 12	1, 4	7, 8
2012 May TZ2	3, 11de	2, 5, 7, 10	1, 4, 9	4, 7
2011 November	3, 5, 10	3, 5, 11	3, 5, 7	2, 9
2011 May TZ1	1, 6	1, 7, 12	4, 8	4, 5, 7
2011 May TZ2	3, 9	6, 12	2, 6	6, 9
2010 November	4	3, 7, 11	4	1, 9
2010 May TZ1	7, 10, 12	8, 12	5	4, 7, 10
2010 May TZ2	1, 4	2, 3, 6, 12	9	1, 3
2009 November	6	5, 6, 13	3, 8	3, 6
2009 May TZ1	12	1, 4	2	4, 7, 8
2009 May TZ2	2, 3	1, 5, 11	9	1, 9
2008 November	3, 8	3, 7, 11	5, 8	3, 5, 7
2008 May TZ1	9	4, 8, 11	10	1, 6, 8
2008 May TZ2	1, 7	1, 4, 7, 11	1, 6	4, 5, 6

Topic **6** Calculus

Throughout this chapter we consider only functions with a finite or infinite interval domain (that may have a finite number of points missing). The definitions and statements use informal language. More precise treatment would require mathematical terminology beyond the level of this course.

6.1 Limit, convergence, continuity (SL 6.1, HL 6.1)

Revised ☐

Limit of a sequence

Revised ☐

Key definition (informal)

The number A is the **limit of the sequence** $a_1, a_2, a_3 \ldots$ if the difference $|A - a_n|$ gets close to 0 as the index n gets large.

In this case we say that the sequence $a_1, a_2, a_3 \ldots$ **converges** to the number A.

We use the notation $\lim_{n \to \infty} a_n = A$, or a bit less formally $a_n \to A$.

If the sequence does not converge to any number A, then it is **divergent**.

Examples

- The limit of the sequence $\frac{1}{2}, \frac{1}{3}, \frac{1}{4}, \ldots$ is 0, or using the limit notation,
  $\lim_{n \to \infty} \frac{1}{n} = 0$.

- For a geometric sequence $a_n = a_1 r^{n-1}$ with common ratio $|r| < 1$, the infinite
  sum is the limit of the finite sums: $\lim_{n \to \infty} S_n = S_\infty \left(= \frac{a}{1-r} \right)$.

  So, the sequence 0.1, 0.11, 0.111, ... converges to $\frac{1}{9}$.

- The sequence 1, 0, 1, 0, ... does not have a limit.
  Not all sequences are convergent.

- The sequence 1, 2, 3, 4, ... does not converge to any finite number; it tends
  to infinity: $\lim_{n \to \infty} n = \infty$.

Limit of a function

Revised ☐

Key definition (informal)

The number A is the **limit of the function** f at $x = a$ if the value $f(x)$ gets close to A as x approaches a.

We use the notation $\lim_{x \to a} f(x) = A$, or $f(x) \to A$ as $x \to a$.

Example

$\lim_{x \to -3} x^2 = 9$

Examples

- The definition extends to the cases when a and/or A is positive or negative infinity.
  - $\lim\limits_{x \to 0} \ln x = -\infty$
  - $\lim\limits_{x \to \infty} \dfrac{2x+5}{3x-6} = \dfrac{2}{3}$
  - $\lim\limits_{x \to -2} \dfrac{1}{(x+2)^2} = \infty$
  - $\lim\limits_{x \to \infty} e^x = \infty$

USING A CALCULATOR

Graphing functions and finding numerical values can enhance the intuition behind limits. For example,

$\dfrac{2 \cdot 100 + 5}{3 \cdot 100 - 6} = 0.697\,278\,911\,6\ldots$

$\dfrac{2 \cdot 1000 + 5}{3 \cdot 1000 - 6} = 0.669\,672\,678\,7\ldots$

$\dfrac{2 \cdot 10000 + 5}{3 \cdot 10000 - 6} = 0.666\,966\,726\,7\ldots$

Examples

- Not all functions have a limit at all points: $\lim\limits_{x \to 2} \dfrac{2x+5}{3x-6}$ does not exist (but the graph of the function $x \mapsto \dfrac{2x+5}{3x-6}$ has a vertical asymptote at $x = 2$).
- A function may have a limit at a point even when the function is not defined at that point: $\lim\limits_{x \to 1} \dfrac{x^2-1}{x-1} = 2$, but $x \mapsto \dfrac{x^2-1}{x-1}$ is not defined at $x = 1$.

CROSS REFERENCE

See also: the concept of horizontal and vertical asymptotes on page 11.

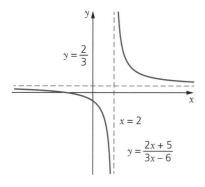

CROSS REFERENCE

The limit of $\dfrac{\sin \theta}{\theta}$ and the limit of $\dfrac{1 - \cos \theta}{\theta}$ as θ approaches 0 are used to establish the derivatives of the sine and cosine functions (see page 54).

- ■ **(HL) Important result:** $\lim\limits_{\theta \to 0} \dfrac{\sin \theta}{\theta} = 1$ (if θ is measured in radians)

Continuity (HL)

Revised ▢

Key definition

A function f is **continuous** at a point $x = a$ if

- $\lim\limits_{x \to a} f(x) = A$ exists and
- $f(a) = A$.

A function is continuous if it is continuous at every point of its domain.

Examples

- The function defined by $f(x) = \begin{cases} x^2 & \text{if } -1 \leq x \leq 0 \\ x & \text{if } 0 < x \leq 1 \end{cases}$

  is continuous on $[-1, 1]$ (including at $x = 0$).

- The function defined by $f(x) = \begin{cases} x^2 & \text{if } -1 \leq x \leq 0 \\ 1-x & \text{if } 0 < x \leq 1 \end{cases}$

  is not continuous at $x = 0$ (but is continuous at any other point).

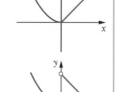

6.2 Differential calculus (SL 6.1, 6.2, 6.3, HL 6.1, 6.2, 6.3)

Revised ☐

Derivative, rules of differentiation

Revised ☐

> **Key definition**
>
> The function $f: x \mapsto f(x)$ is **differentiable** at $x = a$ if there is a number A such that $\lim\limits_{h \to 0} \dfrac{f(a+h) - f(a)}{h} = A$. This limit A is the **derivative (or gradient)** of f at $x = a$. It is also the gradient of the tangent line to the graph of the function at $(a, f(a))$. The function that assigns the derivative (if it exists) of the function to x for every x in the domain is called the **gradient function (or derivative)** of f.

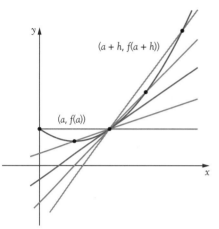

◼ Notation

- There are different notations used to denote the derivative of the function $f: x \mapsto f(x)$. Two of these are:

  - ☐ f' denotes the derivative function and $f'(a)$ the gradient at $x = a$.

  - ☐ $\dfrac{dF}{dx}$ denotes the derivative function and $\dfrac{dF}{dx}(a)$ the gradient at $x = a$.

◼ Higher order derivatives

- The gradient function of the gradient function of f is the second derivative. Usual notations are f'' or $\dfrac{d^2 f}{dx^2}$.

- Similarly, notations for higher order derivatives are $f^{(n)}$ or $\dfrac{d^n f}{dx^n}$.

◼ (HL) Relationship between differentiability and continuity

- If a function is differentiable at $x = a$, then it is defined there and it is also continuous there.

- The converse is not true. A function can be continuous but not differentiable at a point. For example $x \mapsto |x|$ is defined and continuous at $x = 0$, but it is not differentiable there. There is no well-defined tangent line to the graph at $(0, 0)$.

◼ Equation of tangent and normal lines

If f is differentiable at $x = a$, then:

- the equation of the tangent line to the graph of $y = f(x)$ at the point $(a, f(a))$ is $y = f'(a)(x - a) + f(a)$

- if $f'(a) \neq 0$, the equation of the normal line to the graph of $y = f(x)$ at the point $(a, f(a))$ is $y = -\dfrac{1}{f'(a)}(x - a) + f(a)$.

◼ Rules of differentiation (expressed using both notations)

- For $F = kf \pm lg$, $(k, l \in \mathbb{R})$

  - ☐ $F' = kf' \pm lg'$ or $\dfrac{dF}{dx} = k\dfrac{df}{dx} \pm l\dfrac{dg}{dx}$

USING A CALCULATOR

GDCs can graph a derivative function without the need for any algebraic manipulation.

Note

The derivative can also be interpreted as the rate of change of the values of the function f.

CROSS REFERENCE

Higher order derivatives are used in finding Taylor series. This topic is discussed in the HL Calculus option.

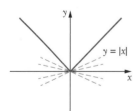

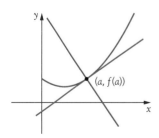

USING A CALCULATOR

GDCs can also work out and draw the tangent line.

- **Product rule.** For $F = fg$,

  - $F' = f'g + fg'$ or $\dfrac{dF}{dx} = \dfrac{df}{dx}g + f\dfrac{dg}{dx}$

- **Quotient rule.** For $F = \dfrac{f}{g}$,

  - $F' = \dfrac{f'g - fg'}{g^2}$ or $\dfrac{dF}{dx} = \dfrac{\dfrac{df}{dx}g - f\dfrac{dg}{dx}}{g^2}$

- **Chain rule.** For $F = f \circ u$,

  - $F' = (f' \circ u)u'$ or $\dfrac{dF}{dx} = \dfrac{df}{du}\dfrac{du}{dx}$

> **IB SYLLABUS**
>
> For simple polynomial functions, you should be able to find the derivative using the definition.

The following table contains the derivatives of some basic functions and the instances of the chain rule related to those functions.

$f(x)$	$f'(x)$	$F(x) = f(u(x))$	$F'(x)$	$\dfrac{dF}{dx}(x)$
x^n	nx^{n-1}	$u^n(x)$	$nu^{n-1}(x)u'(x)$	$nu^{n-1}(x)\dfrac{du}{dx}(x)$
$\ln x$	$\dfrac{1}{x}$	$\ln(u(x))$	$\dfrac{u'(x)}{u(x)}$	$\dfrac{1}{u(x)}\dfrac{du}{dx}(x)$
e^x	e^x	$e^{u(x)}$	$e^{u(x)}u'(x)$	$e^{u(x)}\dfrac{du}{dx}(x)$
$\sin x$	$\cos x$	$\sin u(x)$	$u'(x)\cos u(x)$	$\cos u(x)\dfrac{du}{dx}(x)$
$\cos x$	$-\sin x$	$\cos u(x)$	$-u'(x)\sin u(x)$	$-\sin u(x)\dfrac{du}{dx}(x)$
$\tan x$	$\dfrac{1}{\cos^2 x}$	$\tan u(x)$	$\dfrac{u'(x)}{\cos^2 u(x)}$	$\dfrac{1}{\cos^2 u(x)}\dfrac{du}{dx}(x)$

> **IB SYLLABUS**
>
> The IB Mathematics formula booklet contains the formulae in the first columns, but not the instances of the chain rule.

(HL) Applications of the chain rule

- **Implicit differentiation.** Some curves on the plane (for example, a circle) are not graphs of functions. These curves still may have tangent lines at some points. We may wish to find the gradient of these tangent lines. One way of doing this is using implicit differentiation.

  - First find an implicit description of the curve (most of the time this description is given).

  - In some neighbourhood of the given point, the curve may be considered locally as the graph of a function $x \mapsto y(x)$.

    Hence we are looking for the value of the gradient function $\dfrac{dy}{dx}$ at the given point.

  - Then differentiate both sides of the defining equation with respect to x (thinking of y as a function of x, using a not too precise notation).

> **CROSS REFERENCE**
>
> **(HL)** To use the definition to find the derivative of higher order polynomial functions, the use of the binomial theorem may be helpful (see page 3).

> **Note**
>
> For more complicated functions finding derivatives from first principles is more challenging. Instead, we use the rules of differentiation to help.

> **Note**
>
> An important special case of the chain rule is where the inner function is linear, $u(x) = ax + b$, in which case $u'(x) = a$ (or $\dfrac{du}{dx}(x) = a$) for all x.

> **Note**
>
> It is important to realise the difference between the derivative of $x \mapsto \sin^2 x$ (which is of the form $x \mapsto u^2(x)$, derivative $x \mapsto 2\sin x \cos x$) and $x \mapsto \sin x^2$ (which is of the form $x \mapsto \sin u(x)$, derivative $x \mapsto 2x\cos x^2$).

> **Example**
>
> A circle with its centre at the origin has radius 5. Find the gradient of the tangent to the circle at the point $(3, 4)$.
>
> This circle is the set of points (x, y) on the plane satisfying the equation $x^2 + y^2 = 25$.
>
> $$\frac{d}{dx}(x^2 + y^2) = \frac{d}{dx}(25)$$
>
> $$2x + 2y\frac{dy}{dx} = 0$$
>
> Substituting $x = 3$, $y = 4$, gives
>
> $$6 + 8\frac{dy}{dx} = 0,$$
>
> so the gradient we are looking for is
>
> $$\frac{dy}{dx} = -\frac{3}{4}.$$

- ☐ Substitute the coordinates of the given point.
- ☐ The solution of the resulting equation for $\dfrac{dy}{dx}$ will give the gradient of the tangent to the curve.

- ■ **Related rates**: In some word problems we have some information about the rate of change (in time) of one quantity and we are interested in finding the rate of change of a related quantity at a specified moment. A possible way of solving this type of problem is:

- ☐ Set up an equation that expresses the relationship between the varying quantities.
- ☐ Differentiate (implicitly) both sides of this equation with respect to time (using the chain rule).
- ☐ Substitute the given numerical values for the quantities into the resulting equation.
- ☐ Solve the resulting equation for the rate of change asked for in the problem.

Example

Find the rate of change of the radius of a balloon, when the radius is 5 cm, and the volume is changing at a rate of $12\,cm^3/s$.

$$V = \frac{4}{3}\pi r^3$$

$$\frac{dV}{dt} = 4\pi r^2 \frac{dr}{dt}$$

$$12 = 4\pi 5^2 \frac{dr}{dt}$$

$$\frac{dr}{dt} = 0.0382\,cm/s$$

■ (HL) Some more derivatives

It is important to keep in mind the derivatives of the following functions:

$x \mapsto \sec x$, $x \mapsto \csc x$, $x \mapsto \cot x$, $x \mapsto a^x$, $x \mapsto \log_a x$, $x \mapsto \arcsin x$, $x \mapsto \arccos x$ and $x \mapsto \arctan x$.

The derivatives of these functions are in the IB Mathematics HL formula booklet.

Examples

For $f(x) = \arctan x$, $f'(x) = \dfrac{1}{1 + x^2}$.

For $f(x) = \arctan \left(\dfrac{x}{a}\right)$, $f'(x) = \dfrac{a}{a^2 + x^2}$.

IB SYLLABUS

See also: standard integrals in the IB Mathematics formula booklet.

Graphical behaviour of graphs of functions

Revised ☐

■ Increasing and decreasing behaviour

Key definitions
- A function f is **increasing at a point** $x = a$ if, in some neighbourhood of a, $x < a$ implies $f(x) < f(a)$ and $x > a$ implies $f(x) > f(a)$.
- A function f is **decreasing at a point** $x = a$ if, in some neighbourhood of a, $x < a$ implies $f(x) > f(a)$ and $x > a$ implies $f(x) < f(a)$.
- A function f is **increasing on an interval** $]c, d[$ if, for every $c < x_1 < x_2 < d$, $f(x_1) < f(x_2)$.
- A function f is **decreasing on an interval** $]c, d[$ if, for every $c < x_1 < x_2 < d$, $f(x_1) > f(x_2)$.

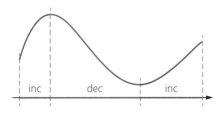

Note

The interval can be closed, $[c, d]$ or even infinite: the definitions and claims are similar.

Claims

- If $f'(x) > 0$ for all $x \in]c, d[$, then f is increasing on $]c, d[$.

- If $f'(x) < 0$ for all $x \in]c, d[$, then f is decreasing on $]c, d[$.

- If f is increasing on $]c, d[$ and differentiable at $a \in]c, d[$, then $f'(a) \geq 0$.

- If f is decreasing on $]c, d[$ and differentiable at $a \in]c, d[$, then $f'(a) \leq 0$.

Note

These claims describe the connection between the local property (gradient) and the global property (increasing/decreasing behaviour on an interval).

Stationary and extremum points

Key definitions

- The point $(a, f(a))$ is a **stationary point** of the graph of f if $f'(a) = 0$.
- The point $(a, f(a))$ is a **local minimum** point of the graph of f if, in some neighbourhood of a, for any $x \neq a$, $f(x) > f(a)$.
- The point $(a, f(a))$ is a **local maximum** point of the graph of f if, in some neighbourhood of a, for any $x \neq a$, $f(x) < f(a)$.
- There are also examples (such as $f(x) = x^3$ at $(0, 0)$) when $f'(a) = 0$, but the stationary point $(a, f(a))$ is neither a local maximum, nor a local minimum point. For the functions we meet, such a point is a horizontal point of inflexion. (The definition of points of inflexion comes a bit later in this section.) It should be noted, however, that there are other possibilities; there are twice differentiable functions, where a stationary point is neither a local maximum point, nor a local minimum point nor a point of inflexion.

Note

Note that the derivative of an increasing function is certainly not negative, but it may be 0 at some points. We will only meet functions where there are a finite number of such points, for example $x \mapsto x^3$.

IB SYLLABUS

For the functions we will meet, a stationary point is either a local maximum point or a local minimum point or a horizontal point of inflexion.

Claims

- If $(a, f(a))$ is a local minimum or maximum point of the graph of $y = f(x)$, and f is differentiable at $x = a$, then $f'(a) = 0$.

- If $f'(a) = 0$ and, in some neighbourhood of a, $f'(x) < 0$ for $x < a$ and $f'(x) > 0$ for $x > a$, then $(a, f(a))$ is a local minimum point of the graph of $y = f(x)$.

- If $f'(a) = 0$ and, in some neighbourhood of a, $f'(x) > 0$, for $x < a$ and $f'(x) < 0$ for $x > a$, then $(a, f(a))$ is a local maximum point of the graph of $y = f(x)$.

USING A CALCULATOR

GDCs have built-in applications to find maximum and minimum points.

For a variety of functions, stationary points can be found and categorised algebraically. A useful tool is a sign diagram for the derivative of the function.

Example

For $f(x) = x^3 - 3x^2 - 9x + 31$, the sign diagram for $f'(x)$ is:

x		-1		3	
$f'(x)$	pos	0	neg	0	pos

Graph sketching

Steps to follow

- Differentiate the function.

- Find the solutions of $f'(x) = 0$ and find the values where $f'(x)$ is not defined. We will only meet functions where there are a finite number of such critical points within the domain, and the derivative function does not change sign on the intervals between neighbouring points.

- Draw a sign diagram for f', indicating the critical points and the sign of $f'(x)$ between neighbouring critical points.

Note

The previous claims give us a basis to use differentiation as a tool for sketching graphs of functions. The steps described here result in a quite accurate sketch of the graph of function f.

- Interpret the sign diagram to find extremum points and intervals where the graph is increasing and decreasing.

- Find the local minimum/maximum values and plot the local extremum points.

- Plot the x- and y-intercepts and values at the endpoints of the domain.

- Find the asymptotes (if any) and sketch the graph.

Example					

For $f(x) = x^3 - 3x^2 - 9x + 31$ on $[-3, 5]$,

x		-1		3	
$f'(x)$	pos	0	neg	0	pos
f	inc	36	dec	4	inc

Concavity and points of inflexion

Key definitions

- The graph of a (twice differentiable) function f is **concave up** on an interval $]c, d[$ if, for all $x \in]c, d[$, $f''(x) > 0$.
- The graph of a (twice differentiable) function f is **concave down** on an interval $]c, d[$ if, for all $x \in]c, d[$, $f''(x) < 0$.
- A point $(a, f(a))$ is a **point of inflexion** on the graph of the (twice differentiable) function f, if
  - $f''(a) = 0$ and
  - the concavity changes at $(a, f(a))$. (In other words, there are intervals $]c, a[$ and $]a, d[$, such that either the graph is concave up on $]c, a[$ and concave down on $]a, d[$, or the graph is concave down on $]c, a[$ and concave up on $]a, d[$).

IB SYLLABUS

Our definition is restricted to graphs of functions with special properties. Concavity is a much more general geometric concept (defined without using the concept of differentiability), but it is beyond the scope of this course.

IB SYLLABUS

In some sources, the condition $f''(a) = 0$ is not always included in the definition, but in this course it needs to be checked when we look for points of inflexion.

Claims

- If the graph of the function is concave up on an interval $]c, d[$, then the graph is above any of its tangent lines drawn at $(a, f(a))$ with $a \in]c, d[$, and the graph is below any line segment connecting points $(a_1, f(a_1))$ and $(a_2, f(a_2))$ with $a_1, a_2 \in]c, d[$.

- If the graph of the function is concave down on an interval $]c, d[$, then the graph is below any of its tangent lines drawn at $(a, f(a))$ with $a \in]c, d[$, and the graph is above any line segment connecting points $(a_1, f(a_1))$ and $(a_2, f(a_2))$ with $a_1, a_2 \in]c, d[$.

- If $(a, f(a))$ is a point of inflexion, then of course $f''(a) = 0$, but $f'(a)$ can be anything. The tangent line to the graph at a point of inflexion can have any gradient.

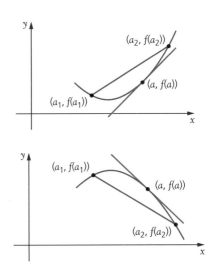

Graph sketching (revisited)

- After finding f', also find f''.

- Identify values where $f''(x)$ is not defined. Solve $f''(x) = 0$ and find the points of inflexion. We will only deal with functions where there are a finite number of such values, and the sign of the second derivative does not change between neighbouring values.

- Identify the intervals where the graph of the function is concave up or down.

- As well as the extremum points and x- and y- intercepts, plot the points of inflexion and use the table to sketch the graph. The table shows the shape of the graph on intervals where neither f' nor f'' change sign.

> **Note**
>
> Besides checking the first derivative, we can also look at the sign of the second derivative. Including these steps in the graph sketching procedure discussed earlier will result in an even more accurate sketch.
>
>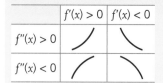

Claims about extremum points (revisited)

- If $(a, f(a))$ is a point on the graph of $y = f(x)$ such that $f'(a) = 0$ and $f''(a) > 0$, then $(a, f(a))$ is a local minimum point.

- If $(a, f(a))$ is a point on the graph of $y = f(x)$ such that $f'(a) = 0$ and $f''(a) < 0$, then $(a, f(a))$ is a local maximum point.

> **Note**
>
> The second derivative test is inconclusive if $f'(x) = 0$ and $f''(x) = 0$.

Summary of the relationship between graphs of f, f' and f''

- This table summarises the connection between the graphs of f, f' and f'' over an interval where none of the functions change sign.

graph of $y = f(x)$	graph of $y = f'(x)$	graph of $y = f''(x)$
increasing	above the x-axis	
decreasing	below the x-axis	
concave up	increasing	above the x-axis
concave down	decreasing	below the x-axis
	concave up	increasing
	concave down	decreasing

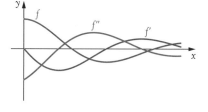

- Special points on the graphs of f, f' and f'' have the following relationships:

  □ Maximum/minimum points of the graph of $y = f(x)$ correspond to x-intercepts of the graph of $y = f'(x)$, where $f'(x)$ changes sign.

  □ Points of inflexion of the graph of $y = f(x)$ correspond to x-intercepts of the graph of $y = f''(x)$, where $f''(x)$ changes sign.

  □ Maximum/minimum points of the graph of $y = f'(x)$ correspond to points of inflexion of the graph of $y = f(x)$.

> **Note**
>
> These statements are true for 'nice' looking functions, where f, f' and f'' are defined on the same interval and there are only a finite number of sign changes of f' and f''. In a more general case they need to be treated with caution.

Tips for solving optimisation problems

Revised

- Set up an expression in one variable expressing the dependent variable to be optimised.

- Find meaningful bounds for the independent variable.

- Find local extrema of the expression within the interval of meaningful values.

- The answer for the optimisation problem is either one of the local extrema or the value of the expression at one of the endpoints of the interval of meaningful values.

IB SYLLABUS

Optimisation can come up in different contexts; for example, area, volume, distance, time, profit optimisation.

> **Example**
>
> To find the rectangle with maximum possible area if the perimeter is fixed at $P = 20\,\text{cm}$, we start with the formulae $P = 2a + 2b$ and $A = ab$, hence $A = a\dfrac{20 - 2a}{2}$, where $0 < a < 10$.
>
> The global maximum point on the graph of A on $]0, 10[$ is $(5, 25)$, the optimal rectangle is a $5\,\text{cm} \times 5\,\text{cm}$ square and the maximum possible area is $25\,\text{cm}^2$.

6.3 Integral calculus (SL 6.4, 6.5, HL 6.4, 6.5, 6.7)

Revised ☐

Indefinite integrals

Revised ☐

Key definition

The family of functions, F, with the property that $F' = f$ (or $\dfrac{dF}{dx} = f$) is called the **antiderivative** (or **indefinite integral**) of f.

The notation for the antiderivative is $\int f(x)\,dx$.

■ Claims

If f is defined on an interval, and F_1 and F_2 both have the property that $F_1' = F_2' = f$, then there is a constant c such that $F_1(x) = F_2(x) + c$ for all x in the domain of f.

CROSS REFERENCE

For the reason behind this fact, see also Rolle's theorem in the Calculus option. **(HL)**

■ Notation

If f is defined on an interval, and $F' = f$, then we can write $\int f(x)\,dx = F + c$

■ Methods of integration

■ $\int kf(x) \pm lg(x)\,dx = k\int f(x)\,dx \pm l\int g(x)\,dx\ \ k, l \in \mathbb{R}$

■ The following table contains some basic integrals and important generalisation of these. In the first line $n \neq -1$ and for the formulae in the right column $a \neq 0$.

Note

There are some rules for integration but, unlike differentiation, we mostly use methods rather than rules to find antiderivatives.

$\int x^n\,dx = \dfrac{x^{n+1}}{n+1} + c$	$\int (ax+b)^n\,dx = \dfrac{1}{a}\dfrac{(ax+b)^{n+1}}{n+1} + c$
$\int \sin x\,dx = -\cos x + c$	$\int \sin(ax+b)\,dx = -\dfrac{1}{a}\cos(ax+b) + c$
$\int \cos x\,dx = \sin x + c$	$\int \cos(ax+b)\,dx = \dfrac{1}{a}\sin(ax+b) + c$
$\int e^x\,dx = e^x + c$	$\int e^{ax+b}\,dx = \dfrac{1}{a}e^{ax+b} + c$
$\int \dfrac{1}{x}\,dx = \ln x + c$	$\int \dfrac{1}{ax+b}\,dx = \dfrac{1}{a}\ln(ax+b) + c$

Examples

It is helpful to remember the connection of the integrals in the second column to the corresponding simpler integral.

$\int \sin(3x-5)\,dx = -\dfrac{1}{3}\cos(3x-5) + c$

$\int e^{2-4x}\,dx = -\dfrac{1}{4}e^{2-4x} + c$

$\int (5x+3)^7\,dx = \dfrac{1}{5}\cdot\dfrac{(5x+3)^8}{8} + c$

$\int \dfrac{1}{(1-x)^2}\,dx = -\dfrac{1}{1}\cdot-\dfrac{1}{1-x} + c$

IB SYLLABUS

The integrals in the first column are in the IB Mathematics SL and HL formula booklets (along with some others for HL).

■ We need to be careful with the integral of the reciprocal function, $x \mapsto \dfrac{1}{x}$. Since it is not defined at $x = 0$, we need to look at the cases $x > 0$ and $x < 0$ separately. The formula in the table is valid for $x > 0$ ($\ln x$ is not even defined otherwise). At Standard level we don't need the $x < 0$ case.

(HL) For $x < 0$, $\int \dfrac{1}{x}\,dx = \ln(-x) + c$. The usual way of expressing this case, and the previous one in one formula, is $\int \dfrac{1}{x}\,dx = \ln|x| + c$. It should be noted, however, that this way of expressing the integral is just a compact way of dealing with the two cases.

We will not really use it, but the most general antiderivative of $x \mapsto \frac{1}{x}$ on the largest possible domain, $\mathbb{R} \setminus \{0\}$, is $x \mapsto \begin{cases} \ln x + c_1 & \text{if } x > 0 \\ \ln(-x) + c_2 & \text{if } x < 0 \end{cases}$

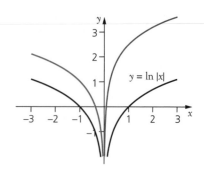

$y = \ln |x|$

- **(HL)** The table shows some integrals related to inverse trigonometric functions. (In the right-hand column, $a \neq 0$.)

$\int \dfrac{1}{1+x^2}\,dx = \arctan x + c$	$\int \dfrac{1}{a^2+x^2}\,dx = \dfrac{1}{a}\arctan\dfrac{x}{a} + c$
$\int \dfrac{1}{\sqrt{1-x^2}}\,dx = \arcsin x + c$	$\int \dfrac{1}{\sqrt{a^2-x^2}}\,dx = \arcsin\dfrac{x}{a} + c$

> **IB SYLLABUS**
>
> The integrals in the right-hand column are in the IB Mathematics HL formula booklet.

- If $F' = f$, then $\int f(u(x))u'(x)\,dx = F \circ u + c$. In simpler cases, these types of integrals can be solved by inspection. For more complicated expressions we can use the substitution $u = u(x)$.

  □ For example:

  - $\int 3x^2(x^3 + 1)^5\,dx = \dfrac{(x^3 + 1)^6}{6} + c$ \qquad $(u(x) = x^3 + 1)$

  - $\int x\cos x^2\,dx = \dfrac{1}{2}\int 2x\cos x^2\,dx = \dfrac{1}{2}\sin x^2 + c$ \qquad $(u(x) = x^2)$

  - **(HL)** $\int \tan x\,dx = \int \dfrac{\sin x}{\cos x}\,dx = -\int \dfrac{-\sin x}{\cos x}\,dx = -\ln|\cos x| + c$

  - $\int \dfrac{u'(x)}{u(x)}\,dx = \ln u(x) + c$ on intervals, where $u(x) > 0$

  - **(HL)** or more generally, $\int \dfrac{u'(x)}{u(x)}\,dx = \ln|u(x)| + c$ on intervals where $u(x) \neq 0$

  - **(HL)** $\int \dfrac{1}{4x^2 + 4x + 10}\,dx = \int \dfrac{1}{9 + (2x+1)^2}\,dx = \dfrac{1}{6}\arctan\dfrac{2x+1}{3} + c$

> **Example**
>
> To find $\int \dfrac{6x+3}{(x^2+x)^3}\,dx$, let us use the substitution $u = x^2 + x$.
>
> $\dfrac{du}{dx} = 2x + 1$, so we can replace $(2x+1)\,dx$ by du and $x^2 + 1$ by u in the integral to
>
> get $\int \dfrac{3}{u^3}\,du = \dfrac{3}{-2}u^{-2} + c$. So the antiderivative is $\dfrac{-3}{2(x^2+x)^2} + c$.

  □ Note the difference between the methods needed to find the following integrals. (Some of these can only be found using HL methods.)

$\int \dfrac{x}{x^2+1}\,dx, \ \int \dfrac{x^2}{x+1}\,dx, \ \int \dfrac{x^2}{x^2+1}\,dx, \ \int \dfrac{x}{x+1}\,dx, \ \int \dfrac{1}{x^2+1}\,dx, \ \int \dfrac{1}{x+1}\,dx$

- **(HL) Integration by parts**: $\int u'(x)v(x)\,dx = u(x)v(x) - \int u(x)v'(x)\,dx$

  □ Typical examples when integration by parts helps to find the integral are:

  $\int x\cos x\,dx, \int xe^x\,dx, \int x^n \ln x\,dx, \int \ln x\,dx, \int \arctan x\,dx.$

  □ Typical cases when repeated application of integration by parts helps are:

  - applying integration by parts twice to evaluate $\int e^x\cos x\,dx$, which results in an equation to solve for the original integral:
  $\int e^x\cos x\,dx = e^x\sin x + e^x\cos x - \int e^x\cos x\,dx$

– applying integration by parts once to $\int x^n e^x \, dx$, which reduces the integral to $\int x^{n-1} e^x \, dx$. Repeated application eventually reduces the integral to $\int e^x \, dx$.

☐ The following integrals need differing methods, two of which can be asked for Standard level exams:

$\int x e^{x^2} \, dx, \; \int x e^x \, dx, \; \int x^2 e^x \, dx, \; \int e^x \, dx.$

Note

A similar looking integral, $\int e^{x^2} \, dx$ is, however, a typical example where the antiderivative cannot be expressed using methods and functions we have learnt.

■ Antidifferentiation with a boundary condition

A typical question is to find f if $F = f'$ and $f(a)$ (for some a) is given. For the solution, first find the antiderivative $\int F(x) \, dx$. Then use the boundary condition (the value of the function at a) to find the value of the integration constant, c.

CROSS REFERENCE

See also: kinematic applications on page 63.

Definite integrals

Revised ☐

In this section we only consider functions which are not too complicated. Our definitions and claims are valid if the function has a finite number of points where it is not continuous, and it has a finite number of x-intercepts. Dealing with more complicated functions is beyond the scope of this course.

Key definitions

- If $f(x) \geq 0$ for all $x \in [a, b]$, then the **definite integral** of $y = f(x)$ on the interval $[a, b]$ is the area between the graph of the function and the x-axis above the interval $[a, b]$.

  The usual notation is $\int_a^b f(x) \, dx$

  a is called the lower limit and b the upper limit of the integral.

- If the function has negative values, then the definite integral is defined as the difference: (area above the x-axis) – (area below the x-axis)

  $\int_a^b f(x) \, dx = A_+ - A_-$

- For $a = b$ we define $\int_a^a f(x) \, dx$ to be 0.

- For $b < a$ we define $\int_a^b f(x) \, dx$ to be $- \int_b^a f(x) \, dx$.

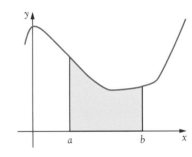

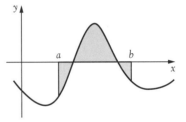

■ Claims

■ $\int_a^b f(x) \, dx = - \int_b^a f(x) \, dx$ for all $a, b \in \mathbb{R}$.

■ $\int_a^b f(x) \, dx + \int_b^c f(x) \, dx = \int_a^c f(x) \, dx$ for all $a, b, c \in \mathbb{R}$.

■ $\int_a^b k f(x) \pm l g(x) \, dx = k \int_a^b f(x) \, dx \pm l \int_a^b g(x) \, dx$ for all $k, l \in \mathbb{R}$.

■ If $f(x) \geq g(x)$ for all $x \in [a, b]$, then the area between the graphs of the functions $x \mapsto f(x)$ and $x \mapsto g(x)$ and the vertical lines $x = a$ and $x = b$ is:

$\int_a^b (f(x) - g(x)) \, dx.$

■ The area between the graphs of two functions (even if the graphs intersect) on the interval $[a, b]$ is given by $\int_a^b |f(x) - g(x)| \, dx$. This is a useful formula for finding areas between graphs using technology.

Note

The equality of the second claim is usually used for $a < b < c$, but this condition is not necessary.

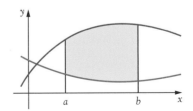

Note

For manual area calculations between intersecting graphs, we need to break up the integral at the intersection points.

- **(HL)** For an increasing or decreasing function $x \mapsto f(x)$, we can also find the area bounded by the graph of the function, the y-axis and two horizontal lines, $y = c$ and $y = d$ ($c < d$).

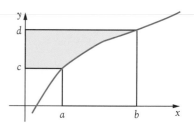

Let $g: y \mapsto f^{-1}(y)$ be the inverse function.

- ☐ If $a, b \geq 0$, then the above mentioned area is

$$\int_c^d g(y)\,dy = \int_c^d f^{-1}(y)\,dy$$

- ☐ In general, even if the graph crosses the y-axis, the area is $\int_c^d |g(y)|\,dy$.

- ☐ For increasing $x \mapsto f(x)$, if $0 \leq a < b$ are such that $0 \leq c = f(a) < d = f(b)$, the diagram (on the right) illustrates the following interesting relationship:

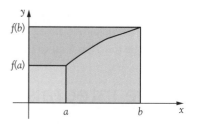

$$\int_a^b f(x)\,dx + \int_{f(a)}^{f(b)} f^{-1}(y)\,dy = bf(b) - af(a).$$

This gives an alternate way of finding the area of the region between the graph of f and the y-axis (without finding and integrating the inverse function).

- ☐ The formula above is actually true without any restriction on a, b, $f(a)$ and $f(b)$, and also for decreasing $x \mapsto f(x)$, but we don't need it in this general form.

Fundamental theorem of calculus

For a continuous function f defined on the interval $[a, b]$, for any $x_0 \in [a, b]$, the area function defined by $A_{x_0}(x) = \int_{x_0}^x f(t)\,dt$ is differentiable at every $]a, b[$, and $A_{x_0}'(x) = f(x)$.

Consequences of the fundamental theorem of calculus

- $\int f(x)\,dx = A_{x_0} + c$

- If f is continuous on $[a, b]$ and $F'(x) = f(x)$ for every $]a, b[$, then $\int_a^b f(x)\,dx = F(b) - F(a)$. Or using a customary notation:

$$\int_a^b f(x)\,dx = \left[\int f(x)\,dx\right]_a^b = [F(x)]_a^b = F(b) - F(a).$$

Volume of revolution

- Let $[a, b]$ be part of the domain of the function f such that $f(x) \geq 0$ for all $x \in [a, b]$. Let us consider the region below the graph of the function and above $[a, b]$. Let us rotate this region about the x-axis by $360°$. The volume of the solid generated is:

$$\text{Volume} = \int_a^b \pi(f(x))^2\,dx$$

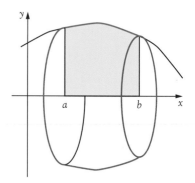

- **(HL)** For an increasing or decreasing function $x \mapsto f(x)$, we can also rotate the region bounded by the graph of the function, the y-axis and two horizontal lines, $y = c$ and $y = d$ ($c < d$) about the y-axis by $360°$.

If $x \mapsto f(x)$ is decreasing, let $a < b$ such that $f(a) = d$ and $f(b) = c$.

Let $g: y \mapsto f^{-1}(y)$ be the inverse function.

The volume of the solid generated is:

$$\text{Volume} = \int_c^d \pi(g(y))^2\,dy = \int_{f(b)}^{f(a)} \pi(f^{-1}(y))^2\,dy$$

For an increasing function the formula is similar.

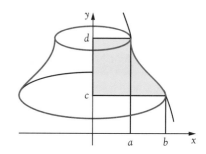

> **Note**
>
> To use the fundamental theorem, we need to find an antiderivative. Sometimes it is not possible to express this antiderivative as a combination of basic functions. Typical examples are $\int \sin x^2\,dx$ or $\int e^{-x^2}\,dx$. To find areas under these curves we use technology.

> **USING A CALCULATOR**
>
> GDCs have built-in applications to find definite integrals. Even if the antiderivative can be found, in a lot of cases it is quicker to use a calculator to find approximate values of definite integrals.

6.4 Kinematics (SL 6.6, HL 6.6)

In this section we consider an object moving along a straight line.

■ Notation

- The position of the object is given by the function $t \mapsto s(t)$, where t represents time. The position is given using an appropriate scale and a fixed number line on the straight line path of the movement. The starting position (also referred to as the initial position) is $s(0)$, the position corresponding to $t = 0$.

- The displacement of the object is the position relative to the starting position. Positive and negative displacement values represent displacement in opposite directions.

- The velocity of the object is given by the function $t \mapsto v(t)$. Velocity is signed: positive velocity means movement in the positive direction; negative velocity means movement in the negative direction. At times, when the movement is changing direction (the object is turning back), the velocity is 0.

- The speed is the magnitude (absolute value) of the velocity. It is always positive or 0.

- Acceleration is given by the function $t \mapsto a(t)$. Acceleration is also signed. When the velocity of the object is positive, positive acceleration means speeding up, negative acceleration means slowing down. When the velocity is negative, positive acceleration means slowing down, negative acceleration means speeding up.

> **Note**
>
> Sometimes the position function is given, but in other cases the motion is described in other ways and we have to specify the scale and number line we are going to use to model the motion.
>
> Often the starting position is assigned to the origin of the number line used to describe the motion, but this is not a strict rule. For example, if we talk about a falling object, we may use ground level as the zero position.

> **IB SYLLABUS**
>
> Sometimes the word displacement is used to describe the position of the object, even if the starting position is not at the origin of the number line.

■ Relationship between position (displacement), velocity and acceleration

- Velocity is the rate of change of the position (displacement): $v = \dfrac{ds}{dt}$.
- Acceleration is the rate of change of the velocity: $a = \dfrac{dv}{dt} = \dfrac{d^2 s}{dt^2}$.
- The diagram illustrates the relationship between position, velocity and acceleration.

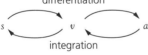

differentiation

$s \qquad v \qquad a$

integration

> **CROSS REFERENCE**
>
> Differentiation with respect to time (especially in physics texts) is often denoted by a dot over the letter: $v = \dot{s}, a = \dot{v} = \ddot{s}$.

■ Important claim

The total distance travelled during the motion between times t_1 and t_2 is given by the formula $\int_{t_1}^{t_2} |v(t)| \, dt$.

- Note that the total distance travelled is not the same as $|s(t_2) - s(t_1)|$, the distance between the positions at the beginning and the end of the motion. For example, if an object is moving away from the starting point for some time, but returning to that point later, then $|s(t_{end}) - s(t_{start})| = 0$, but the total distance travelled is clearly not 0.

> **Note**
>
> This formula is in the IB Mathematics SL formula booklet, but not in the IB Mathematics HL formula booklet. It is useful to find the total distance travelled using a GDC.
>
> The modulus sign is important: the similar integral without the modulus sign calculates the distance between the starting and end positions.

Practice questions for Topic 6

To practice these skills, try these past paper questions. Start with the questions with lower numbers (1–7). In exams, the first questions tend to check your understanding of one specific concept (although this is not a rule, so don't assume this will always be the case). Questions 8–10 on the HL papers are still short questions, but usually you need an imaginative approach to find a solution. The long questions (HL 10–14 and SL 8–10) have multiple parts, often checking understanding of several concepts and connections between these concepts. For more detailed past paper references, see the charts on pages 97–113.

Date	HL Paper 1	HL Paper 2	SL Paper 1	SL Paper 2
2014 November	5, 6, 7, 11cde	4, 8, 10, 13	6, 9	4, 7
2014 May TZ1	5, 6, 8, 9, 11	5, 6b, 10	3, 6, 7	5, 6, 7
2014 May TZ2	8a, 10, 13, 14c	3, 9, 10,12, 14	5, 6, 10	9
2013 November	5, 10	10, 12, 13	4, 6, 10	2, 3, 5, 7
2013 May TZ1	5, 7, 10, 12ef	4, 12, 13	3, 6, 10	5, 9
2013 May TZ2	1, 5, 8	4, 10, 13	6, 7, 9, 10	10
2012 November	4, 8	6, 8, 9	3, 4, 10	3, 7, 9de
2012 May TZ1	2b, 6, 9, 12	8, 10, 11	3, 6, 10	4
2012 May TZ2	7b, 8, 10c, 13a	6bc	3bc, 8c, 10	2, 5, 9
2011 November	4c, 7, 8bc, 11, 13a	1, 9	4, 9cd, 10	7b, 10
2011 May TZ1	7, 9, 12	2, 8	5, 10	6, 8cd, 9
2011 May TZ2	11, 13	3, 7, 9, 10, 13Ba	4, 8, 9d	7
2010 November	12a, 13	4, 10, 13	2, 6, 9d, 10	2, 7, 8
2010 May TZ1	8, 9, 11	10, 13c, 14	6, 8a, 9	3, 6, 9
2010 May TZ2	7, 8, 9, 14b	10, 11f, 14c	5, 7, 8	6, 7, 10
2009 November	7, 9, 10, 12	8, 10	5, 9, 10	2, 5
2009 May TZ1	7, 9, 11, 13Babc	3, 6, 12	3, 4, 7, 10	10
2009 May TZ2	4, 5, 11e, 12fg	3, 6, 9, 10	6, 8	6, 8, 10def
2008 November	5, 6, 7, 9	8, 9, 12	6, 9	9
2008 May TZ1	5, 6, 10, 12abcd, 13a	6, 9, 13	5, 6, 8	5, 10
2008 May TZ2	5, 6, 8, 13	3, 6, 13a	7, 9, 10de	3c, 9

Practice questions

Now have a go at these practice questions. The questions require imaginative application of the concepts you have revised in this book. Read the question first. Try to understand what the question is asking. If you can see a way to work out an answer, go ahead. If not, take a look at the Hints section, which starts on page 75. These may give you a good starting point. If you answered the question, compare your answer to the one in the Answer section that starts on page 119. If you didn't get the answer right, take a look at the Detailed solutions that start on page 126 to see where you went wrong. Even if you got the answer right, you might find this section useful to discover other ways of finding the solution.

Notes

Look for connections between the parts of the questions. Sometimes you need to search for methods rather than mechanically applying formulae.

1 Consider the following sequences:

$u_1 = 1$ and $u_{n+1} = u_n + n + 1$ for $n = 1, 2, 3, \ldots$

$v_1 = 1^3$, $v_2 = 1^3 + 2^3$, $v_3 = 1^3 + 2^3 + 3^3$, $\ldots$, $v_n = \sum_{k=1}^{n} k^3$

a Write down u_1, u_2, u_3, u_4 and u_5.

b There are parameters, a and b, such that u_n can be written as $an^2 + bn$ for all positive integer, n. Find the value of a and b.

c Hence or otherwise find u_{2014}.

d Write down v_1, v_2, v_3, v_4 and v_5.

e Suggest an expression for v_n in terms of n and use your expression to find v_{10}.

f (HL) Use mathematical induction (or any other method) to prove your conjecture for part **e**.

> SL 1.1
>
> HL 1.1, 1.4

2 Consider the function defined by $f(x) = \sin 2x$.

a Find f', f'', f''' and $f^{(4)}$, the first four derivatives of f.

b Find $f^{(14)}, f^{(15)}, f^{(16)}$ and $f^{(17)}$.

c (HL) Suggest an expression for $f^{(n)}(x)$.

d (HL) Use mathematical induction (or any other method) to prove your conjecture for part **c**.

> SL 1.1, 3.2, 6.2
>
> HL 1.1, 1.4, 3.2, 6.2

3 (HL) Let $\omega \neq 1$ be a complex solution of the equation $z^3 = 1$ and let us consider the equation system

$x + y + z = A$
$x + \omega y + \omega^2 z = B$
$x + \omega^2 y + \omega z = C$

a Show that $1 + \omega + \omega^2 = 0$.

b Express $A + B\omega + C\omega^2$ in terms of x, y and z (and ω).

c Solve the equation system, i.e. express $x, y,$ and z in terms of A, B and C (and ω).

d The equation system

$x + y + z = 1$
$x + \omega y + \omega^2 z = 1$
$x + \omega^2 y + az = b$

has infinitely many solutions. Find the value of a and b in the form $p + q\omega$, where p and q are real numbers.

> HL 1.5, 1.7, 1.9

4 **(HL)** Let z_k, $k = 1, \ldots, 5$ be the five (may be complex) solutions of the equation $z^5 = 1$.

HL 1.1, 1.5, 1.7, 2.6

a Find the value of $\displaystyle\sum_{k=1}^{5} z_k$.

b For a complex number w, show that $|w|^2 = ww^*$.

c Find the value of $\displaystyle\sum_{k=1}^{5} |z_1 - z_k|^2$.

d $A_1A_2A_3A_4A_5$ is a regular pentagon inscribed in a circle of radius 1.

Let $a_2\ a_3\ a_4$ and a_5 denote the length of the line segments A_1A_2, A_1A_3, A_1A_4 and A_1A_5 respectively.

Find the value of $a_2^2 + a_3^2 + a_4^2 + a_5^2$.

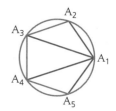

5 The real numbers, a, b, c and A, B, C, are such that

$$a + b + c = A$$
$$4a + 2b + c = B$$
$$16a + 4b + c = C$$

SL 2.2, 2.4

HL 1.9, 2.2, 2.5

a Express:

   i $3a + b$ and $6a + b$ in terms of A, B and C

   ii a in terms of A, B and C

   iii b and c in terms of A, B and C.

b A parabola with equation $y = ax^2 + bx + c$ passes through the points $(1, -2)$, $(2, -1)$ and $(4, 13)$. Find the values of a, b and c.

c There is no parabola through the points $(1, -2)$, $(2, -1)$ and $(4, t)$. Find the value of t.

6 The real numbers, a, b, c and A, B, C, are such that

$$a + b + c = A$$
$$4a + 2b + c = B$$
$$9a + 3b + c = C$$

SL 1.1

HL 1.1, 1.9

a Express:

   i $3a + b$ and $5a + b$ in terms of A, B and C

   ii a in terms of A, B and C

   iii b and c in terms of A, B and C.

b A sequence $\{u_n\}$ starts as $4, 3, 6, 13, 24, \ldots$

   i Show that this is not an arithmetic sequence.

   ii Show that this is not a geometric sequence.

c The general term of the sequence in part **b** can be expressed in the form $u_n = an^2 + bn + c$.

   i Express u_1, u_2 and u_3 in terms of a, b and c.

   ii Find the values of a, b and c.

   iii Check your result of the previous part for u_4 and u_5, and work out the value of u_{15}.

7 The function g is defined by $g(x) = ax^3 + bx^2 + cx + d$.

SL 2.2, 6.2, 6.3

HL 2.2, 2.5, 6.2, 6.3

a Find $g'(x)$.

b Express $g(0)$, $g(1)$, $g'(0)$ and $g'(1)$ in terms of a, b, c and d.

c The graph of the function g has a local minimum at $(0, 0)$ and a local maximum at $(1, 1)$. Find the value of a, b, c and d.

8 **(HL)** The function f is defined by

$$f(x) = \begin{cases} 0 & x \le 0 \\ h(x) & 0 < x < 1 \\ 1 & x \ge 1 \end{cases}$$

for some function $h:(0, 1) \to \mathbb{R}$.

HL 2.2, 2.5, 6.1, 6.2

a Find a linear function, h, that makes f continuous.

b Show that there is no quadratic function, h, that makes f differentiable everywhere.

c Suggest an h for which f is differentiable.

d Using first principles, show that your choice of h is correct.

9 **(HL)** Consider the points P(3, 1, 2), A(7, 2, 9), B(4, 4, 1) and C(5, 0, 1).

HL 4.1, 4.2, 4.6

a Show that the vectors $\overrightarrow{PA}$, $\overrightarrow{PB}$ and $\overrightarrow{PC}$ are perpendicular to each other.

b The plane Π_1 contains the points P, A, B; the plane Π_2 contains the points P, A, C and the plane Π_3 contains the points P, B, C.

 i Which plane has the equation $x + 3y - z = 4$?

 ii Which plane has the equation $2x - y - z = 3$?

 iii Find the equation of the third plane.

c Consider the planes with equation $M(x + 3y - z) + N(2x - y - z) = 4M + 3N$, where M and N are real numbers.

 i The equation above can be rearranged to the form $ax + by + cz = 4M + 3N$. Express a, b and c in terms of M and N.

 ii Show that the line through P and A is in these planes for any M and N.

d Find an equation of the plane through P, A and (0, 0, 0).

e Find an equation of the plane that contains P, A and parallel to $\overrightarrow{BC}$.

10 For the function $f: \mathbb{R} \to \mathbb{R}^+$, we know that $f(1) = 6$ and $f(x + y) = \dfrac{f(x)f(y)}{3}$ for every $x, y \in \mathbb{R}$.

SL 1.2, 2.1, 2.6

HL 1.2, 2.1, 2.4

a Find:

 i $f(2)$ and $f(3)$

 ii $f(0)$

 iii $f(-1)$ and $f(-2)$

 iv $f\left(\dfrac{1}{2}\right)$ and $f\left(\dfrac{1}{3}\right)$.

b Suggest a function that satisfies the properties $f(1) = 6$ and $f(x + y) = \dfrac{f(x)f(y)}{3}$ for every $x, y \in \mathbb{R}$.

c Verify that these properties are indeed true for the function you suggested.

d For given $a, b > 0$, suggest a function that satisfies the properties $g(1) = a$ and $g(x + y) = \dfrac{g(x)g(y)}{b}$ for every $x, y \in \mathbb{R}$.

e Verify that these properties are indeed true for the function you suggested.

SL 1.2, 6.4, 6.5

HL 1.2, 6.4, 6.5

11 a Show that $\dfrac{1}{x-1} - \dfrac{1}{x+1} = \dfrac{2}{x^2 - 1}$.

b Write $\dfrac{1}{x-2} - \dfrac{1}{x+2}$ and $\dfrac{1}{x-3} - \dfrac{1}{x+3}$ as single fractions.

c Write $\dfrac{1}{x-n} - \dfrac{1}{x+n}$ as a single fraction.

d Find $\displaystyle\int_{11}^{12} \dfrac{20}{x^2 - 100} \, dx$ giving your answer in the form $\ln \dfrac{p}{q}$.

12 a Find the sum of the elements in each of the first four rows of Pascal's triangle.

b Find the value of $\sum_{k=0}^{10}\binom{10}{k}$.

c Suggest an expression for $\sum_{k=0}^{n}\binom{n}{k}$.

d (**HL**) Prove your conjecture for part **c**.

e Suggest an expression for $\sum_{k=0}^{n}(-1)^k\binom{n}{k}$.

f (**HL**) Prove your conjecture for part **e**.

g (**HL**) Now consider a new number triangle which is built from the top using the following rules:

- $T_{0,0}=1$ and $T_{n,0}=1$, for all $n\in\mathbb{Z}^+$

- $T_{n,n}=2^n$, for all $n\in\mathbb{Z}^+$

- $T_{n,k}=2T_{n-1,k-1}+T_{n-1,k}$ for all $n\in\mathbb{Z}^+$ and $0<k<n$

  i Write down the first five rows of this new number triangle.

  ii Suggest an expression for $\sum_{k=0}^{n}T_{nk}$.

  iii Suggest an expression for T_{nk}.

13 a Find the equation of the tangent line to the parabola $y=x^2$ at $x=1$, at $x=2$ and at $x=3$.

b Write down the equation of the tangent line to the parabola $y=x^2$ at $x=a$.

c Find the equation of the two tangent lines to the parabola $y=x^2$ with y-intercept $(0, -9)$.

d Find the equation of the two tangent lines to the parabola $y=x^2$ with x-intercept $(1, 0)$.

e Find the equation of the two tangent lines to the parabola $y=x^2$ through the point $(1, -8)$.

14 a Find the x- and y-intercepts of the tangent line to the hyperbola $y=\dfrac{1}{x}$ at $x=1$, at $x=2$ and at $x=3$.

b Write down the x- and y-intercepts of the tangent line to the hyperbola $y=\dfrac{1}{x}$ at $x=a$.

c Find the area of the triangle bounded by the x-axis, the y-axis and the tangent line to the hyperbola $y=\dfrac{1}{x}$ at the point $\left(a, \dfrac{1}{a}\right)$.

d Find the equation of the tangent line to the hyperbola $y=\dfrac{1}{x}$ with y-intercept $(0, 4)$.

e Find the equation of the two tangent lines to the hyperbola $y=\dfrac{1}{x}$ through the point $(0.6, 0.6)$.

15 a   **i** Show that the distance of the point (a, a^2) from the point $(0, 0.25)$ is the same as the distance of (a, a^2) from the line $y=-0.25$.

  ii Show that the distance of the point $(a, 2a^2)$ from the point $(0, 0.125)$ is the same as the distance of $(a, 2a^2)$ from the line $y=-0.125$.

  iii Show that the distance of the point $(a, 4a^2)$ from the point $(0, 0.0625)$ is the same as the distance of $(a, 4a^2)$ from the line $y=-0.0625$.

b Find a similar point and line for the points on the parabola $y=3x^2$.

c Suggest a similar point and line for the points on the parabola $y=kx^2$.

SL 1.3

HL 1.3

$$1$$
$$1\quad 1$$
$$1\quad 2\quad 1$$
$$1\quad 3\quad 3\quad 1$$
$$1\quad 4\quad 6\quad 4\quad 1$$
$$1\quad 5\quad 10\quad 10\quad 5\quad 1$$
$$\cdots\quad\cdots\quad\cdots\quad\cdots\quad\cdots\quad\cdots$$

$$T_{0,0}$$
$$T_{1,0}\quad T_{1,1}$$
$$T_{2,0}\quad T_{2,1}\quad T_{2,2}$$
$$T_{3,0}\quad T_{3,1}\quad T_{3,2}\quad T_{3,3}$$
$$T_{4,0}\quad T_{4,1}\quad T_{4,2}\quad T_{4,3}\quad T_{4,4}$$
$$T_{5,0}\quad T_{5,1}\quad T_{5,2}\quad T_{5,3}\quad T_{5,4}\quad T_{5,5}$$
$$\cdots\quad\cdots\quad\cdots\quad\cdots\quad\cdots\quad\cdots\quad\cdots$$

SL 2.4, 6.1

HL 6.1

SL 2.5, 6.1

HL 6.1

SL 2.4

16 (HL) Consider the following functions defined on the largest possible domain:

$$x \mapsto \cos x, \quad x \mapsto \sin x, \quad x \mapsto x^2, \quad x \mapsto x^3, \quad x \mapsto \frac{1}{x}, \quad x \mapsto \ln|x|,$$

$$x \mapsto e^{-x^2}, \quad x \mapsto \cos x^2, \quad x \mapsto \sin x^2, \quad x \mapsto 1, \quad x \mapsto 0, \quad x \mapsto e^x$$

HL 2.1, 2.4, 2.5, 3.2, 6.1, 6.5

a Which of these functions is both odd and even?

b Which of these functions is neither odd nor even?

c Which of these functions is even but not odd?

d Which of these functions is odd but not even?

e Draw a Venn diagram to illustrate your findings for parts **a–d**.

f The following statements are either true or false. State which are true and which are false. Prove the true statements. For the false statements, give a counter-example.

   i The sum of any two odd functions is an odd function.

   ii The sum of any two odd functions is an even function.

   iii The product of any two odd functions is an odd function.

   iv The product of any two odd functions is an even function.

   v The sum of any two even functions is an odd function.

   vi The sum of any two even functions is an even function.

   vii The product of any two even functions is an odd function.

   viii The product of any two even functions is an even function.

g The following statements are either true or false. State which are true and which are false. Prove the true statements. For the false statements, give a counter-example.

   i The derivative of any odd differentiable function is an odd function.

   ii The derivative of any odd differentiable function is an even function.

   iii The derivative of any even differentiable function is an odd function.

   iv The derivative of any even differentiable function is an even function.

h Without using your calculator, put these integrals in increasing order.

$$\int_{-1}^{1} \tan x \, dx \qquad \int_{-2}^{3} x^3 e^{-x^2} \, dx \qquad \int_{-3}^{2} x^2 \sin x \, dx$$

17 a Consider the parabola with equation $y = x^2 + 4x + 4$ and the line with equation $y = 4x - 1$. Let P be the point on the parabola closest to the line. At point P, the tangent to the parabola is parallel to the line.

SL 2.4, 4.4, 6.1

HL 2.6, 4.4, 6.1

   i Find the x-coordinate of P.

   ii Find the y-coordinate of P.

   iii Find the equation of the normal to the parabola at P.

   iv Find the intersection of this normal and the line $y = 4x - 1$.

   v Suggest a definition for the distance of a parabola and a line.

   vi Using your definition, find the distance of the parabola $y = x^2 + 4x + 4$ and the line $y = 4x - 1$.

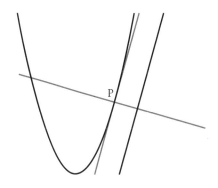

b (HL) Consider the two parabolas with equations $y = x^2 + 4x + 4$ and $y = 4x - 3 - x^2$. We are trying to find points P and Q on the parabolas such that the distance PQ is as small as possible. We say that the smallest such distance is the distance of the parabolas. The coordinates of P and Q are $(p, p^2 + 4p + 4)$ and $(q, 4q - 3 - q^2)$ for some p and q.

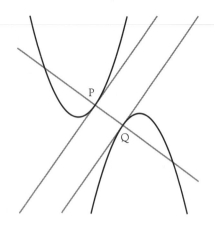

    i If PQ is the smallest distance, then Q is on the normal line to $y = x^2 + 4x + 4$ at P. Write an equation in p and q that expresses this property.

    ii If PQ is the smallest distance, then the tangent lines to the parabolas at P and at Q are parallel. Write an equation in p and q that expresses this property.

    iii You now have two equations in two unknowns. Solve the equation system to find p and q.

    iv Write down the coordinates of P and Q.

    v Find the distance of the two parabolas.

18 Consider a triangle ABC, a point O in the plane and the positive real numbers α, β and γ. Let A_1 be the point on the side BC of the triangle such that $\dfrac{A_1 B}{A_1 C} = \dfrac{\gamma}{\beta}$. Similarly, B_1 is on side AC such that $\dfrac{B_1 A}{B_1 C} = \dfrac{\gamma}{\alpha}$, and C_1 is on side AB such that $\dfrac{C_1 A}{C_1 B} = \dfrac{\beta}{\alpha}$. Let $\overrightarrow{OA} = \boldsymbol{a}$, $\overrightarrow{OB} = \boldsymbol{b}$ and $\overrightarrow{OC} = \boldsymbol{c}$.

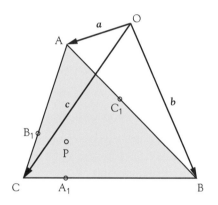

SL 4.1
HL 4.1

    a   **i** Find $\overrightarrow{AB}$ and $\overrightarrow{AC_1}$ in terms of $\boldsymbol{a}$, $\boldsymbol{b}$, α and β.

        ii Show that $\overrightarrow{OC_1} = \dfrac{\alpha \boldsymbol{a} + \beta \boldsymbol{b}}{\alpha + \beta}$.

        iii Write down similar expressions for $\overrightarrow{OA_1}$ and $\overrightarrow{OB_1}$.

    b Let P be the point inside the triangle such that $\overrightarrow{OP} = \dfrac{\alpha \boldsymbol{a} + \beta \boldsymbol{b} + \gamma \boldsymbol{c}}{\alpha + \beta + \gamma}$.

        i Find $\overrightarrow{CP}$ in terms of $\boldsymbol{a}$, $\boldsymbol{b}$, $\boldsymbol{c}$, α, β and γ.

        ii Find $\overrightarrow{CC_1}$ in terms of $\boldsymbol{a}$, $\boldsymbol{b}$, $\boldsymbol{c}$, α, β and γ.

        iii Show that $(\alpha + \beta)\overrightarrow{CC_1} = (\alpha + \beta + \gamma)\overrightarrow{CP}$.

        iv Write down similar relationships between $\overrightarrow{AA_1}$ and $\overrightarrow{AP}$, and also between $\overrightarrow{BB_1}$ and $\overrightarrow{BP}$.

        v Show that the three line segments, AA_1, BB_1 and CC_1 meet at point P.

19 (HL) Consider a triangle ABC with points P on side AC and Q on side BC such that $\dfrac{PC}{PA} = \dfrac{1}{2}$ and $\dfrac{QC}{QB} = \dfrac{1}{3}$. The intersection of AQ and BP is O. The line through C and O intersects AB at point R. Let $\boldsymbol{p} = \overrightarrow{CP}$ and $\boldsymbol{q} = \overrightarrow{CQ}$.

HL 4.1

    a Find $\overrightarrow{CA}$ in terms of $\boldsymbol{p}$ and $\overrightarrow{CB}$ in terms of $\boldsymbol{q}$.

    b Let $\dfrac{OQ}{OA} = \dfrac{3}{x}$ and $\dfrac{OP}{OB} = \dfrac{2}{y}$.

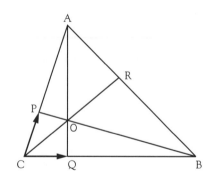

        i Find $\overrightarrow{QA}$, $\overrightarrow{QO}$ and $\overrightarrow{CO}$ in terms of $\boldsymbol{p}$, $\boldsymbol{q}$ and x.

        ii Find $\overrightarrow{PB}$, $\overrightarrow{PO}$ and $\overrightarrow{CO}$ in terms of $\boldsymbol{p}$, $\boldsymbol{q}$ and y.

        iii Show that $xy - 6x - 24 = 0$ and $xy - 6y - 18 = 0$.

        iv Find the values of x and y.

        v Show that $\overrightarrow{CO} = \dfrac{9\boldsymbol{p} + 8\boldsymbol{q}}{11}$.

    c $\overrightarrow{CR} = k\overrightarrow{CO}$ for some $k \in \mathbb{Q}$, and $a\overrightarrow{RA} = -b\overrightarrow{RB}$ for some $a, b \in \mathbb{Z}^+$.

        i Find $\overrightarrow{RA}$ and $\overrightarrow{RB}$ in terms of $\boldsymbol{p}$, $\boldsymbol{q}$ and k.

        ii Show that for $k = \dfrac{11}{5}$, $\overrightarrow{RA}$ and $\overrightarrow{RB}$ are indeed parallel.

        iii Write down possible values for a and b.

        iv Hence, show that $\dfrac{CP}{PA} \dfrac{AR}{RB} \dfrac{BQ}{QC} = 1$.

20 Consider the cubic curve with equation $f(x) = ax^3 + bx^2 + cx + d$, where $a > 0$.

SL 1.3, 2.2, 2.3, 6.3

HL 1.3, 1.9, 2.1, 2.2, 2.3, 2.5, 6.3

  a Show that there is exactly one point of inflexion on this curve. If this point is (p, q), find p and q in terms of a, b, c and d.

  b The graph of f is translated by a vector $\begin{pmatrix} -p \\ -q \end{pmatrix}$. The equation of the translated graph is $y = g(x)$ for some cubic function g.

    i Find $g(x)$ in terms of a, b, c, d and x.

    ii Show that $g(-x) = -g(x)$ for all $x \in \mathbb{R}$.

    iii (**HL**) What symmetry of the graph of g does the previous equality express?

  c **i** Show that $q - f(p - x) = f(p + x) - q$.

    ii (**HL**) The graph of f is symmetric about a point. Write down the coordinates of this point in terms of p and q.

  d **i** Show that if $b^2 - 3ac > 0$, then there is exactly one local maximum, and exactly one local minimum point on the graph of f.

    ii (**HL**) Show that if $b^2 - 3ac > 0$, then on the graph of f, the point of inflexion is the midpoint of the line segment connecting the local maximum and local minimum points.

  e (**HL**) The graph of $y = x^3 + bx^2 + cx + d$ has a local maximum at $(1, 5)$ and a local minimum at $(3, 1)$.

    i Find the coordinates of the point of inflexion of the graph.

    ii Find the values of b, c and d.

21 (**HL**) **a** Match graphs A, B, C, D and E with the functions.

HL 2.2, 2.5, 6.3

    i $x \mapsto x^2$

    ii $x \mapsto x^3 - x^2$

    iii $x \mapsto x^3$

    iv $x \mapsto x^4 - x^3$

    v $x \mapsto x^4 - 2x^3 + x^2$

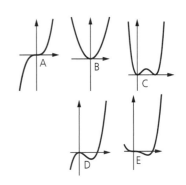

  b Suggest a polynomial function to match the following graphs.

22 Two boats (A and B) start at the same time from different locations and are sailing on straight line paths. Their positions are given by the equations

SL 1.1, 4.1, 4.3

HL 1.1, 4.1, 4.3

$r_A = \begin{pmatrix} -2 \\ 12 \end{pmatrix} + t \begin{pmatrix} 5 \\ -2 \end{pmatrix}$ and $r_B = \begin{pmatrix} 6 \\ 2 \end{pmatrix} + t \begin{pmatrix} 3 \\ 4 \end{pmatrix}$ (distances are measured in kilometres, t represents time in hours and the direction to the east is $\begin{pmatrix} 1 \\ 0 \end{pmatrix}$).

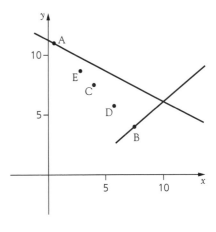

  a A third boat (C) is always halfway between boats A and B.

    i Find the position of boat C at $t = 1$, 2 and 3.

    ii Suggest an expression for the position of boat C at $t = n$.

    iii Check your expression found in part **b** for $t = 10$.

    iv Show that boat C also sails on a straight line path with constant velocity. Find an expression for r_C, the position of boat C.

    v Write down an expression for the velocity of boat C in terms of v_A and v_B, the velocity vectors of boats A and B.

b A fourth boat (D) is always halfway between boats C and B.
Write down an expression for r_D, the position of boat D.

c A fifth boat (E) is always positioned between boats A and B such that
$2AE = EB$. Show that this boat is sailing due east.

23 Consider the quadrilateral ABCD, and points $P_1, P_2, Q_1, Q_2, R_1, R_2, S_1, S_2$ on the
sides such that $AP_1 = P_1P_2 = P_2B$, $BQ_1 = Q_1Q_2 = Q_2C$, $AS_1 = S_1S_2 = S_2D$ and
$DR_1 = R_1R_2 = R_2C$. The intersection of line segments P_1R_1 and S_1Q_1 is M and
the intersection of line segments P_2R_2 and S_2Q_2 is N. Let $\overrightarrow{AP_1} = p$, $\overrightarrow{AS_1} = s$,
$\overrightarrow{BQ_1} = q$ and $\overrightarrow{DR_1} = r$.

a Show that $r - p = q - s$.

b Express $\overrightarrow{S_1Q_1}$ in terms of p and r.

c Show that $\overrightarrow{AS_1} + \dfrac{1}{3}\overrightarrow{S_1Q_1} = \overrightarrow{AP_1} + \dfrac{1}{3}\overrightarrow{P_1R_1}$.

d Show that $3S_1M = S_1Q_1$ and $3P_1M = P_1R_1$.

e Show that MN is parallel to AC.

SL 4.1

HL 4.1

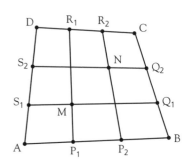

24 a Show that $x \mapsto \dfrac{x + 2}{3x - 1}$ is self-inverse.

b Find the inverse of $x \mapsto \dfrac{2x + 2}{3x - 2}$.

c The function f is defined by $f(x) = \dfrac{3x + 2}{3x - 3}$. Find $(f \circ f)(x)$.

d **i** Suggest infinitely many values for a and d such that $x \mapsto \dfrac{ax + 2}{3x + d}$
is self-inverse.

   ii Show that your suggestions are indeed self-inverse functions.

e **i** For the function defined by $f(x) = \dfrac{ax + b}{cx + d}$, $\left(c \neq 0,\ x \neq -\dfrac{d}{c}\right)$,

express $(f \circ f)(x)$ in the form $\dfrac{Ax + B}{Cx + D}$.

Find A, B, C and D in terms of a, b, c and d.

   ii Find all self-inverse functions of the form $x \mapsto \dfrac{ax + b}{cx + d}$, where $c \neq 0$.

SL 2.1, 2,5

HL 2.1, 2.4

25 Let $\tan \dfrac{x}{2} = t$.

a **i** Find an expression for $\cos^2 \dfrac{x}{2}$ in terms of t.

   ii Show that $\cos x = \dfrac{1 - t^2}{1 + t^2}$.

   iii Find an expression for $\sin x$ in terms of t.

   iv Find an expression for $\tan x$ in terms of t.

   v Check your results for $x = 240°$.

b **(HL)** In this part we assume that $0 < x < \ $.

   i Show that $\dfrac{dx}{dt} = \dfrac{2}{1 + t^2}$.

   ii Use the substitution $\tan \dfrac{x}{2} = t$ to find $\displaystyle\int \dfrac{1}{1 + \cos x}\, dx$.

   iii Find $\displaystyle\int \dfrac{1}{1 + \sin x}\, dx$.

   iv Show that $\displaystyle\int \dfrac{1}{1 + \sin x + \cos x}\, dx = \ln\left(1 + \tan \dfrac{x}{2}\right) + c$.

SL 3.2, 3.3

HL 3.2, 3.3, 6.2, 6.4, 6.7

26 In the diagram, ABCD is a rectangle, AE = 1, AÊF = 90°, 0 < BÂE = $\alpha \le 45°$ and 0 < EÂF = $\beta \le 45°$.

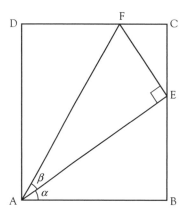

SL 3.2, 3.3

HL 3.2, 3.3

   a Express FÊC and AF̂D in terms of α and β.

   b Express AB and BE in terms of α.

   c Express FE and CE in terms of α and β.

   d Show that $FC = \tan\beta\sin\alpha$.

   e Show that $AD = (\cos\alpha - \tan\beta\sin\alpha)\tan(\alpha + \beta)$.

   f Show that $\tan(\alpha + \beta) = \dfrac{\tan\alpha + \tan\beta}{1 - \tan\alpha\tan\beta}$.

   g Show that $AD = \dfrac{\sin(\alpha + \beta)}{\cos\beta}$.

   h Show that $\sin(\alpha + \beta) = \sin\alpha\cos\beta + \cos\alpha\sin\beta$.

   i Find the exact value of sin 75°, tan 75° and cos 75°.

   j Find the exact value of sin 15°, tan 15° and cos 15°.

27 Blaise and Pierre agree on the following game. They both pay in 10 écu and then they together toss a fair coin ten times. Blaise wins all the 20 écu if five heads come first, Pierre wins all the 20 écu if five tails come first.

SL 5.5

HL 5.2

   a Is this a fair game?

   b After the first seven tosses, they recorded three heads and four tails.

     i Draw a tree diagram to illustrate the possible continuations of the game.

     ii After this start of the game, the chances of winning are changed. Find the new probabilities of winning for both Blaise and Pierre.

   c They suddenly have to finish the game after three heads and four tails. How should they divide the 20 écu they paid in originally?

28 Tom and Martin play the following game. Tom writes a different real number on each of four pieces of paper and puts them in a box. Martin picks a paper randomly from the box and keeps it or gives it to Tom. If Martin does not keep the paper, then he picks another one from the box, and again he either keeps it or gives it to Tom. If Martin keeps a paper, then they stop playing and Tom gets all the remaining papers from the box. Otherwise Martin continues to pick randomly from the box until he decides to keep the paper he just picked. At the end of the game Martin will have one paper with a number written on it and Tom will have the remaining three. Whoever has the largest number wins the game.

SL 5.5

HL 5.2

   a What is the probability of Martin winning the game if he decides to keep the first number he picked?

   b On another occasion Martin uses the following strategy. He decides in advance that he does not keep the first paper, but he looks at the number written on it. He continues to pick and keeps the first paper that has a number written on it that is bigger than the numbers he has seen already.

     i Draw a tree diagram illustrating the possible game flows. Stop a branch when it is clear who the winner is (independent of the continuation).

     ii Find the probability of Martin winning the game if he uses this strategy.

   c On yet another occasion Martin decides to use a different strategy. He now looks at his first two picks, but gives them to Tom. He then keeps the first number which is bigger than the ones he has already seen. Find the probability of Martin winning the game using this strategy.

   d What is the probability of Martin winning the game if he decides in advance not to keep any of his first three picks?

   e Suggest an optimal strategy for Martin.

29 Let the functions S_k and C_k be defined by $S_k(x) = \sin kx$ and $C_k(x) = \cos kx$.

  a Find $\int_{-\pi}^{\pi} S_k^{2}(x)\, dx$ and $\int_{-\pi}^{\pi} C_k^{2}(x)\, dx$.

  b **i** Find $\int_{-\pi}^{\pi} S_1(x)C_1(x)\, dx$ and $\int_{-\pi}^{\pi} S_2(x)C_2(x)\, dx$.

     ii Write down the value of $\int_{-\pi}^{\pi} S_k(x)C_k(x)\, dx$.

     iii **(HL)** Show that for any positive integer, $n \neq m$, $S_n C_m$ is an odd function and hence (or otherwise) find $\int_{-\pi}^{\pi} S_n(x)C_m(x)\, dx$.

  c **(HL)** **i** Show that $2\cos\alpha\cos\beta = \cos(\alpha+\beta) + \cos(\alpha-\beta)$.

     ii For positive integers, $n \neq m$, find $\int_{-\pi}^{\pi} C_n(x)C_m(x)\, dx$.

  d **(HL)** For positive integers, $n \neq m$, find $\int_{-}^{} S_n(x)S_m(x)\, dx$.

  e Find:

     i $\int_{2\pi}^{6\pi} \cos^2(3x)\, dx$

     ii **(HL)** $\int_{2}^{6} \cos(3x)\sin(5x)\, dx$

     iii **(HL)** $\int_{2\pi}^{6} \cos(3x)\cos(5x)\, dx$

     iv **(HL)** $\int_{2\pi}^{6\pi} \sin(3x)\sin(5x)\, dx$

SL 3.3, 3.4, 6.5

HL 3.3, 6.5

30 (HL) A skydiver begins his jump at a height of 4000 metres above the ground. First he falls for 60 seconds then he opens his parachute. His velocity, $v(t)$ is measured in m/s, and time is measured in seconds from the start of the jump. According to a simplified model of the jump, $\dfrac{dv}{dt} = 10 - kv$, where $k = 0.2$ for the free-fall part of the jump, and $k = 2$ when the parachute is open.

HL 6.1, 6.3, 6.4, 6.5, 6.6

  a **i** Give a reason why $0 \leq v(t) \leq 50$ during the free-fall part.

     ii State $\dfrac{dt}{dv}$ and show that the time, T, needed to reach velocity, V (where $0 < V < 50$), is $T = \int_{0}^{V} \dfrac{1}{10 - 0.2v}\, dv$.

     iii Show that $v(t) = 50(1 - e^{-0.2t})$.

  b At the time when the skydiver opens his parachute:

     i What is his velocity?

     ii How far is he from the ground?

  c **i** With the parachute open, $a < v(t) \leq b$. State the value of b and the largest possible a.

     ii Show that the time, T, needed from the point when the parachute is opened to reach velocity, V (where $a < V < b$), is $T = \int_{V}^{b} \dfrac{1}{2v - 10}\, dv$.

     iii Find $v(t)$ for the part where the parachute is open.

  d How long does it take for the skydiver to reach the ground?

  e What is the speed of the skydiver when he reaches the ground?

1 Do you understand the definition of these sequences?

  a Use u_1 to find u_2, then u_2 to find u_3, ...

  b Use the values of u_1 and u_2.

  c Use the result from part **b**.

  d Simply calculate these values.

  e Compare the two sequences.

  f Apply the steps of an inductive proof.

2 A question combining calculus with sequences.

  a Use the chain rule.

  b Can you see the pattern?

  c You need to use cases depending on the remainder of n when it is divided by 4.

  d Apply the steps of an inductive proof.

3 ω is a third root of unity.

  a Factorise $\omega^3 - 1$.

  b Use the result from part **a**.

  c A simplified expression from part **b** gives z.

   y and x can be found similarly.

  d Use row reduction and the result from part **a**.

4 z_1, z_2, z_3, z_4 and z_5 are the fifth roots of unity.

  a Use the Vieta formula.

  b Use the Cartesian form, $w = a + bi$.

  c Use part **b** to expand and use parts **a** and **b** to simplify.

  d Notice the connection to part **c**.

5 Simultaneous linear equations in three unknowns.

  a **i** Eliminate c using two of the given equations.

   ii Use the previous part.

   iii Use the previous parts.

  b Set up equations that express that the parabola goes through the given points.

  c For any t, there is a curve in the form $y = ax^2 + bx + c$ passing through these points. Think about how it can be that this is not a parabola.

6 Can you find the general term of the sequence in part **b** without the help in parts **a** and **c**?

  a **i** Eliminate c using two of the given equations.

   ii Use the previous part.

   iii Use the previous parts.

  b **i** Is the difference common?

   ii Is the ratio common?

c i Substitute $n = 1, 2, 3$ in the formula.

   ii Solve the equation system you got in the previous part.

   iii Substitution again.

7 Cubic curve with specified properties.

   a Use the rules of differentiation.

   b Substitute $x = 0, 1$ in the formulae.

   c At local maximum and minimum the derivative is 0. Set up and solve an equation system in the four unknowns.

8 What does continuity and differentiability mean for a piecewise defined function?

   a Connect the points $(0, f(0))$ and $(1, f(1))$ with a straight line.

   b Can the gradient of a quadratic match the gradient at both endpoints of $[0, 1]$?

   c There are different possibilities here. A cubic polynomial or a trigonometric curve are the simplest to find.

   d A proof here needs to use the limit definition of continuity and the derivative. Consider left and right limits.

9 Part **c** gives a way of using parameters to find the equations of all the (infinitely many) planes containing a given line.

   a Use the dot product.

   b Either substitute the coordinates of the points in the given equations, or check the normal vectors of the given planes and use part **a**.

   c i Rearrange the equation.

    ii Substitute the coordinates of both A and P in the equation.

   d Use part **c** and search for good M and N values. There are infinitely many possibilities; any of these will lead to a solution.

   e Use part **c** and search for M and N for which the normal vector of the plane is perpendicular to $\overrightarrow{BC}$.

10 The functional equation is similar to the index law $z^{x+y} = z^x z^y$.

   a Use $f(1) = 6$ and pick appropriate x- and y-values to substitute in the functional equation formula. For example choosing $x = 1$ and $y = 1$ gives $f(2)$, or choosing $x = y = \frac{1}{2}$ will lead to an equation for $f(\frac{1}{2})$.

   b The values for f at $x = 0, 1, 2, 3$ should give a hint. Check your formula with the other values.

   c Check that $f(1) = 6$ and write an equality chain $f(x + y) = \cdots = \dfrac{f(x)f(y)}{3}$.

   d Generalise your result from the previous parts. You may need to express $g(2), g(3), \ldots$

   e Use the method of part **c**, this time with parameters.

11 Integrating a quotient with a quadratic denominator sometimes involves rewriting the quotient as the sum or difference of two simpler fractions.

   a Use $(x - 1)(x + 1)$ as the common denominator.

   b Similar to part **a**.

   c Generalise from the previous parts.

   d Use the previous part for $n = 10$ and integrate the two simpler fractions.

12 This question generalises a well-known property of Pascal's triangle.

  a Add the numbers carefully.

  b Following the pattern from part **a** is not enough here; you need to calculate all terms involved either using a calculator or by writing Pascal's triangle up to the appropriate row.

  c This is the part where you can write down an expression that is consistent with the pattern in parts **a** and **b**.

  d This can be proved by induction or using the binomial theorem, expanding $(1+1)^n$.

  e Find the values for $n = 1, 2, 3, \ldots$ and generalise.

  f Use the binomial theorem.

  g Build this number triangle from the top using the construction rules given. For suggesting an expression, find the values for $n = 1, 2, 3, 4, 5, \ldots$ and look for a pattern.

13 In parts **c**, **d** and **e** the question asks you to find the tangent lines to a parabola from points not on the curve.

  a Use differentiation to find the gradient.

  b Use the pattern from part **a**.

  c Use the result from part **b** and find the line that goes through the given point.

  d Again, use the general form of the tangent line from part **b**.

  e Again, use the general form of the tangent line from part **b**.

14 Part **c** is an interesting result about hyperbolas and their tangents and asymptotes.

  a Use differentiation to find the gradient first.

  b Use the pattern from part **a**.

  c These are right-angled triangles.

  d Use part **c** to find the x-intercept first.

  e Use the general equation of the tangent line from part **b**.

15 This question investigates a geometric property of parabolas.

  a The distance of a point from a horizontal line is measured vertically.

  b It is not enough to write down the result following the pattern from part **a**; you also need to do the calculation to show that your value is correct.

  c No proof is needed here, just a formula that is consistent with the pattern from parts **a** and **b**.

16 Do you understand the symmetries of the graphs of odd and even functions?

  a There is only one function that is both odd and even.

  b Only one of the listed functions has a graph with no symmetry.

  c Which function satisfies $f(-x) = f(x)$?

  d Which function satisfies $f(-x) = -f(x)$?

  e Summarise the results of parts **a**–**d**.

  f For counter-examples, search among the simple power functions, $x \mapsto x^k$. For proof, write an equality chain. For example, to show that the sum of odd functions is odd, you need a line like $(f + g)(-x) = \cdots = -(f + g)(x)$.

g For counter-examples, search among the simple power functions, $x \mapsto x^k$. For proof, write an equality chain going back to the limit definition of differentiation. To have a feeling for which of the statements is true, draw an odd and an even graph and compare the gradient of the tangent line at $x = a$ and $x = -a$.

h All of these are integrals of odd functions. Use the symmetries of the graphs of odd functions to decide which of these integrals is positive, which one is negative and which one is 0.

17 How would you define the distance of two curves in the plane?

a i Use differentiation and compare gradients.

ii Use the x-coordinate found in part **a i**.

iii The tangent is perpendicular to the normal.

iv Solve the equation system that describes the two lines.

v Can you formulate a definition that is general enough to use for all lines and parabolas? Try to concentrate on stating what the distance is, rather than describing how to find it.

vi Use your definition. You will probably also need the results from the previous parts.

b i Express the gradient of PQ and also the gradient of the normal line at P.

ii Express the gradients of the tangents at P and at Q.

iii This is not a linear system, but you should get a cubic equation in either p or q. This cubic can be factorised as a product of a linear and a quadratic factor with integer coefficients.

iv Use the values you found in the previous part.

v Find the distance of P and Q.

18 Do you remember how to add vectors? For any three points, $\overrightarrow{XY} = \overrightarrow{XZ} + \overrightarrow{ZY}$.

To express $\overrightarrow{XY}$ in terms of given vectors, look for an appropriate Z.

a Parallel vectors are constant multiples of each other.

b To answer the last part, think about what part **iii** tells you about the position of C, C_1 and P.

19 This question is similar to the previous one.

a Parallel vectors are constant multiples of each other.

b i Use vectors $\overrightarrow{CQ}$ and $\overrightarrow{CA}$.

ii Use vectors $\overrightarrow{CP}$ and $\overrightarrow{CB}$.

iii Compare the two expressions you got in the previous two parts for the same vector, $\overrightarrow{CO}$.

iv Solve the equation system from the previous part.

v Substitute your x- or y-value into the expression from part **i** or **ii**.

c i $\overrightarrow{RA} = \overrightarrow{RC} + \overrightarrow{CA}$

ii Parallel vectors are constant multiples of each other.

iii a and b specify the ratio of the length of the vectors.

iv Use a and b to express $\dfrac{\text{AR}}{\text{RB}}$.

20 This question explores the symmetry of a cubic curve.

   a Differentiate f twice.

   b This translation moves the point of inflexion to the origin.

      i $g(x) = f(x + p) - q$

      ii Your previous answer should have neither a quadratic term nor a constant term. If it does, go back and check your calculation.

      iii Think of the symmetry of the graph of an odd function.

   c **i** The right-hand side is $g(x)$.

      ii The graph of f is the translation of the graph of g.

   d **i** Use the derivative and think of the second derivative test.

      ii Think of the symmetry you found earlier.

   e **i** Use the previous part.

      ii Set up an equation system.

21 For a polynomial graph, multiple roots imply horizontal tangent lines at the x-intercept.

   a Factorise the polynomials.

   b Look for a possible expression in factor form.

22 Do you know how to interpret the vectors in the equations describing motion?

   a **i** Use the midpoint formula.

      ii Can you see the pattern from the previous part?

      iii Find the position of boats A, B and C as in part **i**, and see if your formula from part **ii** gives the same position for $t = 10$.

      iv Using part **ii** is not enough here, since that position is only a conjecture from the previous pattern. Instead, use $r_C = \frac{1}{2}(r_A + r_B)$.

      v Look for the velocity, v_C in the form $av_A + bv_B$ for some real numbers, a and b.

   b Use the result and method from part **a iv**.

   c Find the position, r_E, and interpret the result.

23 You will need to carefully manipulate expressions involving vectors.

   a $\overrightarrow{AB} + \overrightarrow{BC} + \overrightarrow{CD} + \overrightarrow{DA} = 0$

   b Write the path from S_1 to Q_1 through A and B as a vector sum.

   c Write both the left-hand side and right-hand side in terms of p, q, r and s and use part **a**.

   d If $\overrightarrow{AX}$ is the vector of the left-hand side of the equality in the previous part, then where is the endpoint, X?

   e The previous part gives you $\overrightarrow{AM}$. Similar method gives $\overrightarrow{AN}$. Use these to express $\overrightarrow{MN}$ in terms of p, q, r and s.

24 This question investigates self-inverse rational functions.

   a Think of asymptotes and the transformation needed to get the graph of the inverse from the graph of a function.

   b Use the usual method.

   c Use the definition and simplify the result.

d i Can you see the pattern in the previous parts?

  ii Use any of the methods from parts **a, b** or **c**.

e i Use the definition and work carefully.

  ii What are the conditions on A, B, C and D so that $(f \circ f)(x) = x$ for all x?

25 This question involves unusual substitution to find integrals involving trigonometric functions.

a i Use the Pythagorean identity involving tangent.

  ii Use the double angle formula for cosine.

  iii Start with the double angle formula for sine.

  iv Either the double angle formula for tangent, or the results from the previous two parts should help.

  v No hint here.

b i Either find $\dfrac{dt}{dx}$ and take the reciprocal, or express x in terms of t first.

  ii After the substitution, simplify the quotient.

  iii Use the same substitution.

  iv Either use the same substitution again or, since the integral is given, checking the result using differentiation is also a good approach.

26 This question leads to the proof of the compound angle formulae for small angles.

a Use the right angles at B, E and D.

b ABE is a right-angled triangle.

c Use the appropriate trigonometric ratios in triangles AEF and ECF.

d Use the same triangles as for part **c**.

e $DF = AB - FC$

f $AD = BE + EC$

g Find AF first.

h $AD = BE + EC$

i Choose appropriate α and β values.

j $15 + 75 = 90$

27 Can you answer part **c** without working out part **b**?

a Think of the symmetry in the description of the game.

b i Think of the possibilities. For example, what happens if the next toss is tails?

  ii Use the tree diagram.

c To be fair, whoever has more chance of winning should get more money.

28 Do you understand the rules of the game?

a What is the chance of picking the largest number at the first pick?

b Do you understand this strategy?

  i Use some symbols to denote the numbers, say $t_1 < t_2 < t_3 < t_4$. Think of what can happen. For example, the first pick can be any of these four numbers with equal probability.

  ii Use the tree diagram.

c Draw a tree, branching first according to the possible first two numbers.

d How many ways can the largest number not be among the first three?

e How would you play if you were Martin? Are there any other meaningful strategies besides the ones mentioned in the previous parts?

29 Definite integrals involving products of trigonometric functions.

   a Express $\sin^2 kx$ in terms of $\cos 2kx$.

   b **i** Use $\sin 2\theta = 2\sin\theta\cos\theta$.

     ii Can you see the pattern in part **i**?

     iii Use the symmetries of odd functions.

   c **i** Use the compound angle identities.

     ii Use part **i**.

   d Find an identity for $2\sin\alpha\sin\beta$.

   e Use the previous parts and the periodicity of the trigonometric functions.

30 This is a kinematics problem, where the acceleration is given as a function of the velocity rather than time.

   a **i** Investigate the sign of $\dfrac{\mathrm{d}v}{\mathrm{d}t}$ for different values of v.

     ii $\dfrac{\mathrm{d}t}{\mathrm{d}v}$ is the reciprocal of $\dfrac{\mathrm{d}v}{\mathrm{d}t}$; t is one of the antiderivatives of $\dfrac{\mathrm{d}t}{\mathrm{d}v}$.

     iii Evaluate the integral in the previous part and solve it for V.

   b Use the formula from part **a iii**.

   c Use similar methods to part **a**. A little care is needed however, because for $v > 5$, $10 - 2v$ is negative, so $\displaystyle\int \frac{1}{10 - 2v}\,\mathrm{d}v$ is not $\ln(10 - 2v)$, rather it is $\ln(2v - 10)$.

   d Use the distance travelled formula and the result from part **c iii**.

   e Use the result from part **d** and the formula from part **c iii**.

Further investigation ideas

The numbering of the ideas in this chapter corresponds to the numbering of the Practice questions. These are not problems that would appear on exams, rather some open-ended questions related to the exercises. Answers are deliberately not given, because these are not problems to solve, rather ideas to think about.

1 In this question we came up with the formulae $\sum_{k=1}^{n} k = \frac{1}{2}n^2 + \frac{1}{2}n$ and

$\sum_{k=1}^{n} k^3 = \frac{1}{4}n^4 + \frac{1}{2}n^3 + \frac{1}{4}n^2.$

   ■ Can you show that $\sum_{k=1}^{n} k^2 = \frac{1}{3}n^3 + \frac{1}{2}n^2 + \frac{1}{6}n$?

   ■ Can you see a pattern in these formulae?

   ■ Can you find a formula for $\sum_{k=1}^{n} k^4$?

   ■ Can you generalise your work to suggest a method to find formulae for

     $\sum_{k=1}^{n} k^p$ for natural numbers $p \geq 5$?

2 The statements in this question rely on the fact that for $g(x) = \sin x$ and for $g(x) = \cos x$, $g^{(4)}(x) = g(x)$.

   ■ You already know a function for which $g'(x) = g(x)$ for all $x \in \mathbb{R}$. Can you find all such functions?

   ■ Can you think of a function with property $g''(x) = g(x)$ for all $x \in \mathbb{R}$ (but $g'(x) \neq g(x)$ for at least one x)?

   ■ It is more tricky to find a function with property $g'''(x) = g(x)$ for all $x \in \mathbb{R}$ (but $g'(x) \neq g(x)$ for at least one x). Try to find a function like this, or use technology to help your search.

   ■ What about higher order derivatives?

   ■ If $g''(x) = g(x)$ and $g'''(x) = g(x)$, then it is not difficult to show that $g'(x) = g(x)$.

     □ Is the same conclusion true if $g^{(n)}(x) = g(x)$ and $g^{(m)}(x) = g(x)$?

     □ If not, then can you find n and m for which it is not true, and can you find a condition on n and m under which the conclusion is true?

3 It was not asked in the question, but the relationship $\omega^2 = -1 - \omega$ can be used to express ω^n in the form $p_n + q_n \omega$, where p_n and q_n are real numbers.

   ■ Can you find p_n and q_n?

   ■ In fact, if ω is a complex or real number and $\omega^2 = P + Q\omega$, then ω^n can still be expressed in the form $p_n + q_n \omega$, where p_n and q_n are expressions in P and Q.

     □ Investigate this for different P and Q values.

     □ Find a recursive formula for p_n and q_n.

     □ The closed form for p_n and q_n can be found using linear recursion. This topic is covered in the discrete mathematics option of the HL syllabus.

4 This question is based on an older HL internal assessment task, 'Patterns from complex numbers'. There are other areas of elementary geometry where an approach using complex numbers can be useful. Multiplication by a complex number corresponds to enlargement and rotation on the complex plane. This can be used, for example, to solve the following problems (and many more).

- Let ABC be a triangle and O_C, O_A and O_B be the centres of the equilateral triangles ABC_1, BCA_1 and CBA_1 respectively. Then $O_AO_BO_C$ is an equilateral triangle.

- Let ABCD be a quadrilateral, and O_1, O_2, O_3, O_4 the centres of the squares drawn above the sides AB, BC, CD and DA respectively. Then O_1O_3 is perpendicular to O_2O_4, and these two line segments have equal lengths.

- If $A_1 A_2 A_3 A_4 A_5 A_6 A_7$ is a regular polygon with seven vertices, then
$$\frac{1}{A_1A_2} = \frac{1}{A_1A_3} + \frac{1}{A_1A_4}.$$

- If A, $i=1,\ldots,15$ are vertices of a regular polygon with fifteen sides, then
$$\frac{1}{A_1A_2} = \frac{1}{A_1A_3} + \frac{1}{A_1A_5} + \frac{1}{A_1A_8}.$$

5　The choice of points in part **b** was not important. For any three points (x_1, y_1), (x_2, y_2), (x_3, y_3), if x_1, x_2 and x_3 are all different, then there is a unique function in the form $f: x \mapsto ax^2 + bx + c$, such that $f(x_1) = y_1$, $f(x_2) = y_2$ and $f(x_3) = y_3$.

- You can experiment with different points. Set up an equation system like the one in the question and investigate the number of solutions.

- Can you prove that the solution is unique for any three points?

  □ It can be done using row reduction, which is part of the HL syllabus.

  □ The calculation is simpler if you use matrices. The study of matrices is no longer in the core syllabus; it is now part of the linear algebra topic of the further mathematics syllabus.

- Can you generalise from three to four or more points?

  □ Can you find four points where there is no parabola going through all of these?

  □ What type of curve do we need in order to go through four points?

  □ Pick four points and find a curve passing through all of them.

  □ Can you prove that there is always a unique cubic curve through four points with different x-coordinates?

6　The difference sequence of the sequence in part **b** is $-1, 3, 7, 11, \ldots$

The difference sequence of this difference sequence is $4, 4, 4, \ldots$

- It is generally true that if the second difference sequence is constant, then the general term of the original sequence is of the form $u_n = an^2 + bn + c$.

  □ Can you find examples to this claim other than the one in the question?

  □ Given u_1 and u_2 (the first two terms of the sequence) and $d, d, d, \ldots$ the constant second difference sequence, can you find u_3, u_4 and the general term u_n?

- The converse of the previous claim is also true. If the general term is of the form $u_n = an^2 + bn + c$, then the second difference sequence is constant.

  □ Check this claim with different values of a, b and c.

  □ Express $u_{n+1} - u_n$, the nth term of the difference sequence, in terms of a, b, c and n.

  □ Can you find the nth term of the second difference sequence? Does it depend on n?

- Can you generalise? What happens if the third, fourth, etc. difference sequence is constant?

7 In this question, we had to find a cubic polynomial function with given value and gradient 0 at $x = 0$ and $x = 1$.

- Was it important that the gradient is 0? Was it important that the values were given at $x = 1$ and $x = 0$? These values made the calculation easy, but do we always get a unique cubic polynomial function if we specify the value and gradient for two different x-values?

- In the question, four conditions were given (the values of $g(0)$, $g(1)$, $g'(0)$, $g'(1)$) that translated to four equations in the four unknowns. Can these conditions be changed to four other conditions so that the resulting equation system has a unique solution? For example,

  ☐ the value of the polynomial at four different x-values

  ☐ the value of the polynomial at three different x-values, and the gradient at another x-value

  ☐ the value of the polynomial at two different x-values, and the gradient at another two x-values

  ☐ the value of the polynomial for an x-value, and the gradient at another three x-values

  ☐ the gradient at four different x-values.

- If more conditions need to be satisfied, then can it always be done with a cubic polynomial, or do we need higher order polynomials? For example, if we are looking for a function when the values are known for several different x-values, what strategy can be used?

  ☐ We can look for higher order polynomials.

  ☐ We can look at piecewise defined functions, where the pieces are lower order polynomials.

  ☐ We can look at lower order polynomials that may not match the values exactly, but are close enough for practical purposes.

8 This question is related to the last investigation idea for question **7**.

- Suppose we have some points on the plane, (x_1, y_1), (x_2, y_2), ..., such that $x_1 < x_2 < ...$ The goal is to find a function such that $f(x_i) = y_i$.

- Pick four points to start with and find the cubic polynomial that goes through these four points. Use technology to experiment with the shape of the curve when the positions of the points change.

- Add a fifth point and try to find a cubic polynomial that goes through all the points. In most cases you will not succeed. Either you need a higher order polynomial or a piecewise defined function.

- To find a piecewise defined function, you can simply find the linear functions connecting (x_1, y_1) to (x_2, y_2), and so on, but this will not give a nice graph.

- It looks better if the curves defined on different intervals join 'smoothly'.

  ☐ Try to use quadratic curves on intervals $[x_1, x_2]$, $[x_2, x_3]$, ... Can you find curves that join smoothly at the endpoints?

  ☐ Modifying the result of the exercise, you can find cubic curves with given values at the endpoints of the intervals, and with 0 derivatives at the endpoints. If you put these curves together, you will get a smooth curve passing through all the points, but the resulting graph will still not look nice.

  ☐ Can you see the problem with the previous approach? Can you suggest a way to improve on the construction of the function?

- You can also investigate how to find curves through given points on the plane, when the x-coordinates are not in increasing order.

  ☐ Can you think of a way to deal with this more general situation?

  ☐ If you want to do some research, you can look for the key words 'parametric curves' or 'Bézier curves'.

9 In linear algebra, an expression of the form $M\boldsymbol{v} + N\boldsymbol{w}$ (where M and N are real numbers) is called the linear combination of vectors $\boldsymbol{v}$ and $\boldsymbol{w}$. In part **c** of this question we can view the plane constructed as $M\Pi_2 + N\Pi_1$, the 'linear combination' of planes Π_1 and Π_2 (even though planes are not vectors). In part **c** we showed that all planes of this form pass through P and A.

- Can you show the converse of the claim in part **c**? In other words, can you show that all the planes passing through P and A are of the form $M\Pi_2 + N\Pi_1$?

- Which planes correspond to positive M and N values?

- Can you suggest a meaningful way of defining 'linear combination' of lines in 2D or 3D?

10 This question is related to the general concept of functional equations when a function is given by its properties, rather than a formula. It was not asked in the question, but in fact the answer for part **b** is the only continuous function satisfying the conditions of the question. There are different ways of doing further investigation in this area.

- We can start with a function.

  □ For example, if a function is defined by $f(x) = e^x$, then one of the index laws tells us that $f(x+y) = f(x)f(y)$. Can you find other functions satisfying this functional equation?

  □ Can you find a functional equation satisfied by $f : x \mapsto \ln x$? Can you find other functions satisfying the same functional equation?

  □ Can you show that for $l : x \mapsto \ln\left(1 + \dfrac{1}{x}\right)$, $l(x) = l(2x+1) + l(2x)$?

  □ Can you show that for $L : x \mapsto x \ln x$, $L(xy) = xL(y) + yL(x)$?

  □ Can you show that for $t : x \mapsto \tan^{-1}\left(\dfrac{1}{x}\right)$, $t(x) = t(x+1) + t(x^2 + x + 1)$?

- We can start with an equation.

  □ Can you find functions satisfying the following equations? All of these look similar to the ones mentioned before. In some of these you may need to restrict the set of possible x- and y-values.

  - $f(x+y) = f(x) + f(y)$

  - $f(xy) = f(x)f(y)$

  - $f(xy) = f(x) + f(y)$

  □ What happens if you modify these a bit?

  □ Here are some other equations. Can you find a function satisfying these?

  - $f(x+y) + f(x-y) = 2f(x)f(y)$
  - $f(x+y) = \dfrac{f(x)f(y)}{f(x) + f(y)}$
  - $f(x+y) = f(x) + f(y) + f(x)f(y)$
  - $f(xy) = f(x)f(y) - f(x+y) + 1$

11 In part **a** of this question we wrote $\dfrac{2}{x^2 - 1}$ as a difference of two fractions with simpler denominators as $\dfrac{1}{x-1} - \dfrac{1}{x+1}$. This is called the partial fraction decomposition of $\dfrac{2}{x^2 - 1}$. The study of partial fractions used to be part of the HL syllabus, so you may find older past paper exercises that use this technique.

- If you can answer the following questions, then you are on a right track to discover a general statement about partial fraction decomposition.
  - ☐ Can you write $\dfrac{1}{(x+1)(2x-3)}$ in the form $\dfrac{A}{x+1}+\dfrac{B}{2x-3}$?

    How about $\dfrac{4x+5}{(x+1)(2x-3)}$ or $\dfrac{x^3-x^2+1}{(x+1)(2x-3)}$?
  - ☐ Can you write $\dfrac{1}{x^2+1}$ as a sum or difference of two fractions with simpler

    denominators? What is the difference between $\dfrac{1}{x^2+1}$ and $\dfrac{1}{x^2-1}$?
  - ☐ Can you write $\dfrac{1}{(x-1)^2}$ as a sum or difference of two fractions with simpler

    denominators? What is the difference between $\dfrac{1}{(x-1)^2}$ and $\dfrac{1}{x^2-1}$?
  - ☐ Can you write $\dfrac{1}{(x+1)^2(2x-3)}$ as a sum of fractions with simpler

    denominators? How many fractions do you need and what are the denominators? Using the partial fraction decomposition, can you integrate this expression?

- Partial fraction decomposition can also be useful for simplifying certain sums.
  - ☐ Can you show that $\displaystyle\sum_{k=2}^{n}\dfrac{1}{k^2-1}=\dfrac{3n^2-n-2}{4n^2+4n}$?
  - ☐ Can you give a meaning and find the infinite sum $\displaystyle\sum_{k=2}^{\infty}\dfrac{1}{k^2-1}$?
  - ☐ Can you give a meaning and find the infinite sum $\displaystyle\sum_{k=2}^{\infty}\dfrac{1}{k^3-k}$?

12 The generating rule of Pascal's triangle is simply adding the two numbers above a certain position in the triangle.

- There are several ways of modifying this generating rule. One was mentioned in the question. Here are some other possibilities. Can you find the sum of the numbers in the rows of these new triangles? You can also try to think of other ways of modifying the generating rule.
  - ☐ In the question, a number was the weighted sum of the numbers above it. What happens if the weight changes, for example the recursive rule of the question changes to $T_{n,k}=3T_{n-1,k-1}+2T_{n-1,k}$ or $T_{n,k}=2T_{n-1,k-1}-T_{n-1,k}$? Of course the numbers on the borders of the triangle needs to be changed accordingly. Can you build a triangle following the general rule $T_{n,k}=AT_{n-1,k-1}+BT_{n-1,k}$?

  - ☐ We can add more than two numbers, for example, three or four:

			1										1					
		1	1	1							1	1	1	1				
	1	2	3	2	1					1	2	3	4	3	2	1		
1	3	6	7	6	3	1		1	3	6	10	12	12	10	6	3	1	

    ... ...

  - ☐ We can add two numbers, but change the numbers on the border:

		1					1					a		
	1		2			1		-1			a		b	
1		3		2	1		0		-1	a		...		b
1	4		5	2	1	1	-1		-1	a		...	...	b

    ... ...

- Can you suggest a way to build Pascal's pyramid, a 3D version of Pascal's triangle, and find some interesting properties of it?

13 In part **e** of this question we found the tangents to the parabola with equation $y = x^2$ from a point not on the graph. Can you think of a way of finding the tangents to a general parabola $y = ax^2 + bx + c$ from a general point (x_0, y_0)?

■ First look at the case when the point (x_0, y_0) is on the graph.

    ☐ Start with some numerical examples, for example, using $y = 3x^2 - 2x + 5$ and several points on the graph, for example, (0, 5), (1, 6), ... In general, find the equation of the tangent at the point (x_0, y_0) on the graph.

    ☐ After some more numerical examples, you can try to write up the equation of the tangent line to $y = ax^2 + bx + c$ at the point (x_0, y_0) on the graph.

    ☐ If your calculation is correct, you should get an equation equivalent to $\dfrac{y + y_0}{2} = axx_0 + b\dfrac{x + x_0}{2} + c$. If you did not succeed, can you prove that this line is indeed a tangent to $y = ax^2 + bx + c$ if the point (x_0, y_0) is on the graph?

■ Now turn to the case when (x_0, y_0) is not on the parabola.

    ☐ Use technology (for example Geogebra) to investigate the relationship between the parabola $y = ax^2 + bx + c$, the point (x_0, y_0) and the line $\dfrac{y + y_0}{2} = axx_0 + b\dfrac{x + x_0}{2} + c$.
Investigate different parabolas and several points.

        • In some cases the line intersects the parabola, in some cases it does not. When does the line intersect the curve? Can you formulate a conjecture?

        • In the case where the line intersects the parabola, connect the intersection points with (x_0, y_0). Do you notice something interesting?

        • Can you prove what you have noticed during your investigation?

14 Part **c** of this question asks about an interesting property of the graph of $y = \dfrac{1}{x}$.

The area of the triangle bounded by the coordinate axes and the tangent line to this hyperbola is independent of the tangent line. Can you find other graphs with this property?

■ In particular, is there a differentiable function f, other than $x \mapsto \dfrac{1}{x}$, defined for all positive real numbers, such that the area of the triangle bounded by any tangent line to the graph of f and the coordinate axes is 2?

    ☐ One way of looking for an answer to this question is to translate the area condition to an equation to solve:

        • find the equation of the tangent line to f at the point $(x_0, f(x_0))$, using the slope $f'(x_0)$

        • express the x- and y-intercepts of this tangent line in terms of x_0, $f(x_0)$ and $f'(x_0)$

        • express the area of the triangle bounded by the tangent and the coordinate axes in terms of x_0, $f(x_0)$ and $f'(x_0)$

        • use this expression to set up a differential equation that the function defined by $y = f(x)$ needs to satisfy. If your calculations are correct, this equation is equivalent to $2xy - \dfrac{y^2}{y'} - x^2 y' = 4$. If you have access to computer algebra systems that can solve differential equations, you can try to solve this equation. Can you interpret the solutions you get?

■ What happens if you change the area to another value? Can you guess a solution without setting up a new differential equation?

Part **e** of this question leads to an investigation similar to finding tangents to parabolas (see the previous question).

- After investigating numerical examples, can you find the equation of the tangent line to $y = \dfrac{1}{x}$ at the point (x_0, y_0) on the graph? Did you get $\dfrac{x_0 y + x y_0}{2} = 1$ (or an equivalent form)?

- As with the previous investigation with parabolas, use technology to experiment with what happens if the point (x_0, y_0) is not on the hyperbola. When does the line $\dfrac{x_0 y + x y_0}{2} = 1$ intersect the hyperbola $y = \dfrac{1}{x}$? If there are intersection points, connect them to (x_0, y_0). What do you notice? Can you prove your conjecture?

- In the case of the parabola $y = ax^2 + bx + c$, we got the equation of the tangent line at the point (x_0, y_0) on the graph by replacing y with $\dfrac{y + y_0}{2}$, x with $\dfrac{x + x_0}{2}$ and x^2 with xx_0. In the case of the hyperbola $y = \dfrac{1}{x}$, we get the equation of the tangent line by first rewriting the equation of the hyperbola as $xy = 1$, then replacing xy with $\dfrac{x_0 y + x y_0}{2}$.
  - ☐ Can you generalise to suggest the equation of the tangent line to the hyperbola $y = \dfrac{ax + b}{cx + d}$ at the point (x_0, y_0)?
  - ☐ Check your suggestion using technology.
  - ☐ Investigate what happens when the point is not on the hyperbola.

- A common generalisation of the parabola in the previous example, and of the hyperbola in this example, is the quadratic curve $Ax^2 + By^2 + Cxy + Dx + Ey + F = 0$.
  - ☐ Investigate the shape of this curve with the use of technology. Investigate what happens if any of the parameters are 0.
  - ☐ Can you generalise from the previous examples to suggest the equation of the tangent line to this curve at the point (x_0, y_0) on the curve?
  - ☐ Can you prove your suggestion?
  - ☐ Investigate what happens to the curve and the line if the point is not on the curve. When do they intersect? What is the special property of the lines when you connect the intersection points to (x_0, y_0)?

15 Let $d(P, Q)$ denote the distance between points P and Q, and let $d(P, l)$ denote the distance of the point P from the line l. In this question we have seen that the locus of the points $P(x, y)$ with the property that $d(P, F) = d(P, l)$ (where $F\left(0, \dfrac{1}{4}\right)$ is a point on the y-axis, and l is the line with equation $y = -\dfrac{1}{4}$) is the parabola $y = x^2$.

- Change the position of the point F and the line l (for example to $(3, 4)$ and $2x + y = 2$, or any other point and line) and use technology to investigate the locus. Can you find the equation of this curve? It will not be a graph of a function; you will need an implicit equation.

- Can you find the equation for a general point and line?

- Go back to the original point and line and investigate the locus if the condition is changed to:
  - ☐ $d(P, F) = 2d(P, l)$
  - ☐ $2d(P, F) = d(P, l)$
  - ☐ $d(P, F) = kd(P, l)$

for different positive k-values.
  - ☐ Can you find the equation of the curve for a general point and line for any k-value?

16 Not every function is even or odd. However, here is an interesting fact about even and odd functions:

- Any function defined on a symmetric interval $[-a, a]$ can be uniquely written as a sum of an even and an odd function. Can you prove this?

The following set of polynomials (the Legandre polynomials) have several interesting properties, some of which are related to symmetries:

- Let $Q_n(x) = \dfrac{1}{2^n n!} \dfrac{d^n}{dx^n}(x^2 - 1)^n$ (the nth derivative of $(x^2 - 1)^n$).

  ☐ What is the order of $Q_n(x)$?

  ☐ Can you show that for odd n, $Q_n(x)$ is odd, and for even n, $Q_n(x)$ is even?

  ☐ Can you find $Q_1(x), Q_2(x), Q_3(x), ...$, the first few of these polynomials? You can calculate a few by hand, but for larger values of n use technology. Computer algebra systems can find derivatives of functions.

  ☐ Find $\int_{-1}^{1} Q_1(x)Q_2(x)\,dx$, $\int_{-1}^{1} Q_1(x)Q_3(x)\,dx$, $\int_{-1}^{1} Q_2(x)Q_3(x)\,dx$.

    • Can you formulate a conjecture?

    • Check your conjecture on integrals involving $Q_n(x)$ for larger n values. Use technology.

    • It is not easy but, by using integration by parts, you can prove your conjecture. Try it!

- We define the polynomials, $P_n(x)$, recursively as follows: Let $P_0(x) = 1$ and $P_1(x) = x$, and for $n > 1$ the following relationship holds: $(n+1)P_{n+1}(x) = (2n+1)xP_n(x) - nP_{n-1}(x)$.

  ☐ What is the order of $P_n(x)$?

  ☐ Can you show that for odd n, $P_n(x)$ is odd, and for even n, $P_n(x)$ is even?

  ☐ Can you find $P_1(x), P_2(x), P_3(x), ...$, the first few of these polynomials? You can calculate a few by hand, but for larger values of n use technology.

  ☐ Did you notice the connection between $Q_n(x)$ and $P_n(x)$?

17 This question discussed ways of defining distances of curves. Here we suggest a way of investigating a simpler concept, the distance of a point to a curve.

- Start with a simple curve, for example, the graph of $y = x^2$.

  ☐ Which point of this graph is closest to $(0, 0.1)$? How about the point $(0, 1)$? To investigate this question, use technology to draw circles centred at these points and change the radius.

  ☐ For some $r > 0$, the vertex of the parabola $(0, 0)$ will be the closest to the point $(0, r)$. Can you find these r-values?

  ☐ The point $(1, 1)$ is on this parabola.

    • Find a circle with radius 1 that touches the parabola at this point. There are two such circles. Are either of these inside the parabola?

    • Find circles with radius r that touch the parabola at this point. For any $r > 0$, there are two such circles. For some r-value, one of these will be 'inside' the parabola. Can you find these r-values?

    • Can you find points (x, y) for which $(1, 1)$ is the closest point on the parabola?

  ☐ Pick points other than $(1, 1)$ on the parabola.

    • Find circles that touch the parabola at that point, and are 'inside' the parabola. There is an upper bound for the radius that depends on how fast the parabola is turning at that point. Can you find this upper bound?

- Can you find points (x, y) for which $(2, 4)$ is the closest point on the parabola? Can you do this for a general point on the parabola?

■ Even with the simple $y = x^2$, we have seen that finding a point on the graph closest to a given point is not easy. You can also experiment with other curves.

18 The point P we found in this question is the centre of mass of the three point system, when mass α is placed at position A, mass β is placed at position B and mass γ is placed at position C.

■ Students who are interested in physics might come up with a justification of the statement in part **b v** using arguments involving properties of the centre of mass.

■ There are similar statements in 3D involving vertices of a tetrahedron, A, B, C and D, and corresponding weights α, β, γ and δ.

□ Can you find point P_{AB} on edge AB (defined in terms of A, B, α and β) and similar points on the other edges of the tetrahedron so that the line segments $P_{AB}P_{CD}$, $P_{AC}P_{BD}$ and $P_{AD}P_{BC}$ intersect?

□ If you connect this intersection point with the vertices of the tetrahedron, where does this line intersect the opposite face of the tetrahedron?

19 There are other, more elegant, ways of proving the statement of part **c iv**. For example, the physics analogue using centres of mass can lead to an intuitive justification. The following approach uses areas. On the diagram a, b, c, d, e and f denote the areas of the corresponding triangle.

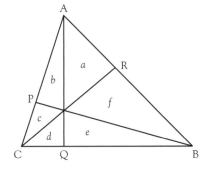

■ Using the notation of the diagram, $\dfrac{b}{c} = \dfrac{AP}{PC}$. (Can you see why?)
Also, $\dfrac{b+a+f}{c+d+e} = \dfrac{AP}{PC}$.

Combining these two equalities gives $\dfrac{a+f}{d+e} = \dfrac{AP}{PC}$.

□ Can you write similar quotients and finish the proof for part c iv?

□ As you can see from this approach, the value of $\dfrac{AP}{PC}$ and $\dfrac{QC}{QB}$ is not important. The statement of part **c iv** is true for any ratios.

There is an interesting generalisation of this claim if the three lines do not meet in one point. If $\dfrac{AP}{PC} = x$, $\dfrac{CQ}{QB} = y$ and $\dfrac{BR}{RA} = z$, then the area of the triangle in the middle of the diagram can be expressed in terms of x, y, z as a proportion of the area of the triangle ABC.

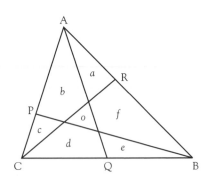

■ Using the notation from the second diagram, you can set up an equation system for the unknown areas a, b, c, d, e, f and o. For example, $\dfrac{d+e+f+o}{a+b+c} = \dfrac{BR}{RA} = z$. Can you write two other similar equations?

■ Another equation can be written for the ratio of the area $a + f$ and the total area of the triangle. This is not easy. Try to use the previous claim, where the line segments meet at one point. If you are successful, you should get $\dfrac{a+f}{a+b+c+d+e+f+o} = 1+y+\dfrac{1}{x}$ (or an equivalent form). Can you write two other similar equations?

■ If we also assume that the area of ABC is 1, then we have $a+b+c+d+e+f+o=1$.

■ Altogether this is a linear equation system in seven unknowns with seven equations. For specific x, y and z ratios, you can use any GDC to solve this system. For the general solution, you need some powerful software with computer algebra capabilities. You should get $o = \dfrac{(1 - xyz)^2}{(1+ x + xy)(1+ y + yz)(1+ z + zx)}$ (or an equivalent form).

20 The symmetry of any quadratic curve is part of the syllabus. In this question we proved that any cubic curve is symmetric about a point. It is natural to investigate higher order polynomials.

- Is there a quartic polynomial with a graph symmetric about a point? If you think that the answer is yes, give an example. If you think that there is no such quartic polynomial, give a convincing argument to justify this.

- The graph of $y = x^4$ is symmetric about the y-axis. Are all quartic graphs symmetric about a line?

  □ If you think that the answer is yes, try to prove it.

  □ If the answer is no, give a counter-example.

  □ If the answer is no, can you find some conditions on a, b, c, d and e in $y = ax^4 + bx^3 + cx^2 + dx + e$ so that the resulting graph is symmetric about a line? Start with a condition such that the resulting graph is symmetric about the y-axis.

- Is there a quintic polynomial with a graph symmetric about a line? If you think that the answer is yes, give an example. If you think that there is no such quintic polynomial, give a convincing argument to justify this.

- The graph of $y = x^5$ is symmetric about $(0, 0)$. Are all quintic graphs symmetric about a point?

  □ If you think that the answer is yes, try to prove it.

  □ If the answer is no, give a counter-example.

  □ If the answer is no, can you find some conditions on a, b, c, d, e and f in $y = ax^5 + bx^4 + cx^3 + dx^2 + ex + f$ so that the resulting graph is symmetric about a point? Start with a condition such that the resulting graph is symmetric about the origin.

Another natural direction for an investigation is to look at symmetries of surfaces that are graphs of two variable functions.

- If the surface is the graph of a linear expression $z = Ax + By + D$, then the graph is a plane and the question is not too interesting.

- On the other hand, quadratic surfaces with equation $z = Ax^2 + By^2 + Cxy$ have interesting shapes with some symmetries.

  □ Draw some of these using a 3D graphing software package and find symmetries.

  □ What happens if we change the equation to $z = Ax^2 + By^2 + Cxy + Dx + Ey + F$?

21 All graphs in this exercise have the property that at $(0, 0)$, the tangent line is horizontal.

- The graphs of $f_n : x \mapsto x^n$ have the same property for all $n \in \mathbb{Z}^+$. In addition, for all these functions, $f_n(0) = 0$ and $f_n(1) = 1$.

  □ Graph f_n on $[0, 1]$ for some n and observe the behaviour around $(0, 0)$.

  □ Find the first ten derivatives of f_1, f_2, ..., f_{10} at $x = 0$.

  □ Do you see a pattern? Find $f_n^{(k)}(0)$ for all n, $k \in \mathbb{Z}^+$.

- Now consider the following interesting function defined by $f(x) = \mathrm{e} \mathrm{e}^{-x^{-2}}$ for $x \neq 0$ and $f(0) = 0$.

  □ Graph this function, and notice that it also has the property that $f(0) = 0$ and $f(1) = 1$.

  □ Find $f'(0)$. Note that you need to use the limit definition of the derivative to find this gradient.

☐ Find $f''(0)$. For this, you will need $f'(x)$ for $x \neq 0$ and the limit definition of the derivative.

☐ Find $f'''(0)$.

☐ Can you find all derivatives of f at $x = 0$?

22 In this question, points A and B were moving, and points C and D were on the line connecting them. In the following investigation, we fix points A and B, and consider possible positions of point P satisfying certain conditions. The solutions of these questions use elementary geometry. It is only relevant to the geometry topic of the further mathematics syllabus, but still interesting enough to be considered by others who miss the elementary geometry from the syllabus.

■ For fixed A and B:

☐ Find the locus of the points P with the property AP = PB. If you don't know the answer, experiment with graphing software, for example, Geogebra.

☐ Find the locus of the points P with the property 2AP = PB. Experimenting with graphing software is again helpful here.

☐ Can you also find the locus if you change the condition to kAP = PB, for different values of k?

■ Now fix the three points A, B and C.

☐ Find point P with the property PA = PB = PC.

☐ Can you find a point P, with property PA = 2PB = 3PC?

☐ Is your method general enough to apply if the condition is changed to PA = mPB = nPC for any m and n?

■ Here are some other interesting questions, although they are not closely related to this exercise. The solutions are not easy. Think them through, or try to look for the answers in books or online.

☐ For fixed A, B, C, find the point P for which PA + PB + PC is as small as possible.

☐ For fixed A, B, C and D, find a system of line segments with minimal total length that connects the points.

☐ Can you do the same for five or more points?

23 In this question the points A, B, C and D were in a plane. You can investigate what happens if we change the positions of these points so that they are not coplanar.

■ In a planar case, the line segments P_1R_1 and S_1Q_1 clearly intersect. When the points are not coplanar, this is not automatic.

☐ Can you show that P_1R_1 and S_1Q_1 intersect even if A, B, C and D are not coplanar? Can you see that the vector proof used in the question works even in the non-planar case?

☐ Now consider arbitrary points P, Q, R and S on sides AB, BC, CD and DA respectively.

    • Is it still true that PR and SQ always intersect?

    • If the answer to the previous question is no, then give a counter-example, and try to find a condition on the position of the points P, Q, R and S on sides AB, BC, CD and DA that guarantees that PR and SQ do intersect.

■ Now consider points A(0, 0, 0), B(1, 0, 0), C(1, 1, 1) and D(0, 1, 0):

☐ Can you find a two-variable function $f(x, y)$ so that points A, B, C and D are on the graph?

☐ Can you find this function so that points P_1 and R_1 are also on the graph?

- ☐ Can you find this function so that not only these points, but also the line segments AB, BC, CD, DA and P_1R_1 are on the graph?

- ☐ Can you find this function so that in addition to these, the line segments P_2R_2, Q_1S_1 and Q_2S_2 are also on the graph?

- ☐ Can you find other line segments on the graph of the function you found?

- ☐ If you are interested in physics, you can do some research into the following question: What will be the form of the soap film suspended on the wire frame ABCD? Will the graph of the function you found be the shape of the soap film?

- ■ Can you answer the previous questions if you move the points around? First change the z-coordinates, then you can try it with arbitrary points.

24 In the solution to this question, we used the fact that if we need to write $f \circ f$ in the form $\dfrac{Ax+B}{Cx+D}$, and we already know that $(f \circ f)(x) = \dfrac{(a^2+bc)x+(ab+bd)}{(ac+dc)x+(cb+d^2)}$, then we can choose $A = a^2 + bc$, $B = ab + bd$, $C = ac + dc$ and $D = cb + d^2$. These are certainly possible expressions for A, B, C and D, but are these the only ones?

- ■ From the equality $\dfrac{A_1x+B_1}{C_1x+D_1} = \dfrac{A_2x+B_2}{C_2x+D_2}$, which holds for every x-value where the denominator is not 0, can we conclude that

  $A_1 = A_2$, $B_1 = B_2$, $C_1 = C_2$ and $D_1 = D_2$?

  - ☐ If we can, prove it.

  - ☐ If we cannot, what is the correct conclusion we can draw from the equality of the two quotients?

- ■ There are other families of functions where similar questions can be asked. Can you think of families other than the ones listed here? If the answer to any of these questions is yes, try to prove it. If the answer is no, try to modify the family to get a 'yes'.

  - ☐ If $A_1 B_1^{C_1x} = A_2 B_2^{C_2x}$ for all x, does it follow that $A_1 = A_2$, $B_1 = B_2$ and $C_1 = C_2$?

  - ☐ If $A_1 \log_{B_1} C_1x = A_2 \log_{B_2} C_2x$ for all positive x, does it follow that $A_1 = A_2$, $B_1 = B_2$ and $C_1 = C_2$?

  - ☐ If $A_1 \cos x + B_1 \sin x = A_2 \cos x + B_2 \sin x$, does it follow that $A_1 = A_2$ and $B_1 = B_2$?

  - ☐ If $A_1 \cos x + B_1 \cos 2x = A_2 \cos x + B_2 \cos 2x$, does it follow that $A_1 = A_2$ and $B_1 = B_2$?

  - ☐ If $A_1 \sin x + B_1 \sin 2x + C_1 \sin 3x = A_2 \sin x + B_2 \sin 2x + C_2 \sin 3x$, does it follow that $A_1 = A_2$, $B_1 = B_2$ and $C_1 = C_2$?

  - ☐ If $A_1x^2 + B_1x + C_1 = A_2x^2 + B_2x + C_2$, does it follow that $A_1 = A_2$, $B_1 = B_2$ and $C_1 = C_2$?

  - ☐ If $A_1x^3 + B_1x^2 + C_1x + D_1 = A_2x^3 + B_2x^2 + C_2x + D_2$, does it follow that $A_1 = A_2$, $B_1 = B_2$, $C_1 = C_2$ and $D_1 = D_2$?

25 In part **a** of this question, some trigonometric identities were found. You have already met some other trigonometric identities in the syllabus. We introduce here two other functions, defined by $\sinh x = \dfrac{e^x - e^{-x}}{2}$ and $\cosh x = \dfrac{e^x + e^{-x}}{2}$. These are called the hyperbolic sine and hyperbolic cosine functions. These are not periodic, but the properties are quite similar to the trigonometric identities.

- ■ Can you find an identity involving the hyperbolic sine and cosine functions, similar to $\sin^2 x + \cos^2 x = 1$?

- ■ Suggest a definition for the hyperbolic tangent and secant functions.

- Find an identity connecting the hyperbolic tangent and secant.

- Find identities involving hyperbolic functions, similar to the trigonometric identities found in the IB Mathematics formula booklet.

- Can you suggest a general rule of how to obtain identities involving hyperbolic sine and cosine from the trigonometric identities?

- Can you express $\sinh x$ and $\cosh x$ in terms of $\tanh \dfrac{x}{2}$?

- Find the derivatives of the hyperbolic functions. Can you see the similarities to the derivatives of trigonometric functions?

Hyperbolic functions have a lot of useful applications. For example, it can be shown that the shape of a hanging chain (with uniform weight distribution) is the scaled version of the graph of the hyperbolic cosine function.

26 This exercise gives an expression for the sine and cosine value of the angles 15° and 75° involving only the four basic operations and the square root (and integer numbers). We already know that the sine and cosine values of 30°, 45° and 60° also only involve these operations. What other acute angles have similar trigonometric ratios?

- This is closely related to the question: what acute angles can be constructed with only a ruler and compass?

   □ Can you construct the angles mentioned already?

   □ Can you construct any other acute angle with integer degree measure? This is not easy; the diagram of a regular pentagon might help.

   □ Assume 1° cannot be constructed with a ruler and compass (this is true but it is a difficult result to prove), and find all acute angles with integer degree measure that *can* be constructed using a ruler and compass.

- Pick any of the acute angles that you can construct with a ruler and compass, and find the exact sine and cosine value of this angle.

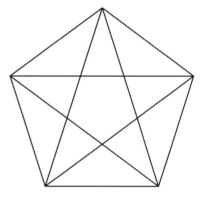

27 The problem in this question is often referred to as the 'problem of points' or the 'unfinished game'. In our question we considered a game where the goal was to reach five heads or tails and where the game ended after three heads and four tails. Experiment with different numerical parameters and find out how you would divide the money put in after the interruption.

- Consider these games:

   □ the goal is to reach 10 heads or tails; the game is interrupted after 8 heads and 9 tails

   □ the goal is to reach 20 heads or tails; the game is interrupted after 18 heads and 19 tails

   □ the goal is to reach 5 heads or tails; the game is interrupted after 3 heads and 3 tails

   □ the goal is to reach 5 heads or tails; the game is interrupted after 3 heads and 2 tails

   □ the goal is to reach 10 heads or tails; the game is interrupted after 8 heads and 7 tails

   □ the goal is to reach 10 heads or tails; the game is interrupted after 7 heads and 5 tails

- Try to find a method that is applicable to any such game.

28 This game can also be modified by changing the number of papers they start with.

- Consider the game with 5 papers, instead of the 4 in the question.

   □ How should Martin play?

- □ What is the probability of Martin getting the largest number, if he plays with the optimal strategy?

- ■ Can you answer these questions if they start with 6, 7 or 10 papers?

- ■ Is there a pattern? Can you answer the question if they start with 100 papers?

29 The properties of the sine and cosine functions proved in this question are the foundations of an important area of mathematics, where the aim is to approximate and investigate periodic functions.

- ■ Choose any periodic function, f, with period 2π.

  - □ Find $a_0 = \dfrac{1}{2\pi}\displaystyle\int_{-\pi}^{\pi} f(x)\,\mathrm{d}x$. If f is simple, you might find this integral algebraically, but a GDC or computer algebra software can find this definite integral easily.

  - □ Find $a_1 = \dfrac{1}{\pi}\displaystyle\int_{-\pi}^{\pi} f(x)\cos x\,\mathrm{d}x$ and $b_1 = \dfrac{1}{\pi}\displaystyle\int_{-\pi}^{\pi} f(x)\sin x\,\mathrm{d}x$.

  - □ Graph $y = a_0 + a_1\cos x + b_1\sin x$. Is this graph close to the graph of f?

  - □ Find $a_2 = \dfrac{1}{\pi}\displaystyle\int_{-\pi}^{\pi} f(x)\cos 2x\,\mathrm{d}x$ and $b_2 = \dfrac{1}{\pi}\displaystyle\int_{-\pi}^{\pi} f(x)\sin 2x\,\mathrm{d}x$.

  - □ Graph $y = a_0 + a_1\cos x + b_1\sin x + a_2\cos 2x + b_2\sin 2x$. Is this a better approximation of the graph of f?

  - □ Do you see the pattern? Continue calculating a_3, b_3, ... and graph better and better approximations for the graph of f.

- ■ You might ask why you should calculate an approximation for a known function. This is a valid point so, instead of choosing a periodic function, continue now with drawing a curve over $[-\pi, \pi]$ and try to approximate this curve using graphs of the form $y = a_0 + a_1\cos x + b_1\sin x + a_2\cos 2x + b_2\sin 2x \ldots$

  - □ The first problem is to find $a_0 = \dfrac{1}{2\pi}\displaystyle\int_{-\pi}^{\pi} f(x)\,\mathrm{d}x$. Since f is unknown now, we cannot use a GDC to find this integral directly. You will need to approximate this integral, for example, using a division of the interval $[-\pi, \pi]$.

  - □ Similarly, numerical integration can give you approximate values of a_1, b_1, a_2, b_2, ... Calculate as many as you need so that the resulting graph of $y = a_0 + a_1\cos x + b_1\sin x + a_2\cos 2x + b_2\sin 2x \ldots$ is close enough to the original curve.

30 The differential equation used in this question is a very simplified description of a free fall. A more realistic model uses the square of the velocity instead of the velocity: $m\dfrac{\mathrm{d}v}{\mathrm{d}t} = mg - \tfrac{1}{2}\rho C_d A v^2$, where m is the mass of the body, g is the gravitational acceleration, ρ is the air density, C_d is the drag coefficient and A is the cross sectional area of the falling body.

- ■ An example of a differential equation of this type is $\dfrac{\mathrm{d}v}{\mathrm{d}t} = 10 - 0.4v^2$.

  - □ The solutions, $v(t)$, of this differential equation, like the solutions of the one in the question, have horizontal asymptotes. The velocity of the skydiver will approach a so-called terminal velocity. Draw a slope field and find this terminal velocity.

  - □ Using technology, or by hand, find the general solution of this differential equation.

- ■ Usually, a skydiver starts the jump with the parachute closed and then opens it.

- ■ Do some research and find realistic values for g and ρ.

- ■ Find realistic values for C_d. This drag coefficient will be different with the parachute closed and open.

- Find a realistic value for A when the parachute is closed.

  ☐ What is the terminal velocity of the skydiver with the parachute closed?

  ☐ How long does it take for the skydiver to reach close to this terminal velocity?

- Experiment with different A-values for the parachute.

  ☐ Is there an optimal size? Is there a size which is too small to be safe? How would you describe what safe is?

- With a safe size of parachute, experiment with different jumping heights.

  ☐ When should the skydiver open the parachute? Is there a time that is too late?

  ☐ What is the shortest time needed for the skydiver to safely reach the ground?

  ☐ Is there a height that is too low for a safe jump?

Past IB questions reference charts

Working on past paper questions is a good way to prepare for an exam. The tables on the next pages allow you to find questions on specific papers from 2008–2014. Remember that there are two types of paper. Calculator use is not allowed on Paper 1 and you are expected to have access to a calculator with certain graphical abilities on Paper 2. Since this guide is concentrating on the core content of the syllabus, these tables don't cover the option paper 3 of the HL exams.

TZ1 and TZ2 refer to the papers for the two timezones in the May exams.

HL specimen	P1	P2
1.1 Sequences, sigma notation	2	2, 11
1.2 Exponents, logarithms	9	
1.3 Counting principles, binomial theorem		
1.4 Proof by induction	12	
1.5 Complex numbers, cartesian form	10	4
1.6 Complex numbers, polar form	10	4
1.7 de Moivre's theorem		4
1.8 Conjugate roots of real polynomials		
1.9 Systems of linear equations	7	
2.1 Functions	5, 13	
2.2 Graphs of functions		13
2.3 Graph transformations		
2.4 Graphs of rational, exponential and logarithm functions		6
2.5 Polynomial functions, factor and remainder theorem		1
2.6 Quadratic and polynomial equations, Viete formulae	2	
2.7 Inequalities		
3.1 Radian measure, arc length, sector area		
3.2 Trigonometric functions and identities, special angles	1, 10, 12	
3.3 Compound angle identities	1	
3.4 Composite trigonometric functions		
3.5 Inverse trigonometric functions	11	
3.6 Trigonometric equations		
3.7 Triangle trigonometry	6	7
4.1 Vectors, vector algebra	8	8
4.2 Scalar product		
4.3 Equation of a line		10
4.4 Relative position of lines in 2D and 3D		10
4.5 Vector product	8	10, 13
4.6 Equation of a plane		10
4.7 Relative position of planes and lines		
5.1 Descriptive statistics		3
5.2 Elementary probability	3	
5.3 Combined events, mutually exclusive events		
5.4 Conditional probability, independent events	3	12
5.5 General probability distributions	4	
5.6 Binomial distribution, Poisson distribution		12
5.7 Normal distribution		12
6.1 Limit, continuity, derivative, tangent, normal	13	13
6.2 Rules of differentiation, related rates, implicit differentiation	9, 12	9, 13
6.3 Graph properties, optimisation	4, 5, 9	13
6.4 Indefinite integrals	11	
6.5 Definite integrals, area, volume	4, 11	5
6.6 Kinematics and similar rates of change problems		5
6.7 Integration techniques (substitution, by parts)	11	

HL 2014	May	May	May	May	Nov	Nov
	P1 TZ1	**P2 TZ1**	**P1 TZ2**	**P2 TZ2**	**P1**	**P2**
1.1 Sequences, sigma notation	13	12	9	1, 6		7, 9
1.2 Exponents, logarithms	3, 11		2, 13		11	
1.3 Counting principles, binomial theorem		3, 8		5	10	
1.4 Proof by induction		7		13	8	
1.5 Complex numbers, cartesian form	13		7	13		
1.6 Complex numbers, polar form	13		7	13	13	
1.7 de Moivre's theorem	13				13	
1.8 Conjugate roots of real polynomials		1		13	13	
1.9 Systems of linear equations		4	3			
2.1 Functions		12	14	7	11	
2.2 Graphs of functions	6	5, 10, 12	5, 13	3, 7, 14	11	
2.3 Graph transformations		12	8			
2.4 Graphs of rational, exponential and logarithm functions				7	1	
2.5 Polynomial functions, factor and remainder theorem	1		13			6
2.6 Quadratic and polynomial equations, Viete formulae	4		4		2	
2.7 Inequalities		6		6		
3.1 Radian measure, arc length, sector area				4		
3.2 Trigonometric functions and identities, special angles	9, 12		5, 9, 10		13	14
3.3 Compound angle identities	5, 10		9		13	
3.4 Composite trigonometric functions			5			
3.5 Inverse trigonometric functions	9		9, 13, 14			
3.6 Trigonometric equations	10					
3.7 Triangle trigonometry	7			4, 12, 13		9, 10
4.1 Vectors, vector algebra	12		6		3, 12	
4.2 Scalar product	12		6			
4.3 Equation of a line	12		12			5
4.4 Relative position of lines in 2D and 3D			12			
4.5 Vector product			12			
4.6 Equation of a plane	12		12			5
4.7 Relative position of planes and lines	12		3, 12			1, 5
5.1 Descriptive statistics	2	2		2	9	3
5.2 Elementary probability		8, 9	11	6		12
5.3 Combined events, mutually exclusive events			1		4	
5.4 Conditional probability, independent events			1, 11	11	4	
5.5 General probability distributions		11	11	11	9	
5.6 Binomial distribution, Poisson distribution		9		2, 8		11
5.7 Normal distribution		2		2		2
6.1 Limit, continuity, derivative, tangent, normal	11	10	8	10		
6.2 Rules of differentiation, related rates, implicit differentiation	8, 9, 11	10	13, 14	9, 10, 12, 14	7	4
6.3 Graph properties, optimisation	6, 11		13	12	3, 5, 11	4, 10
6.4 Indefinite integrals	5, 11	6	13, 14		11	
6.5 Definite integrals, area, volume	5, 6, 11	5	13	3, 11	11	13
6.6 Kinematics and similar rates of change problems				14		8, 13
6.7 Integration techniques (substitution, by parts)	5, 11		10, 13	11, 14	6, 11, 13	

HL 2013	May P1 TZ1	May P2 TZ1	May P1 TZ2	May P2 TZ2	Nov P1	Nov P2
1.1 Sequences, sigma notation	8		6	5, 11	7	2
1.2 Exponents, logarithms	8		9		3, 9	
1.3 Counting principles, binomial theorem	13	8	3	11	12	
1.4 Proof by induction				8	6	
1.5 Complex numbers, cartesian form			7			6
1.6 Complex numbers, polar form	1		13			
1.7 de Moivre's theorem	1		13		12	
1.8 Conjugate roots of real polynomials		6	13			
1.9 Systems of linear equations		2			11	
2.1 Functions		13	12		3	13
2.2 Graphs of functions	12	6, 12	12	7, 13	3, 10	3, 8, 12
2.3 Graph transformations	12				10	
2.4 Graphs of rational, exponential and logarithm functions			12			
2.5 Polynomial functions, factor and remainder theorem	11, 12	6			1	
2.6 Quadratic and polynomial equations, Viete formulae	11	9	9	6	5, 7	
2.7 Inequalities		13	9	5, 11		2, 3
3.1 Radian measure, arc length, sector area		5		1		8
3.2 Trigonometric functions and identities, special angles	10, 11			6	8, 12	
3.3 Compound angle identities	11, 12		10, 13		8	
3.4 Composite trigonometric functions						
3.5 Inverse trigonometric functions	12	4	10			
3.6 Trigonometric equations		7		6		7
3.7 Triangle trigonometry			11	13		
4.1 Vectors, vector algebra						
4.2 Scalar product		11	11			7
4.3 Equation of a line		11	11		11	9
4.4 Relative position of lines in 2D and 3D		11				9
4.5 Vector product	2		11		11	
4.6 Equation of a plane			11		11	
4.7 Relative position of planes and lines					11	
5.1 Descriptive statistics		1				
5.2 Elementary probability	13	10	4			5
5.3 Combined events, mutually exclusive events	9					
5.4 Conditional probability, independent events	9					5
5.5 General probability distributions	4, 13			7	2	11
5.6 Binomial distribution, Poisson distribution	13	3, 10		9, 11		11
5.7 Normal distribution		3		3		4
6.1 Limit, continuity, derivative, tangent, normal	7	13	5			13
6.2 Rules of differentiation, related rates, implicit differentiation	5, 7, 13	13	5, 8	13	5, 10	13
6.3 Graph properties, optimisation		7, 12	7, 12	13	10	3, 12
6.4 Indefinite integrals	10, 12		1	4		10, 12
6.5 Definite integrals, area, volume	4, 10, 12	4	1	4, 7	10, 12	11, 12, 13
6.6 Kinematics and similar rates of change problems		12		10		12
6.7 Integration techniques (substitution, by parts)	4, 12			4	10	10
Not in the core syllabus from 2014	3, 6		2		4	1
Not in the core syllabus from 2014, but can be reworded		12(e, f)		2, 10		12(b)(iii)
Not in the core syllabus from 2014, but in the calculus option				12		

HL 2012	May P1 TZ1	May P2 TZ1	May P1 TZ2	May P2 TZ2	Nov P1	Nov P2
1.1 Sequences, sigma notation	1			1, 8		1, 5
1.2 Exponents, logarithms	6, 8	6			4	
1.3 Counting principles, binomial theorem		3, 9	4	4	2	
1.4 Proof by induction			13		12	
1.5 Complex numbers, cartesian form	7		6, 12		10	
1.6 Complex numbers, polar form	3		12		10	10
1.7 de Moivre's theorem	3				10	
1.8 Conjugate roots of real polynomials			12			
1.9 Systems of linear equations				11	6	
2.1 Functions			11		12	
2.2 Graphs of functions	2	10	7, 10	6	3	9, 12
2.3 Graph transformations	4	6			3, 12	
2.4 Graphs of rational, exponential and logarithm functions	4					
2.5 Polynomial functions, factor and remainder theorem			1, 12		3	
2.6 Quadratic and polynomial equations, Viete formulae		1				2
2.7 Inequalities						
3.1 Radian measure, arc length, sector area				9		
3.2 Trigonometric functions and identities, special angles	5		9, 10		1, 7	10
3.3 Compound angle identities	5		2, 9		1, 8	10
3.4 Composite trigonometric functions						
3.5 Inverse trigonometric functions	12					
3.6 Trigonometric equations	10		2			
3.7 Triangle trigonometry	10			3, 9	7	12
4.1 Vectors, vector algebra						
4.2 Scalar product		13	2			
4.3 Equation of a line		13		11	9	13
4.4 Relative position of lines in 2D and 3D					9, 11c	13
4.5 Vector product						
4.6 Equation of a plane		13		11	6	13
4.7 Relative position of planes and lines		4		11		13
5.1 Descriptive statistics		5				4
5.2 Elementary probability		3	3			7
5.3 Combined events, mutually exclusive events						
5.4 Conditional probability, independent events		12	3			7
5.5 General probability distributions		2	11	7	5	
5.6 Binomial distribution, Poisson distribution		7, 12		2, 5		11
5.7 Normal distribution		12		10		11
6.1 Limit, continuity, derivative, tangent, normal	2, 9	11	13	6	8	
6.2 Rules of differentiation, related rates, implicit differentiation	6, 9, 12	11	13		8	6, 12
6.3 Graph properties, optimisation	12	1, 10, 11	7, 8		4	12
6.4 Indefinite integrals	12	8	10			8
6.5 Definite integrals, area, volume	2, 6	2, 8	10			9
6.6 Kinematics and similar rates of change problems						6
6.7 Integration techniques (substitution, by parts)	12		10			8
Not in the core syllabus from 2014	11		5		11a, b	3
Not in the core syllabus from 2014, but can be reworded				12		
Not in the core syllabus from 2014, but in the calculus option						

HL 2011	May P1 TZ1	May P2 TZ1	May P1 TZ2	May P2 TZ2	Nov P1	Nov P2
1.1 Sequences, sigma notation	3		10	2		7, 12, 14
1.2 Exponents, logarithms		9	8			8
1.3 Counting principles, binomial theorem	13	5	9			
1.4 Proof by induction				13A	6	
1.5 Complex numbers, cartesian form	2, 13		4			10
1.6 Complex numbers, polar form	13		12a, b		2	6, 14
1.7 de Moivre's theorem	13		12a, b		2	
1.8 Conjugate roots of real polynomials						
1.9 Systems of linear equations		11				2
2.1 Functions	8, 10, 12		8	7	9	8
2.2 Graphs of functions	8, 10, 12	2	5	5		1
2.3 Graph transformations	10		1, 13			
2.4 Graphs of rational, exponential and logarithm functions						
2.5 Polynomial functions, factor and remainder theorem	13	4	1		7	
2.6 Quadratic and polynomial equations, Viete formulae		5, 8, 9			9	10
2.7 Inequalities	12	8			9	7
3.1 Radian measure, arc length, sector area		6	7	1	1, 8	
3.2 Trigonometric functions and identities, special angles	5, 13		13		4, 8, 10, 12	4, 14
3.3 Compound angle identities	5		13		4	
3.4 Composite trigonometric functions						
3.5 Inverse trigonometric functions	7		13	7		4
3.6 Trigonometric equations	13		13			4
3.7 Triangle trigonometry		3, 6	4, 7	8	8	
4.1 Vectors, vector algebra	4		6	11	12	
4.2 Scalar product	4		6		12	
4.3 Equation of a line	11	10, 11		11		13
4.4 Relative position of lines in 2D and 3D						
4.5 Vector product				11	12	
4.6 Equation of a plane	11	11		11		13
4.7 Relative position of planes and lines	11	11		11		13
5.1 Descriptive statistics		1				
5.2 Elementary probability	6		9	12	3, 5	
5.3 Combined events, mutually exclusive events	1					
5.4 Conditional probability, independent events	1, 6	12	9	6	3	11
5.5 General probability distributions		7	3	12	5, 10	
5.6 Binomial distribution, Poisson distribution		12		6, 12		3, 5
5.7 Normal distribution		12		6		11
6.1 Limit, continuity, derivative, tangent, normal	9		11	7, 10		
6.2 Rules of differentiation, related rates, implicit differentiation	9, 12		11	3, 9, 10	6, 8, 11	9
6.3 Graph properties, optimisation	12	2			8, 11	
6.4 Indefinite integrals		7, 8	3, 13		4, 10	
6.5 Definite integrals, area, volume	7	7, 14a	3, 13	3	4, 7, 10	1
6.6 Kinematics and similar rates of change problems		8		3		
6.7 Integration techniques (substitution, by parts)	7		13	13Ba	10	
Not in the core syllabus from 2014		13	2, 12c, d	4		
Not in the core syllabus from 2014, but can be reworded		14b, c				
Not in the core syllabus from 2014, but in the calculus option				13Bb, c	13	

HL 2010	May P1 TZ1	May P2 TZ1	May P1 TZ2	May P2 TZ2	Nov P1	Nov P2
1.1 Sequences, sigma notation		6		1, 13	5, 6	
1.2 Exponents, logarithms	4			4	13	5, 13
1.3 Counting principles, binomial theorem		7		8	3	
1.4 Proof by induction	13		11		12b	
1.5 Complex numbers, cartesian form		4		9	11	
1.6 Complex numbers, polar form		4	13	9	11	
1.7 de Moivre's theorem		4	13	9		
1.8 Conjugate roots of real polynomials						6
1.9 Systems of linear equations		2		7		
2.1 Functions	2	9	10	14	9	
2.2 Graphs of functions	2, 5, 11	10		11		8, 10, 13
2.3 Graph transformations			2			
2.4 Graphs of rational, exponential and logarithm functions	5					
2.5 Polynomial functions, factor and remainder theorem	1		2	8		6
2.6 Quadratic and polynomial equations, Viete formulae						
2.7 Inequalities		9		8, 11	1, 9	
3.1 Radian measure, arc length, sector area				13		
3.2 Trigonometric functions and identities, special angles		4	6, 14b	9	11	
3.3 Compound angle identities	13		6			
3.4 Composite trigonometric functions		1				
3.5 Inverse trigonometric functions	9				9	
3.6 Trigonometric equations	13	13	6			9
3.7 Triangle trigonometry		3, 13ab		5		1
4.1 Vectors, vector algebra	6		3		10	12
4.2 Scalar product	3, 6	11	12		7, 10	9
4.3 Equation of a line				7		
4.4 Relative position of lines in 2D and 3D						
4.5 Vector product		11	12			9, 12
4.6 Equation of a plane	3	11	12	7		12
4.7 Relative position of planes and lines		11	12	7	7	12
5.1 Descriptive statistics	10	8		12	5	
5.2 Elementary probability	7				4	11
5.3 Combined events, mutually exclusive events						
5.4 Conditional probability, independent events	12			12	4	11
5.5 General probability distributions	12		1	2		11
5.6 Binomial distribution, Poisson distribution		12	4	6		7
5.7 Normal distribution		8		3		3
6.1 Limit, continuity, derivative, tangent, normal			8		13	4, 10
6.2 Rules of differentiation, related rates, implicit differentiation	11		7, 8	10, 14	12, 13	4, 13
6.3 Graph properties, optimisation	11	13c	7	14		13
6.4 Indefinite integrals	8, 9, 12		9, 14b			
6.5 Definite integrals, area, volume	8, 12	10	1, 9, 14b	11	13	13
6.6 Kinematics and similar rates of change problems		14		14	12a	
6.7 Integration techniques (substitution, by parts)	8, 9		9, 14b		13	
Not in the core syllabus from 2014		5	5	12bii		2
Not in the core syllabus from 2014, but can be reworded					2	
Not in the core syllabus from 2014, but in the calculus option			14a		8	

HL 2009	May P1 TZ1	May P2 TZ1	May P1 TZ2	May P2 TZ2	Nov P1	Nov P2
1.1 Sequences, sigma notation				13	11	13
1.2 Exponents, logarithms	3, 7, 12, 13A		4	13	4, 10, 12	
1.3 Counting principles, binomial theorem	10		12			4
1.4 Proof by induction			8		11	
1.5 Complex numbers, cartesian form	1				13	7
1.6 Complex numbers, polar form	13A		7, 12		2, 13	
1.7 de Moivre's theorem			12		2, 13	
1.8 Conjugate roots of real polynomials		2	7			7
1.9 Systems of linear equations		7		7		
2.1 Functions	11		11		4	9, 10
2.2 Graphs of functions	9	12	11	12, 13	9	1, 3, 9
2.3 Graph transformations				4	5	9
2.4 Graphs of rational, exponential and logarithm functions				4, 13	12	
2.5 Polynomial functions, factor and remainder theorem	10		1, 7		1	7
2.6 Quadratic and polynomial equations, Viete formulae				7		
2.7 Inequalities		3	9	4		
3.1 Radian measure, arc length, sector area	6					3
3.2 Trigonometric functions and identities, special angles	2, 5, 11	12	9, 12			
3.3 Compound angle identities	5				13	
3.4 Composite trigonometric functions	2					
3.5 Inverse trigonometric functions	5, 11	9		3, 9, 12	4	
3.6 Trigonometric equations				2	13	
3.7 Triangle trigonometry			9	12		12
4.1 Vectors, vector algebra	8	11				
4.2 Scalar product		5		2		
4.3 Equation of a line		5, 11	10	2		2, 11
4.4 Relative position of lines in 2D and 3D			10	2		11
4.5 Vector product	8		10			
4.6 Equation of a plane		7, 11	10			2, 11
4.7 Relative position of planes and lines		7, 11	10			2
5.1 Descriptive statistics	12	1	2			
5.2 Elementary probability				1, 5	6	13
5.3 Combined events, mutually exclusive events				1		
5.4 Conditional probability, independent events				1, 5	6	6
5.5 General probability distributions			3			5, 13
5.6 Binomial distribution, Poisson distribution		4		11		
5.7 Normal distribution		1		11		6
6.1 Limit, continuity, derivative, tangent, normal	7, 13B	12	5, 11	3, 13	12	8
6.2 Rules of differentiation, related rates, implicit differentiation	7, 11	3, 9	5, 11	3, 7, 10, 13	12	8, 10, 12
6.3 Graph properties, optimisation	11	11, 12		7, 12, 13	9	9, 10
6.4 Indefinite integrals		6, 12	3, 4, 11, 12	9	7, 10	
6.5 Definite integrals, area, volume	9	6, 12	3, 4, 5, 11, 12		7, 10	5
6.6 Kinematics and similar rates of change problems				6		
6.7 Integration techniques (substitution, by parts)		6, 12		9	7, 10	
Not in the core syllabus from 2014	4	10	6		3	
Not in the core syllabus from 2014, but can be reworded	13B TZ1			8		
Not in the core syllabus from 2014, but in the calculus option		8			8	

HL 2008	May P1 TZ1	May P2 TZ1	May P1 TZ2	May P2 TZ2	Nov P1	Nov P2
1.1 Sequences, sigma notation	3, 7		12		4	2
1.2 Exponents, logarithms	7, 8				2, 5	8, 9
1.3 Counting principles, binomial theorem		1				11
1.4 Proof by induction	12		12			
1.5 Complex numbers, cartesian form	1	10	14	9	13	
1.6 Complex numbers, polar form	1	14	14		13	
1.7 de Moivre's theorem	1	14	14		13	
1.8 Conjugate roots of real polynomials						
1.9 Systems of linear equations		5				5
2.1 Functions	8		4			12
2.2 Graphs of functions		2	9	3, 8	11	6, 12
2.3 Graph transformations		2				
2.4 Graphs of rational, exponential and logarithm functions						9
2.5 Polynomial functions, factor and remainder theorem			2		1	
2.6 Quadratic and polynomial equations, Viete formulae	6					4
2.7 Inequalities				10		6
3.1 Radian measure, arc length, sector area						
3.2 Trigonometric functions and identities, special angles		10	6, 14		11	12
3.3 Compound angle identities	4, 9	10	3	13	11	
3.4 Composite trigonometric functions		2		2	11	
3.5 Inverse trigonometric functions		7	8, 9	13	7	12
3.6 Trigonometric equations	4, 9	7	9		11	
3.7 Triangle trigonometry	4	12		5	9	1
4.1 Vectors, vector algebra	11		11		10	
4.2 Scalar product		3	10, 11		10	4
4.3 Equation of a line	11	3, 5	11			10
4.4 Relative position of lines in 2D and 3D			11			10
4.5 Vector product	11		10			
4.6 Equation of a plane	11	3	11			5, 10
4.7 Relative position of planes and lines	11	3, 5				5, 10
5.1 Descriptive statistics	9			1, 4	3	
5.2 Elementary probability		8			8	11
5.3 Combined events, mutually exclusive events			7			
5.4 Conditional probability, independent events		8	7			7, 11
5.5 General probability distributions	9		1	4	8	3
5.6 Binomial distribution, Poisson distribution		11		7, 11		7, 11
5.7 Normal distribution		4		11		11
6.1 Limit, continuity, derivative, tangent, normal		6, 13	5, 8		6	
6.2 Rules of differentiation, related rates, implicit differentiation	5, 12, 13a	6, 13	5, 8, 13	6	6, 7, 9, 11	8, 12
6.3 Graph properties, optimisation	5, 12	13	13	4, 6	9, 11	12
6.4 Indefinite integrals	6, 9, 10	9	6		5	9
6.5 Definite integrals, area, volume	6, 9, 10		6	3, 4	5	3, 12
6.6 Kinematics and similar rates of change problems	13b			13		9
6.7 Integration techniques (substitution, by parts)	10	9	6		5	
Not in the core syllabus from 2014	2			12	12	
Not in the core syllabus from 2014, but can be reworded	13b			13		
Not in the core syllabus from 2014, but in the calculus option						

SL specimen	P1	P2
1.1 Sequences, sigma notation		1
1.2 Exponents, logarithms		
1.3 Binomial theorem, binomial coefficients		
2.1 Functions		9, 10
2.2 Graphs of functions	3, 8	2, 9
2.3 Graph transformations	8	
2.4 Quadratic functions	8	
2.5 Reciprocal function, rational functions		9
2.6 Exponential and logarithmic functions		
2.7 Solving equations	8	2, 7, 10
2.8 Applications to real life situations		10
3.1 Radian measure, arc length, sector area		7
3.2 Trigonometric ratios, special angles	6	
3.3 Trigonometric identities	5, 6	
3.4 Trigonometric functions, composite functions, applications	10	
3.5 Trigonometric equations	6	
3.6 Solution of triangles, applications		6
4.1 Vectors, vector algebra	1	
4.2 Scalar product		4
4.3 Equation of a line		4
4.4 Relative position of lines in 2D and 3D		4
5.1 Presentation of statistical data		
5.2 Statistical measures	4	
5.3 Cumulative frequency		
5.4 Linear correlation of bivariate data	2	8
5.5 Elementary probability	9	
5.6 Combined events, conditional probability, independence	9	
5.7 Discrete random variable	9	
5.8 Binomial distribution		5
5.9 Normal distribution		3
6.1 Limit, derivative, tangent, normal	3	2
6.2 Rules of differentiation, higher derivatives	7, 10	
6.3 Graph properties, optimisation	10	
6.4 Indefinite integrals	5	
6.5 Definite integrals, area, volume		9
6.6 Kinematics problems	3	

SL 2014	May P1 TZ1	May P2 TZ1	May P1 TZ2	May P2 TZ2	Nov P1	Nov P2
1.1 Sequences, sigma notation	2, 10		7		2	9
1.2 Exponents, logarithms	4		2, 10		4	9
1.3 Binomial theorem, binomial coefficients		2		7		6
2.1 Functions			3			1
2.2 Graphs of functions		9, 10	3	9	5, 9	4
2.3 Graph transformations			8		9	
2.4 Quadratic functions	1, 7		8	2	1	
2.5 Reciprocal function, rational functions		10			5	
2.6 Exponential and logarithmic functions				8		
2.7 Solving equations	4, 7, 8, 10	9	8, 9, 10	6, 8	1, 4, 9, 10	1, 4, 9
2.8 Applications to real life situations				8		
3.1 Radian measure, arc length, sector area				1		3
3.2 Trigonometric ratios, special angles	6		1, 5			
3.3 Trigonometric identities			1		7	
3.4 Trigonometric functions, composite functions, applications		5, 9		6		5
3.5 Trigonometric equations	6					
3.6 Solution of triangles, applications		1		5	7	
4.1 Vectors, vector algebra	8	4				
4.2 Scalar product		4	9		7	
4.3 Equation of a line	8		4, 9		10	
4.4 Relative position of lines in 2D and 3D	8		9			
5.1 Presentation of statistical data						
5.2 Statistical measures		8				8
5.3 Cumulative frequency		8				8
5.4 Linear correlation of bivariate data		3		3		2
5.5 Elementary probability	5, 9			4, 10	8	8, 10
5.6 Combined events, conditional probability, independence	9			4, 10	8	8, 10
5.7 Discrete random variable					3	
5.8 Binomial distribution		8		10	8	
5.9 Normal distribution		8		10		10
6.1 Limit, derivative, tangent, normal		5, 7				
6.2 Rules of differentiation, higher derivatives	7	7	10	9		
6.3 Graph properties, optimisation			6	9		
6.4 Indefinite integrals	3, 6		5, 10		6	
6.5 Definite integrals, area, volume	3, 6	6	5, 10	2, 9	6, 9	4, 7
6.6 Kinematics problems		6		9		7

SL 2013	May	May	May	May	Nov	Nov
	P1 TZ1	P2 TZ1	P1 TZ2	P2 TZ2	P1	P2
1.1 Sequences, sigma notation		1		5	9	
1.2 Exponents, logarithms	7, 10		3		10	
1.3 Binomial theorem, binomial coefficients		3		6		
2.1 Functions	5	9	1		8	
2.2 Graphs of functions		5, 9, 10	4		8, 10	5, 7
2.3 Graph transformations		6			4, 5	
2.4 Quadratic functions	2		9			2
2.5 Reciprocal function, rational functions					8	
2.6 Exponential and logarithmic functions					6	5
2.7 Solving equations	8	5, 9, 10		4, 5, 7, 8, 10	7, 9, 10	2, 5, 9, 10
2.8 Applications to real life situations						
3.1 Radian measure, arc length, sector area		8	7	7		8
3.2 Trigonometric ratios, special angles				7	5	
3.3 Trigonometric identities						
3.4 Trigonometric functions, composite functions, applications		10	5		5	
3.5 Trigonometric equations						
3.6 Solution of triangles, applications		8		3		8
4.1 Vectors, vector algebra	1, 8			8	1	
4.2 Scalar product	8			8		9
4.3 Equation of a line	8			4		9
4.4 Relative position of lines in 2D and 3D	8			4		9
5.1 Presentation of statistical data		2	8			
5.2 Statistical measures		2, 7				
5.3 Cumulative frequency		2	8		3	
5.4 Linear correlation of bivariate data						
5.5 Elementary probability	9	10	8	9		10
5.6 Combined events, conditional probability, independence	9			9		4, 10
5.7 Discrete random variable	9			9		
5.8 Binomial distribution				9		10
5.9 Normal distribution		7		2		6
6.1 Limit, derivative, tangent, normal	3		9, 10	10	6	7
6.2 Rules of differentiation, higher derivatives	3, 10	9	9, 10	10	6, 10	3
6.3 Graph properties, optimisation	10	9	10	10	10	5, 7
6.4 Indefinite integrals	6		6		10	3
6.5 Definite integrals, area, volume	6	5	6, 7	10	4, 10	2, 5
6.6 Kinematics problems		5	6			5
Not in the syllabus from 2014	4	4	2	1	2	1

SL 2012	May P1 TZ1	May P2 TZ1	May P1 TZ2	May P2 TZ2	Nov P1	Nov P2
1.1 Sequences, sigma notation		1		3		1
1.2 Exponents, logarithms	6				10	
1.3 Binomial theorem, binomial coefficients		6	7			4
2.1 Functions	9		2	9		
2.2 Graphs of functions	7, 9	10	10	2, 10		3, 7
2.3 Graph transformations	7		5			9
2.4 Quadratic functions		2	8			9
2.5 Reciprocal function, rational functions						
2.6 Exponential and logarithmic functions	3, 9					
2.7 Solving equations	8, 9	2, 4, 9	6	3, 9, 10	7, 10	3, 4, 9
2.8 Applications to real life situations						
3.1 Radian measure, arc length, sector area		9		10		8
3.2 Trigonometric ratios, special angles	5					
3.3 Trigonometric identities	7				5	
3.4 Trigonometric functions, composite functions, applications	5		3			5
3.5 Trigonometric equations	10					
3.6 Solution of triangles, applications		9, 10		1, 10		8
4.1 Vectors, vector algebra				8	9	
4.2 Scalar product	8			8	9	
4.3 Equation of a line	8			8	6	
4.4 Relative position of lines in 2D and 3D	8				6	
5.1 Presentation of statistical data	1	8			8	
5.2 Statistical measures	1	8	1		8	
5.3 Cumulative frequency	1		1		8	
5.4 Linear correlation of bivariate data						
5.5 Elementary probability	4	7, 8	9	7		10
5.6 Combined events, conditional probability, independence	4		9	7		10
5.7 Discrete random variable			4		2	
5.8 Binomial distribution		7		7		
5.9 Normal distribution		8		4		6
6.1 Limit, derivative, tangent, normal	3		3		4	3
6.2 Rules of differentiation, higher derivatives	3, 10		10	2, 9	4, 10	7
6.3 Graph properties, optimisation	10		3, 10	9		7
6.4 Indefinite integrals	6		8		3	
6.5 Definite integrals, area, volume	6, 10	4	8	5	3	9
6.6 Kinematics problems	10			5	10	7
Not in the syllabus from 2014	2	3, 5		6	1	2

SL 2011	May	May	May	May	Nov	Nov
	P1 TZ1	P2 TZ1	P1 TZ2	P2 TZ2	P1	P2
1.1 Sequences, sigma notation		3	1			8
1.2 Exponents, logarithms	5	10	5		10	10
1.3 Binomial theorem, binomial coefficients				3		5
2.1 Functions	1	10		1		1
2.2 Graphs of functions	7	6, 8, 10		2, 10		6, 10
2.3 Graph transformations		2	5		10	7
2.4 Quadratic functions	7	2	9		1	
2.5 Reciprocal function, rational functions						
2.6 Exponential and logarithmic functions						6
2.7 Solving equations	5, 7	8, 9		2, 8, 10	5, 7, 8	6, 8
2.8 Applications to real life situations						
3.1 Radian measure, arc length, sector area						3
3.2 Trigonometric ratios, special angles	6, 10				6	
3.3 Trigonometric identities	6				6	
3.4 Trigonometric functions, composite functions, applications		8	10	10	9	
3.5 Trigonometric equations	6			10		
3.6 Solution of triangles, applications		1		5, 10		4
4.1 Vectors, vector algebra	2, 9		3	8	8	
4.2 Scalar product	9		3	8	8	
4.3 Equation of a line	2			8	8	
4.4 Relative position of lines in 2D and 3D				8	8	
5.1 Presentation of statistical data			6			
5.2 Statistical measures			6			2
5.3 Cumulative frequency			6			2
5.4 Linear correlation of bivariate data						
5.5 Elementary probability	8	7	2	9	3, 7	
5.6 Combined events, conditional probability, independence	8					9
5.7 Discrete random variable	4			9	5	
5.8 Binomial distribution		5		9		9
5.9 Normal distribution		4		6		9
6.1 Limit, derivative, tangent, normal			8		9, 10	
6.2 Rules of differentiation, higher derivatives	5, 10	8, 9	4, 8, 9		9	10
6.3 Graph properties, optimisation	5, 10	9	9			10
6.4 Indefinite integrals			8	7	4, 10	
6.5 Definite integrals, area, volume	10	6	8	7	4, 10	7
6.6 Kinematics problems	10		9			7
Not in the syllabus from 2014	3		7	4	2	

SL 2010	May P1 TZ1	May P2 TZ1	May P1 TZ2	May P2 TZ2	Nov P1	Nov P2
1.1 Sequences, sigma notation		2		2	1	3
1.2 Exponents, logarithms	7		6			8
1.3 Binomial theorem, binomial coefficients	3			4		
2.1 Functions	7		4		9	
2.2 Graphs of functions		3	7	5, 6, 10	10	2, 5, 8
2.3 Graph transformations	8		10		9	
2.4 Quadratic functions	1		1		9	
2.5 Reciprocal function, rational functions						
2.6 Exponential and logarithmic functions		9		7		
2.7 Solving equations	1, 8, 10	5, 7, 8, 9	6	5, 9, 10	5, 9	5, 7, 9, 10
2.8 Applications to real life situations				7		
3.1 Radian measure, arc length, sector area				8	3	
3.2 Trigonometric ratios, special angles	4, 9		4		2	10
3.3 Trigonometric identities	4		4, 10		5	
3.4 Trigonometric functions, composite functions, applications		5	10			10
3.5 Trigonometric equations			10		5	
3.6 Solution of triangles, applications		8		8		6
4.1 Vectors, vector algebra	10		2		8	
4.2 Scalar product	10		2	9	8	4
4.3 Equation of a line	10			9	8	
4.4 Relative position of lines in 2D and 3D	10				8	
5.1 Presentation of statistical data		4		1		1
5.2 Statistical measures		4		1		1
5.3 Cumulative frequency				1		
5.4 Linear correlation of bivariate data						
5.5 Elementary probability	5	10	9	3	4	9
5.6 Combined events, conditional probability, independence	5	10	9		4	
5.7 Discrete random variable			9			9
5.8 Binomial distribution		7		3		9
5.9 Normal distribution		10				
6.1 Limit, derivative, tangent, normal			5		2, 9, 10	
6.2 Rules of differentiation, higher derivatives	8, 9	3, 9	5	7, 10	2, 10	7
6.3 Graph properties, optimisation	8, 9	9	7, 8	10		7
6.4 Indefinite integrals	6	6	8, 10		6, 10	
6.5 Definite integrals, area, volume	6	6	8, 10	6	6, 10	2, 8
6.6 Kinematics problems		6				2
Not in the syllabus from 2014	2	1	3		7	

SL 2009	May P1 TZ1	May P2 TZ1	May P1 TZ2	May P2 TZ2	Nov P1	Nov P2
1.1 Sequences, sigma notation		1, 6		5		1
1.2 Exponents, logarithms	6, 10		4	6	1, 7	
1.3 Binomial theorem, binomial coefficients		10	3			
2.1 Functions	6	3	1		1, 7, 9	
2.2 Graphs of functions	10			10	9	5, 9
2.3 Graph transformations	5, 10			2	4	
2.4 Quadratic functions						9
2.5 Reciprocal function, rational functions						
2.6 Exponential and logarithmic functions						
2.7 Solving equations	6, 7	5, 6, 10	7, 10, 11	3, 7, 8, 10	2, 5	1, 5, 9
2.8 Applications to real life situations						7
3.1 Radian measure, arc length, sector area		2				8
3.2 Trigonometric ratios, special angles	3, 8, 9		7, 8		6	
3.3 Trigonometric identities	8, 9				6	
3.4 Trigonometric functions, composite functions, applications		3		10		9
3.5 Trigonometric equations	8		7		6	
3.6 Solution of triangles, applications	9			4		8
4.1 Vectors, vector algebra	9		10		2	10
4.2 Scalar product	9		2		2	10
4.3 Equation of a line		5	10			10
4.4 Relative position of lines in 2D and 3D		5	10			
5.1 Presentation of statistical data		8		1		
5.2 Statistical measures		8		1		
5.3 Cumulative frequency		8				
5.4 Linear correlation of bivariate data						
5.5 Elementary probability	2	7	9		8	
5.6 Combined events, conditional probability, independence	2	7			8	6
5.7 Discrete random variable		8	9			
5.8 Binomial distribution				9		3
5.9 Normal distribution		4		9	3	
6.1 Limit, derivative, tangent, normal	3	10		6	10	5
6.2 Rules of differentiation, higher derivatives	3, 8		6, 8	6, 10	5, 9, 10	2, 5
6.3 Graph properties, optimisation	4, 8, 10	10	6	10	9	
6.4 Indefinite integrals	7		11	8	10	
6.5 Definite integrals, area, volume	7, 10		11	8	10	9
6.6 Kinematics problems	4		11			
Not in the syllabus from 2014	1	9	5			4

SL 2008	May P1 TZ1	May P2 TZ1	May P1 TZ2	May P2 TZ2	Nov P1	Nov P2
1.1 Sequences, sigma notation	3			1, 10	1	
1.2 Exponents, logarithms	5, 7				4	
1.3 Binomial theorem, binomial coefficients				2		2
2.1 Functions	7				4	
2.2 Graphs of functions	9	4		3, 8, 9	4, 10	4
2.3 Graph transformations	9		5		10	
2.4 Quadratic functions	9		2			1
2.5 Reciprocal function, rational functions						
2.6 Exponential and logarithmic functions					4	
2.7 Solving equations	4, 8, 9	4, 8, 10	2	3, 4, 7, 9, 10		4, 9
2.8 Applications to real life situations				8, 10		
3.1 Radian measure, arc length, sector area		3	10			
3.2 Trigonometric ratios, special angles			4, 10			
3.3 Trigonometric identities	2		4		7	
3.4 Trigonometric functions, composite functions, applications	4		9	8	10	
3.5 Trigonometric equations			9			
3.6 Solution of triangles, applications		2	10			6
4.1 Vectors, vector algebra		7, 9	8		2	8
4.2 Scalar product		7, 9	8			8
4.3 Equation of a line		9		7	2	
4.4 Relative position of lines in 2D and 3D				7		
5.1 Presentation of statistical data		1	1			3
5.2 Statistical measures		1	1			3
5.3 Cumulative frequency		1				3
5.4 Linear correlation of bivariate data						
5.5 Elementary probability	10		6		8	
5.6 Combined events, conditional probability, independence			6		5, 8	
5.7 Discrete random variable	10			4	8	
5.8 Binomial distribution		6		6		5
5.9 Normal distribution		8		5		7
6.1 Limit, derivative, tangent, normal	8			3, 9		9
6.2 Rules of differentiation, higher derivatives	8	10	9, 10	9		9
6.3 Graph properties, optimisation	8	5	10	8	6	
6.4 Indefinite integrals	5, 6		9		9	
6.5 Definite integrals, area, volume	5, 6	10	7, 9	9	9	4, 9
6.6 Kinematics problems	6				9	
Not in the syllabus from 2014	1		3		3	10

Are you ready?

Use this checklist to record progress as you revise. Tick each box when you have:

- Revised and understood a topic
- Tested yourself using the **Practice questions** and several past paper questions
- Checked your answers and compared your approach with the **detailed solution**

	Revised	Tested	Exam ready
Topic 1 Algebra			
1.1 Sequences and series	☐	☐	☐
1.2 Exponents and logarithms	☐	☐	☐
1.3 Binomial theorem	☐	☐	☐
1.4 Polynomials (HL)	☐	☐	☐
1.5 Proof by mathematical induction (HL)	☐	☐	☐
1.6 Complex numbers (HL)	☐	☐	☐
1.7 Systems of linear equations (HL)	☐	☐	☐
Topic 2 Functions and equations			
2.1 Functions in general	☐	☐	☐
2.2 Transformation of graphs	☐	☐	☐
2.3 Basic functions	☐	☐	☐
2.4 Equation solving	☐	☐	☐
Topic 3 Circular functions and trigonometry			
3.1 Radian measure	☐	☐	☐
3.2 Circular functions	☐	☐	☐
3.3 Trigonometric equations	☐	☐	☐
3.4 Triangle trigonometry	☐	☐	☐
Topic 4 Vectors			
4.1 Vector algebra	☐	☐	☐
4.2 Equations of lines and planes	☐	☐	☐

	Revised	Tested	Exam ready
Topic 5 Statistics and probability			
5.1 One variable statistics	☐	☐	☐
5.2 Two variable statistics (SL)	☐	☐	☐
5.3 Elementary probability	☐	☐	☐
5.4 Probability distributions	☐	☐	☐
Topic 6 Calculus			
6.1 Limit, convergence, continuity	☐	☐	☐
6.2 Differential calculus	☐	☐	☐
6.3 Integral calculus	☐	☐	☐
6.4 Kinematics	☐	☐	☐

My revision notes

Answers

1 a 1, 3, 6, 10, 15

b $a = 0.5, b = 0.5$

c 2 029 105

d 1, 9, 36, 100, 225

e $v_n = \dfrac{n^2(n+1)^2}{4}$, $v_{10} = 3025$

f no numerical answer

2 a $f'(x) = 2\cos 2x \quad f''(x) = -4\sin 2x$

$f'''(x) = -8\cos 2x \quad f^{(4)}(x) = 16\sin 2x$

b $f^{(14)}(x) = -2^{14}\sin 2x \quad f^{(15)}(x) = -2^{15}\cos 2x$

$f^{(16)}(x) = 2^{16}\sin 2x \quad f^{(17)}(x) = 2^{17}\cos 2x$

c $f^{(4k)}(x) = 2^{4k}\sin 2x \quad f^{(4k+1)}(x) = 2^{4k+1}\cos 2x$

$f^{(4k+2)}(x) = -2^{4k+2}\sin 2x \quad f^{(4k+3)}(x) = -2^{4k+3}\cos 2x$

d no numerical answer

3 a no numerical answer

b $3z$

c $x = \dfrac{A+B+C}{3}$, $y = \dfrac{A+B\omega^2+C\omega}{3}$, $z = \dfrac{A+B\omega+C\omega^2}{3}$

d $a = -2\omega, b = 1$

4 a 0

b no numerical answer

c 10

d 10

5 a i $3a+b = B-A$, $6a+b = \dfrac{1}{6}C - \dfrac{1}{2}B$

ii $a = \dfrac{1}{3}A - \dfrac{1}{2}B + \dfrac{1}{6}C$

iii $b = -2A + \dfrac{5}{2}B - \dfrac{1}{2}C$, $c = \dfrac{8}{3}A - 2B + \dfrac{1}{3}C$

b $a = 2, b = -5, c = 1$

c $t = 1$

6 a i $3a + b = B - A, 5a + b = C - B$

ii $a = \dfrac{1}{2}A - B + \dfrac{1}{2}C$

iii $b = -\dfrac{5}{2}A + 4B - \dfrac{3}{2}C$, $c = 3A - 3B + C$

b i no numerical answer

ii no numerical answer

c i $u_1 = a + b + c, u_2 = 4a + 2b + c, u_3 = 9a + 3b + c$

ii $a = 2, b = -7, c = 9$

iii $u_{15} = 354$

7 a $g'(x) = 3ax^2 + 2bx + c$

   b $g(0) = d, g(1) = a + b + c + d, g'(0) = c, g'(1) = 3a + 2b + c$

   c $a = -2, b = 3, c = 0, d = 0$

8 a $h(x) = x$

   b no numerical answer

   c either $h(x) = -2x^3 + 3x^2$, or $h(x) = \dfrac{1}{2} - \dfrac{1}{2}\cos(\pi x)$, or ...

   d no numerical answer

9 a no numerical answer

   b **i** Π_2

      ii Π_1

      iii $4x + y + 7z = 27$

   c **i** $a = M + 2N, b = 3M - N, c = -M - N$

      ii no numerical answer

   d $5x - 13y - z = 0$

   e $28x + 7y - 17z = 57$

10 a **i** $f(2) = 12, f(3) = 24$

      ii $f(0) = 3$

      iii $f(-1) = \dfrac{3}{2}, f(-2) = \dfrac{3}{4}$

      iv $f\left(\dfrac{1}{2}\right) = \sqrt{18}, f\left(\dfrac{1}{3}\right) = \sqrt[3]{54}$

   b $f(t) = 3 \cdot 2^t$

   c no numerical answer

   d $g(t) = b\left(\dfrac{a}{b}\right)^t$

   e no numerical answer

11 a no numerical answer

   b $\dfrac{1}{x-2} - \dfrac{1}{x+2} = \dfrac{4}{x^2 - 4}, \dfrac{1}{x-3} - \dfrac{1}{x+3} = \dfrac{6}{x^2 - 9}$

   c $\dfrac{1}{x-n} - \dfrac{1}{x+n} = \dfrac{2n}{x^2 - n^2}$

   d $\ln\dfrac{21}{11}$

12 a (1), 2, 4, 8, 16

   b 1024

   c 2^n

   d no numerical answer

   e 0

   f no numerical answer

   g **i**

```
                      1
                   1     2
                1     4     4
             1     6    12     8
          1     8    24    32    16
       1    10    40    80    80    32
```

      ii 3^n

      iii $T_{n,k} = \begin{pmatrix} n \\ k \end{pmatrix} 2^k$

13 a $y = 2x - 1, y = 4x - 4, y = 6x - 9$

b $y = 2ax - a^2$

c $y = 6x - 9$ and $y = -6x - 9$

d $y = 0$ and $y = 4x - 4$

e $y = 8x - 16$ and $y = -4x - 4$

14 a At $x = 1$, $(2, 0)$ and $(0, 2)$

At $x = 2$, $(4, 0)$ and $(0, 1)$

At $x = 3$, $(6, 0)$ and $\left(0, \dfrac{2}{3}\right)$

b $(2a, 0)$ and $\left(0, \dfrac{2}{a}\right)$

c 2

d $y = -4x + 4$

e $y = -\dfrac{1}{9}x + \dfrac{2}{3}$ and $y = -9x + 6$

15 a i no numerical answer

ii no numerical answer

iii no numerical answer

b $\left(0, \dfrac{1}{12}\right)$ and $y = -\dfrac{1}{12}$

c $\left(0, \dfrac{1}{4k}\right)$ and $y = -\dfrac{1}{4k}$

16 a $x \mapsto 0$

b $x \mapsto e^x$

c $x \mapsto \cos x, x \mapsto x^2, x \mapsto \ln|x|, x \mapsto e^{-x^2}, x \mapsto \cos x^2, x \mapsto \sin x^2, x \mapsto 1$

d $x \mapsto \sin x, x \mapsto x^3, x \mapsto \dfrac{1}{x}$

e

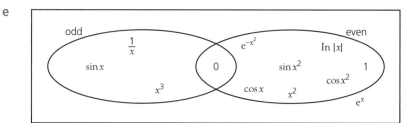

f i True

ii False

iii False

iv True

v False

vi True

vii False

viii True

g i False

ii True

iii True

iv False

h $\displaystyle\int_{-3}^{2} x^2 \sin x \, dx < \int_{-1}^{1} \tan x \, dx < \int_{-2}^{3} x^3 e^{-x^2} \, dx$

17 a **i** 0

　　ii 4

　　iii $y = -\dfrac{1}{4}x + 4$

　　iv $\left(\dfrac{20}{17}, \dfrac{63}{17}\right)$

　　v The distance of the closest point on the parabola from the line.

　　vi $\dfrac{5}{\sqrt{17}}$

b **i** $\dfrac{-1}{2p+4} = \dfrac{p^2 + 4p - 4q + q^2 + 7}{p - q}$

　　ii $p = -q$

　　iii $p = -1, q = 1$

　　iv $P(-1, 1),\ Q(1, 0)$

　　v $\sqrt{5}$

18 a **i** $\overrightarrow{AB} = \mathbf{b} - \mathbf{a},\ \overrightarrow{AC_1} = \dfrac{\beta}{\alpha + \beta}(\mathbf{b} - \mathbf{a})$

　　ii no numerical answer

　　iii $\overrightarrow{OA_1} = \dfrac{\beta \mathbf{b} + \gamma \mathbf{c}}{\beta + \gamma},\ \overrightarrow{OB_1} = \dfrac{\alpha \mathbf{a} + \gamma \mathbf{c}}{\alpha + \gamma}$

b **i** $\overrightarrow{CP} = \dfrac{\alpha \mathbf{a} + \beta \mathbf{b} - (\alpha + \beta)\mathbf{c}}{\alpha + \beta + \gamma}$

　　ii $\overrightarrow{CC_1} = \dfrac{\alpha \mathbf{a} + \beta \mathbf{b} - (\alpha + \beta)\mathbf{c}}{\alpha + \beta}$

　　iii no numerical answer

　　iv $(\beta + \gamma)\overrightarrow{AA_1} = (\alpha + \beta + \gamma)\overrightarrow{AP},\ (\alpha + \gamma)\overrightarrow{BB_1} = (\alpha + \beta + \gamma)\overrightarrow{BP}$

　　v no numerical answer

19 a $\overrightarrow{CA} = 3\mathbf{p},\ \overrightarrow{CB} = 4\mathbf{q}$

b **i** $\overrightarrow{QA} = 3\mathbf{p} - \mathbf{q},\ \overrightarrow{QO} = \dfrac{9\mathbf{p} - 3\mathbf{q}}{3 + x},\ \overrightarrow{CO} = \dfrac{9\mathbf{p} + x\mathbf{q}}{3 + x}$

　　ii $\overrightarrow{PB} = 4\mathbf{q} - \mathbf{p},\ \overrightarrow{PO} = \dfrac{8\mathbf{q} - 2\mathbf{p}}{2 + y},\ \overrightarrow{CO} = \dfrac{y\mathbf{p} + 8\mathbf{q}}{2 + y}$

　　iii no numerical answer

　　iv $x = 8, y = 9$

　　v no numerical answer

c **i** $\overrightarrow{RA} = \dfrac{(33 - 9k)\mathbf{p} - 8k\mathbf{q}}{11},\ \overrightarrow{RB} = \dfrac{-9k\mathbf{p} + (44 - 8k)\mathbf{q}}{11}$

　　ii no numerical answer

　　iii $a = 3, b = 2$ (There are other possibilities: $a = 3n, b = 2n$)

　　iv no numerical answer

20 a $p = -\dfrac{b}{3a},\ q = \dfrac{2b^3}{27a^2} - \dfrac{bc}{3a} + d$

b **i** $g(x) = ax^3 + (c - \dfrac{b^2}{3a})x$

　　ii no numerical answer

　　iii Symmetry to the point $(0, 0)$

c **i** no numerical answer

　　ii (p, q)

   d **i** no numerical answer

       ii no numerical answer

   e **i** $(2, 3)$

       ii $b = -6, c = 9, d = 1$

21 a **i** B

       ii D

       iii A

       iv E

       v C

   b F: $x \mapsto x^3(x-1)^2$, G: $x \mapsto x^3(x-1)^3$, H: $x \mapsto x^2(x-1)^3$

22 a **i** $t = 1$: $(6, 8)$, $t = 2$: $(10, 9)$, $t = 3$: $(14, 10)$

       ii $(2 + 4n, 7 + n)$

       iii no numerical answer

       iv $\mathbf{r}_C = \begin{pmatrix} 2 \\ 7 \end{pmatrix} + t \begin{pmatrix} 4 \\ 1 \end{pmatrix}$

       v $\mathbf{v}_C = \dfrac{1}{2}\mathbf{v}_A + \dfrac{1}{2}\mathbf{v}_B$

   b $\mathbf{r}_D = \begin{pmatrix} 4 \\ 4.5 \end{pmatrix} + t \begin{pmatrix} 3.5 \\ 2.5 \end{pmatrix}$

   c no numerical answer

23 a no numerical answer

   b $\overrightarrow{S_1Q_1} = 2\mathbf{p} + \mathbf{r}$

   c no numerical answer

   d no numerical answer

   e no numerical answer

24 a no numerical answer

   b $x \mapsto \dfrac{2x + 2}{3x - 2}$

   c $(f \circ f)(x) = x$

   d **i** $d = -a$ for any real number a

       ii no numerical answer

   e **i** $A = a^2 + bc, B = ab + bd, C = ac + dc, D = cb + d^2$

       ii $x \mapsto \dfrac{ax + b}{cx - a}$, for any real a, b, c where c $\neq$ 0 and $a^2 + bc \neq 0$

25 a **i** $\cos^2 \dfrac{x}{2} = \dfrac{1}{1 + t^2}$

       ii no numerical answer

       iii $\sin x = \dfrac{2t}{1 + t^2}$

       iv $\tan x = \dfrac{2t}{1 - t^2}$

       v no numerical answer

b   **i**   no numerical answer

    ii $x \mapsto \tan\dfrac{x}{2} + c$

    iii $x \mapsto \dfrac{-2}{1 + \tan\dfrac{x}{2}} + c$

    iv   no numerical answer

26 a $F\hat{E}C = \alpha$, $A\hat{F}D = \alpha + \beta$

   b $AB = \cos\alpha$, $BE = \sin\alpha$

   c $FE = \tan\beta$, $CE = \tan\beta\cos\alpha$

   d   no numerical answer

   e   no numerical answer

   f   no numerical answer

   g   no numerical answer

   h   no numerical answer

   i $\sin 75° = \dfrac{\sqrt{6}+\sqrt{2}}{4}$, $\tan 75° = \dfrac{\sqrt{3}+1}{\sqrt{3}-1}$, $\cos 75° = \dfrac{\sqrt{6}-\sqrt{2}}{4}$

   j $\sin 15° = \dfrac{\sqrt{6}-\sqrt{2}}{4}$, $\tan 15° = \dfrac{\sqrt{3}-1}{\sqrt{3}+1}$, $\cos 15° = \dfrac{\sqrt{6}+\sqrt{2}}{4}$

27 a   yes, it is

   b   **i**

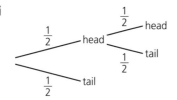

    ii $P(\text{Blaise wins}) = \dfrac{1}{4}$, $P(\text{Pierre wins}) = \dfrac{3}{4}$

   c   Pierre should get 15 écu and Blaise should get 5 écu.

28 a $\dfrac{1}{4}$

   b   **i**   If the numbers are $t_1 < t_2 < t_3 < t_4$:

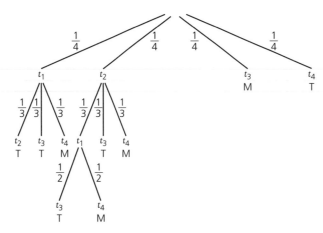

    ii $\dfrac{11}{24}$

   c $\dfrac{5}{12}$

   d $\dfrac{1}{4}$

   e   The strategy in part **b**.

29 a The value of both integrals is π.

   b **i** The value of both integrals is 0.

     ii 0

     iii 0

   c **i** no numerical answer

     ii 0

   d 0

   e **i** 2π

     ii 0

     iii 0

     iv 0

30 a **i** no numerical answer

     ii no numerical answer

     iii no numerical answer

   b **i** 50.0 m/s (3 s.f.)

     ii 1250 metres

   c **i** $a = 5, b = 50$

     ii no numerical answer

     iii $v(t) = 5 + 45e^{-2(t-60)}$

   d 306 seconds (3 s.f.)

   e 5.00 m/s

Detailed solutions

1 a $u_1 = 1$ is given

$u_2 = 1+1+1 = 3$

$u_3 = 3+2+1 = 6$

$u_4 = 6+3+1 = 10$

$u_5 = 10+4+1 = 15$

b for $n = 1$, $1 = a \cdot 1^2 + b \cdot 1 = a + b$

for $n = 2$, $3 = a \cdot 2^2 + b \cdot 2 = 4a + 2b$

two equations, two unknowns, the solution is $a = 0.5$, $b = 0.5$

c $u_n = 0.5n^2 + 0.5n$, so $u_{2014} = 0.5 \cdot 2014^2 + 0.5 \cdot 2014 = 2\,029\,105$

d $v_1 = 1$

$v_2 = 1+8 = 9$

$v_3 = 1+8+27 = 36$

$v_4 = 1+8+27+64 = 100$

$v_5 = 1+8+27+64+125 = 225$

e From the first five terms:

$1^2 = 1$, $3^2 = 9$, $6^2 = 36$, $10^2 = 100$, $15^2 = 225$
so the suggested formula is:

$$v_n = u_n^{\ 2} = (0.5n^2 + 0.5n)^2 = \frac{n^2(n+1)^2}{4}$$

$$v_{10} = \frac{10^2 11^2}{4} = 3025$$

f First term: $1 = v_1 = \dfrac{1^2(1+1)^2}{4}$, this is true.

Induction step: Assume that $v_k = \dfrac{k^2(k+1)^2}{4}$

$$v_{k+1} = 1^3 + \cdots + k^3 + (k+1)^3 = v_k + (k+1)^3$$

$$= \frac{k^2(k+1)^2}{4} + (k+1)^3 = \frac{k^2(k+1)^2 + 4(k+1)^3}{4}$$

$$= \frac{(k^2 + 4(k+1))(k+1)^2}{4} = \frac{(k+1)^2(k+2)^2}{4}$$

Conclusion: Since $v_1 = \dfrac{1^2(1+1)^2}{4}$, and if $v_k = \dfrac{k^2(k+1)^2}{4}$, then

$v_{k+1} = \dfrac{(k+1)^2((k+1)+1)^2}{4}$, so by the principle of mathematical

induction, $v_n = \dfrac{n^2(n+1)^2}{4}$ for all $n \in \mathbb{Z}^+$.

2 a $f'(x) = 2\cos 2x$

$f''(x) = -4\sin 2x$

$f'''(x) = -8\cos 2x$

$f^{(4)}(x) = 16\sin 2x$

b From part **a** we see that $f^{(4)}(x) = 2^4 f(x)$, so in higher order

derivatives, $\sin 2x$, $\cos 2x$, $-\sin 2x$ and $-\cos 2x$ will alternate.

$$f^{(14)}(x) = -2^{14}\sin 2x$$

$$f^{(15)}(x) = -2^{15}\cos 2x$$

$$f^{(16)}(x) = 2^{16}\sin 2x$$

$$f^{(17)}(x) = 2^{17}\cos 2x$$

c The pattern in part **b** suggests that

$$f^{(4k)}(x) = 2^{4k}\sin 2x$$

$$f^{(4k+1)}(x) = 2^{4k+1}\cos 2x$$

$$f^{(4k+2)}(x) = -2^{4k+2}\sin 2x$$

$$f^{(4k+3)}(x) = -2^{4k+3}\cos 2x$$

d For $n = 4k$ we use induction on k to show that

$$f^{(4k)}(x) = 2^{4k}f(x).$$

For $k = 1$, in part **a**: $f^{(4)}(x) = 2^4 f(x)$

Induction step: Assuming $f^{(4m)}(x) = 2^{4m}f(x)$,

$$f^{(4(m+1))}(x) = (f^{(4m)})''''(x) = (2^{4m}f)''''(x)$$

$$= 2^{4m}f^{(4)}(x) = 2^{4m}2^4 f(x) = 2^{4(m+1)}f(x)$$

Conclusion: Since $f^{(4)}(x) = 2^4 f(x)$, and if $f^{(4m)}(x) = 2^{4m}f(x)$, then

$f^{(4(m+1))}(x) = 2^{4(m+1)}f(x)$, hence by the principle of mathematical

induction, $f^{(4k)}(x) = 2^{4k}f(x)$ for all $k \in \mathbb{Z}^+$.

Hence $f^{(4k)}(x) = 2^{4k}\sin 2x$

Differentiating this three times we get:

$$f^{(4k+1)}(x) = 2^{4k}2\cos 2x = 2^{4k+1}\cos 2x$$

$$f^{(4k+2)}(x) = -2^{4k+1}2\sin 2x = -2^{4k+2}\sin 2x$$

$$f^{(4k+3)}(x) = -2^{4k+2}2\cos 2x = -2^{4k+3}\cos 2x$$

3 a $0 = \omega^3 - 1 = (\omega - 1)(\omega^2 + \omega + 1)$

Since $\omega - 1 \neq 0$, $1 + \omega + \omega^2 = 0$

b $A + B\omega + C\omega^2 =$

$(x + y + z) + (x + \omega y + \omega^2 z)\omega + (x + \omega^2 y + \omega z)\omega^2 =$

$x(1 + \omega + \omega^2) + y(1 + \omega^2 + \omega^4) + z(1 + \omega^3 + \omega^3) =$

$y(1 + \omega^2 + \omega) + z(1 + 1 + 1) = 3z$

c Similarly,

$A + B\omega^2 + C\omega =$

$(x + y + z) + (x + \omega y + \omega^2 z)\omega^2 + (x + \omega^2 y + \omega z)\omega =$

$x(1 + \omega^2 + \omega) + y(1 + \omega^3 + \omega^3) + z(1 + \omega^4 + \omega^2) = 3y$

$A + B + C =$

$(x + y + z) + (x + \omega y + \omega^2 z) + (x + \omega^2 y + \omega z) =$

$x(1 + 1 + 1) + y(1 + \omega + \omega^2) + z(1 + \omega^2 + \omega) = 3x$

so $x = \dfrac{A + B + C}{3}$

$y = \dfrac{A + B\omega^2 + C\omega}{3}$

$z = \dfrac{A + B\omega + C\omega^2}{3}$

> **Note**
>
> Since the derivative in the previous part is given using different formulae, we use induction to prove one of these and deduce the others from this one.

> **Note**
>
> ω is a third root of unity, the property in part **a** is well-known. It can also be rearranged as $\omega^2 = -1 - \omega$.
>
> We also need to use the property that $\omega^3 = 1$ and, as a consequence, $\omega^4 = \omega$, $\omega^5 = \omega^2$, etc.

d
$$\begin{pmatrix} 1 & 1 & 1 & | & 1 \\ 1 & \omega & \omega^2 & | & 1 \\ 1 & \omega^2 & a & | & b \end{pmatrix} \begin{array}{l} R_2 - R_1 \to R_2 \\ R_3 - R_1 \to R_3 \end{array}$$

$$\begin{pmatrix} 1 & 1 & 1 & | & 1 \\ 0 & \omega-1 & \omega^2-1 & | & 0 \\ 0 & \omega^2-1 & a-1 & | & b-1 \end{pmatrix} R_3 - (\omega+1)R_2 \to R_3$$

$$\begin{pmatrix} 1 & 1 & 1 & | & 1 \\ 0 & \omega-1 & \omega^2-1 & | & 0 \\ 0 & 0 & a-1-(\omega^2-1)(\omega+1) & | & b-1 \end{pmatrix}$$

$$(\omega^2-1)(\omega+1) = \omega^3 + \omega^2 - \omega - 1 = \omega^2 - \omega = -1 - 2\omega$$

$$\begin{pmatrix} 1 & 1 & 1 & | & 1 \\ 0 & \omega-1 & \omega^2-1 & | & 0 \\ 0 & 0 & a+2\omega & | & b-1 \end{pmatrix}$$

The system has infinitely many solutions if $a+2\omega = 0$ and $b-1 = 0$, so $a = -2\omega$ and $b = 1$.

4 a sum of roots is $\dfrac{-a_{n-1}}{a_n} = \dfrac{-a_4}{a_5} = \dfrac{0}{1} = 0$

b $ww^* = (a+bi)(a-bi) = a^2 - b^2 i^2 = a^2 + b^2 = |w|^2$

c
$$|z_1 - z_k|^2 = (z_1 - z_k)(z_1 - z_k)^*$$
$$= (z_1 - z_k)(z_1^* - z_k^*)$$
$$= z_1 z_1^* - z_1 z_k^* - z_k z_1^* + z_k z_k^*$$
$$= |z_1|^2 - z_1 z_k^* - z_k z_1^* + |z_k|^2$$
$$= 2 - z_1 z_k^* - z_k z_1^*$$

$$\sum_{k=1}^{5} |z_1 - z_k|^2 = 5 \cdot 2 - z_1 \sum_{k=1}^{5} z_k^* - z_1^* \sum_{k=1}^{5} z_k$$
$$= 10 - z_1 (\textstyle\sum_{k=1}^{5} z_k)^* - z_1^* \cdot 0$$
$$= 10 - z_1 \cdot 0^* = 10$$

d Place the regular pentagon on the unit circle centred at the origin of the Argand diagram so that A_1 is on the positive real axis. Then A_k can be considered z_k, the fifth roots of unity of the previous parts.

Also, $a_k = |A_1 A_k| = |z_1 - z_k|$

Since $|z_1 - z_1| = 0$, $a_2^2 + a_3^2 + a_4^2 + a_5^2 = \displaystyle\sum_{k=1}^{5} |z_1 - z_k|^2 = 10$

5 a **i** $3a+b = (4a+2b+c) - (a+b+c) = B - A$

$12a + 2b = (16a+4b+c) - (4a+2b+c) = C - B$

$6a + b = \dfrac{1}{2}C - \dfrac{1}{2}B$

ii $3a = (6a+b) - (3a+b) = (\dfrac{1}{2}C - \dfrac{1}{2}B) - (B-A) = A - \dfrac{3}{2}B + \dfrac{1}{2}C$

$a = \dfrac{1}{3}A - \dfrac{1}{2}B + \dfrac{1}{6}C$

iii $b = (6a+b) - 6a = (\dfrac{1}{2}C - \dfrac{1}{2}B) - 6(\dfrac{1}{3}A - \dfrac{1}{2}B + \dfrac{1}{6}C)$

$b = -2A + \dfrac{5}{2}B - \dfrac{1}{2}C$

$c = (a+b+c) - a - b = A - (\dfrac{1}{3}A - \dfrac{1}{2}B + \dfrac{1}{6}C) - (-2A + \dfrac{5}{2}B - \dfrac{1}{2}C)$

$c = \dfrac{8}{3}A - 2B + \dfrac{1}{3}C$

Note

For the last part of the question, careful row reduction is needed. A good start is to find the augmented matrix corresponding to the equation system.

Note

This question can be answered by considering the fifth roots of unity as powers of one of them ($1, \omega, \omega^2, \omega^3$ and ω^4) but we look at another approach. The first step is to use the Vieta formula about the relationship between the sum of roots and the coefficients of a polynomial. This can be read from expanding the factor form

$z^5 - 1 = (z-z_1)(z-z_2)(z-z_3)$
$(z-z_4)(z-z_5)$.

In part **c** several properties of the conjugate operation are used, besides the one asked in part **b**. We also use the fact that $|z_k| = 1$ for the fifth roots of unity.

Note

The last part can be solved using elementary geometry, but it takes time. Noticing the connection to part **c** significantly reduces the calculation (in fact the calculation is already done). The key observation here is that the fifth roots of unity form a regular pentagon inscribed in the unit circle.

Note

Solving an equation system in three unknowns is part of the HL syllabus, but it is not expected in the SL exam. However, with guidance, it is not beyond the level of the SL syllabus.

b $(1, -2)$ is on the graph of $y = ax^2 + bx + c$, so $a \cdot 1^2 + b \cdot 1 + c = -2$, or
$a + b + c = -2$

$(2, -1)$ is on the graph, so $4a + 2b + c = -1$

$(4, 13)$ is on the graph, so $16a + 4b + c = 13$

Using the results of part **a** with $A = -2$, $B = -1$ and $C = 13$ gives
$a = 2$, $b = -5$ and $c = 1$.

Note

The information given in the question translates to an equation system similar to that in part **a**.

c $a + b + c \quad = -2$

$4a + 2b + c = -1$

$16a + 4b + c = t$

According to part **a**, there is always a solution.
It does not give a parabola, if $a = 0$.

$a = \dfrac{1}{3}(-2) - \dfrac{1}{2}(-1) + \dfrac{1}{6}t = 0$, $-4 + 3 + t = 0$, so $t = 1$

Note

This part seemingly contradicts part **a**, where we found a solution for any A, B, C.

The key here is to notice that not all graphs of the form $y = ax^2 + bx + c$ are parabolas

6 a i $3a + b = (4a + 2b + c) - (a + b + c) = B - A$

$5a + b = (9a + 3b + c) - (4a + 2b + c) = C - B$

ii $2a = (5a + b) - (3a + b) = (C - B) - (B - A) = A - 2B + C$

$a = \dfrac{1}{2}A - B + \dfrac{1}{2}C$

Note

As in the previous question, this part gives guidance to solve an equation system in three unknowns of a specific form.

iii $b = (3a + b) - 3a = (B - A) - 3(\dfrac{1}{2}A - B + \dfrac{1}{2}C)$

$b = -\dfrac{5}{2}A + 4B - \dfrac{3}{2}C$

$c = (a + b + c) - a - b = A - (\dfrac{1}{2}A - B + \dfrac{1}{2}C) - (-\dfrac{5}{2}A + 4B - \dfrac{3}{2}C)$

$c = 3A - 3B + C$

b i $3 - 4 \neq 6 - 3$, there is no common difference

ii $\dfrac{3}{4} \neq \dfrac{6}{3}$, there is no common ratio

c i $u_1 = a + b + c$

$u_2 = 4a + 2b + c$

$u_3 = 9a + 3b + c$

Note

This is not a sequence we meet in the syllabus, so a hint is given about the form of the general term. Comparing this hint with the known terms of the sequence helps to set up an equation system, which is of the form we solved in general in part **a**.

ii Using part **a** with $A = u_1 = 4$, $B = u_2 = 3$ and $C = u_3 = 6$, we get
$a = 2$, $b = -7$ and $c = 9$.

iii $u_4 = 2 \cdot 4^2 - 7 \cdot 4 + 9 = 13$

$u_5 = 2 \cdot 5^2 - 7 \cdot 5 + 9 = 24$

$u_{15} = 2 \cdot 15^2 - 7 \cdot 15 + 9 = 354$

7 a $g'(x) = 3ax^2 + 2bx + c$

b $g(0) = d$

$g(1) = a + b + c + d$

$g'(0) = c$

$g'(1) = 3a + 2b + c$

c $(0, 0)$ is a local minimum, so $g(0) = 0$ and $g'(0) = 0$

$(1, 1)$ is a local maximum, so $g(1) = 1$ and $g'(1) = 0$

so (using part **b**), $d = 0$, $a + b + c + d = 1$, $c = 0$ and $3a + 2b + c = 0$

Solving this equation system gives $a = -2$, $b = 3$, $c = 0$, $d = 0$.

Note

The key here is to translate the information given into an equation for the four unknowns.

8 a Since linear functions are continuous, we need

$$h(0) = f(0) = 0 \text{ and } h(1) = f(1) = 1$$

hence $h(x) = x$

b Since the derivative of quadratic functions are continuous,

- if f is differentiable at $x = 0$, then $h'(0)$ must be the same as the left derivative of f at $x = 0$, which is 0

- if f is differentiable at $x = 1$, then $h'(1)$ must also be 0, the right derivative of f at $x = 1$.

There is no quadratic with 0 derivative at two different places, so there is no quadratic $h(x)$ that makes f differentiable everywhere.

c We look for a function with $h(0) = 0$, $h'(0) = 0$, $h(1) = 1$, $h'(1) = 0$

- a cubic polynomial like this is $h(x) = -2x^3 + 3x^2$

- a trigonometric example is $h(x) = \dfrac{1}{2} - \dfrac{1}{2}\cos(\pi x)$.

d Since the defining functions are differentiable everywhere, we only need to show differentiability at the endpoints of the defining intervals.

For the polynomial example:

$$\lim_{x \to 0^-} \frac{f(x) - f(0)}{x - 0} = \lim_{x \to 0^-} \frac{0 - 0}{x - 0} = 0$$

$$\lim_{x \to 0^+} \frac{f(x) - f(0)}{x - 0} = \lim_{x \to 0^+} \frac{h(x) - 0}{x - 0}$$

$$= \lim_{x \to 0^+} \frac{-2x^3 + 3x^2 - 0}{x}$$

$$= \lim_{x \to 0^+} -2x^2 + 3x = -2 \cdot 0^2 + 3 \cdot 0 = 0$$

Since the two limits are the same, f is differentiable at $x = 0$.

$$\lim_{x \to 1^+} \frac{f(x) - f(1)}{x - 1} = \lim_{x \to 1^+} \frac{1 - 1}{x - 1} = 0$$

$$\lim_{x \to 1^-} \frac{f(x) - f(1)}{x - 1} = \lim_{x \to 1^-} \frac{h(x) - 1}{x - 1}$$

$$= \lim_{x \to 1^-} \frac{-2x^3 + 3x^2 - 1}{x - 1}$$

$$= \lim_{x \to 1^-} \frac{(x - 1)(-2x^2 + x + 1)}{x - 1}$$

$$= \lim_{x \to 1^-} (-2x^2 + x + 1) = -2 \cdot 1^2 + 1 + 1 = 0$$

Since the two limits are the same, f is differentiable at $x = 1$.

For the trigonometric example:

$$\lim_{t \to 0^+} \frac{f(0 + t) - f(0)}{t} = \lim_{h \to 0^+} \frac{h(0 + t) - 0}{t}$$

$$= \lim_{t \to 0^+} \frac{1 - \cos(\pi t) - 2 \cdot 0}{2t} =$$

$$= \lim_{t \to 0^+} \frac{(1 - \cos(\pi t))(1 + \cos(\pi t))}{2(1 + \cos(\pi t))t}$$

$$= \lim_{t \to 0^+} \frac{\sin(\pi t)}{t} \frac{\sin(\pi t)}{2(1 + \cos(\pi t))} = \pi \frac{0}{4} = 0$$

Note

Informally, continuity means that the parts of the graph join together.

Note

Informally, the function is differentiable at the joining point. If the curve is smooth, it does not instantly change direction.

Note

There are other types of curves with given values and horizontal tangents at two different points. According to parts **a** and **b**, if we look for a polynomial, the order has to be at least three.

Note

To show differentiability of a piecewise defined function, we either go back to the derivative (like in this solution), or we use facts about the defining functions (for example, that the derivatives are continuous).

$$\lim_{t \to 0^-} \frac{f(1+t)-f(1)}{t} = \lim_{t \to 0^-} \frac{h(1+t)-1}{t}$$

$$= \lim_{t \to 0^-} \frac{1-\cos(\pi(1+t))-2}{2t}$$

$$= \lim_{t \to 0^-} \frac{-\cos(\pi t)\cos\pi - 1}{2t} + \frac{\sin(\pi t)\sin\pi}{2t}$$

$$= \lim_{t \to 0^-} \frac{\cos(\pi t)-1}{2t} + \frac{\sin(\pi t) \cdot 0}{2t} = 0 + 0 = 0$$

9 **a** $\overrightarrow{PA} = \begin{pmatrix} 4 \\ 1 \\ 7 \end{pmatrix}$, $\overrightarrow{PB} = \begin{pmatrix} 1 \\ 3 \\ -1 \end{pmatrix}$, $\overrightarrow{PC} = \begin{pmatrix} 2 \\ -1 \\ -1 \end{pmatrix}$

> **Note**
>
> Perpendicularity is characterised by the 0 dot product.

$\overrightarrow{PA} \cdot \overrightarrow{PB} = 4 \cdot 1 + 1 \cdot 3 + 7 \cdot (-1) = 0$, hence $\overrightarrow{PA}$ is perpendicular to $\overrightarrow{PB}$.

$\overrightarrow{PA} \cdot \overrightarrow{PC} = 4 \cdot 2 + 1 \cdot (-1) + 7 \cdot (-1) = 0$, hence $\overrightarrow{PA}$ is perpendicular to $\overrightarrow{PC}$.

$\overrightarrow{PC} \cdot \overrightarrow{PB} = 2 \cdot 1 + (-1) \cdot 3 + (-1) \cdot (-1) = 0$, hence $\overrightarrow{PC}$ is perpendicular to $\overrightarrow{PB}$.

b **i** From the equation we see that $\overrightarrow{PB} = \begin{pmatrix} 1 \\ 3 \\ -1 \end{pmatrix}$ is perpendicular to this

> **Note**
>
> The key here is to notice the relationship of the normal vector of the plane given by this equation, and the relative positions of points A, B, C and P.

plane. Since $\overrightarrow{PA}$ and $\overrightarrow{PC}$ are both perpendicular to $\overrightarrow{PB}$, both of these vectors are parallel to the plane.

$3 + 3 \cdot 1 - 2 = 4$, so P is on this plane. Therefore A and C are on the plane. This is the equation of Π_2.

ii Similarly, since the normal vector is $\overrightarrow{PC}$, this plane is Π_1.

iii $\overrightarrow{PA}$ can be chosen as the normal vector, so a possible equation is

$4x + y + 7z = 4 \cdot 3 + 1 + 7 \cdot 2 = 27$.

> **Note**
>
> In this part we are constructing planes in a special way from two planes both containing points P and A.

c **i** $a = M + 2N$, $b = 3M - N$, $c = -M - N$

ii For P:

$(M+2N) \cdot 3 + (3M-N) \cdot 1 + (-M-N) \cdot 2 = M(3+3-2) + N(6-1-2) = 4M + 3N$

For A :

$(M+2N) \cdot 7 + (3M-N) \cdot 2 + (-M-N) \cdot 9 = M(7+6-9) + N(14-2-9) = 4M + 3N$

Since both P and A are on these planes, all of these planes contain the line through P and A.

d Looking for the plane in the form of part **c i**, we need an M and N so that $4M + 3N = 0$. For example, $M = -3$ and $N = 4$ works, so the equation is: $(-3+8)x + (3(-3)-4)y + (-(-3)-4)z = 0$

After simplification: $5x - 13y - z = 0$

e Again, using the form of part **c i**, the normal vector, $\begin{pmatrix} M+2N \\ 3M-N \\ -M-N \end{pmatrix}$ should

be perpendicular to $\overrightarrow{BC} = \begin{pmatrix} 1 \\ -4 \\ 0 \end{pmatrix}$.

$(M+2N)+(3M-N)(-4)=0$, so $-11M+6N=0$

For example, $M=6$ and $N=11$ works, so the equation is:

$(6+22)x+(18-11)y+(-6-11)z=24+33$

$28x+7y-17z=57$

10 a **i** $f(2)=f(1+1)=\dfrac{f(1)f(1)}{3}=\dfrac{6\cdot6}{3}=12$

$f(3)=f(2+1)=\dfrac{f(2)f(1)}{3}=\dfrac{12\cdot6}{3}=24$

Note

A typical method of finding a function satisfying a functional equation is to use the defining equation with different x- and y-values.

ii $f(0+1)=\dfrac{f(0)f(1)}{3}$

$6=\dfrac{f(0)\cdot6}{3}$, so $f(0)=3$

iii $f(0)=f(-1+1)=\dfrac{f(-1)f(1)}{3}$

$3=\dfrac{f(-1)\cdot6}{3}$, so $f(-1)=\dfrac{3}{2}$

$f(0)=f(-2+2)=\dfrac{f(-2)f(2)}{3}$

$3=\dfrac{f(-2)\cdot12}{3}$, so $f(-2)=\dfrac{3}{4}$

iv $f(1)=f\left(\dfrac{1}{2}+\dfrac{1}{2}\right)=\dfrac{f\left(\frac{1}{2}\right)f\left(\frac{1}{2}\right)}{3}$, so $6=\dfrac{\left(f\left(\frac{1}{2}\right)\right)^2}{3}$

Since $f\left(\dfrac{1}{2}\right)>0$, $f\left(\dfrac{1}{2}\right)=\sqrt{18}=3\sqrt{2}$

$f(1)=f\left(\dfrac{1}{3}+\dfrac{2}{3}\right)=\dfrac{f\left(\frac{1}{3}\right)f\left(\frac{2}{3}\right)}{3}$

$6=\dfrac{f\left(\frac{1}{3}\right)f\left(\frac{1}{3}+\frac{1}{3}\right)}{3}=\dfrac{f\left(\frac{1}{3}\right)\dfrac{f\left(\frac{1}{3}\right)f\left(\frac{1}{3}\right)}{3}}{3}$

$6=\dfrac{\left(f\left(\frac{1}{3}\right)\right)^3}{9}$, so $f\left(\dfrac{1}{3}\right)=\sqrt[3]{54}=3\sqrt[3]{2}$

b $f(t)=3\cdot2^t$

c $f(1)=3\cdot2^1=6$

Note

It may be useful to organise the results from part **a** in a table to help formulate a conjecture.

$f(x+y)=3\cdot2^{x+y}=3\cdot2^x2^y=\dfrac{3\cdot2^x3\cdot2^y}{3}=\dfrac{f(x)f(y)}{3}$

d $g(t)=b\left(\dfrac{a}{b}\right)^t$

Note

Careful analysis of parts **a** and **b** is needed for this generalisation.

e $g(1)=b\left(\dfrac{a}{b}\right)^1=a$

$g(x+y)=b\left(\dfrac{a}{b}\right)^{x+y}=b\left(\dfrac{a}{b}\right)^x\left(\dfrac{a}{b}\right)^y=\dfrac{b\left(\frac{a}{b}\right)^x b\left(\frac{a}{b}\right)^y}{b}=\dfrac{g(x)g(y)}{b}$

11 a $\dfrac{1}{x-1}-\dfrac{1}{x+1}=\dfrac{(x+1)-(x-1)}{(x-1)(x+1)}=\dfrac{2}{x^2-1}$

b $\dfrac{1}{x-2}-\dfrac{1}{x+2}=\dfrac{(x+2)-(x-2)}{(x-2)(x+2)}=\dfrac{4}{x^2-4}$

$\dfrac{1}{x-3}-\dfrac{1}{x+3}=\dfrac{(x+3)-(x-3)}{(x-3)(x+3)}=\dfrac{6}{x^2-9}$

c $\dfrac{1}{x-n}-\dfrac{1}{x+n}=\dfrac{(x+n)-(x-n)}{(x-n)(x+n)}=\dfrac{2n}{x^2-n^2}$

d $\displaystyle\int_{11}^{12}\dfrac{20}{x^2-100}\,\mathrm{d}x=\int_{11}^{12}\dfrac{1}{x-10}-\dfrac{1}{x+10}\,\mathrm{d}x$

$=[\ln(x-10)-\ln(x+10)]_{11}^{12}$

$=(\ln 2-\ln 22)-(\ln 1-\ln 21)$

$=\ln 2-\ln 22+\ln 21=\ln\dfrac{2\cdot 21}{22}=\ln\dfrac{21}{11}$

12 a $1+1=2$

$1+2+1=4$

$1+3+3+1=8$

$1+4+6+4+1=16$

b $1+10+45+120+210+252+210+120+45+10+1=1024$

c $\displaystyle\sum_{k=0}^{n}\binom{n}{k}=2^n$

d $\displaystyle\sum_{k=0}^{n}\binom{n}{k}=\sum_{k=0}^{n}\binom{n}{k}1^{n-k}1^k=(1+1)^n=2^n$

e $\displaystyle\sum_{k=0}^{n}(-1)^k\binom{n}{k}=0$

f $\displaystyle\sum_{k=0}^{n}(-1)^k\binom{n}{k}=\sum_{k=0}^{n}\binom{n}{k}1^{n-k}(-1)^k=(1+(-1))^n=0$

g **i**

$$
\begin{array}{ccccccccccc}
&&&&&1&&&&&\\
&&&&1&&2&&&&\\
&&&1&&4&&4&&&\\
&&1&&6&&12&&8&&\\
&1&&8&&24&&32&&16&\\
1&&10&&40&&80&&80&&32\\
\end{array}
$$

ii $\displaystyle\sum_{k=0}^{n}T_{n,k}=3^n$

iii $T_{n,k}=\binom{n}{k}2^k$

13 a $\dfrac{\mathrm{d}y}{\mathrm{d}x}=2x$

■ For $x=1$, gradient: 2, point: (1, 1), equation of the tangent: $y=2x-1$

■ For $x=2$, gradient: 4, point: (2, 4), equation of the tangent: $y=4x-4$

■ For $x=3$, gradient: 6, point: (3, 9), equation of the tangent: $y=6x-9$

b Following the pattern: $y=2ax-a^2$

c

Note

Noticing the connection to the previous parts is essential in past **d**. Without hints, the evaluation of this integral is not part of the syllabus. However, after rewriting the quotient as the difference of simpler quotients, the integral becomes accessible.

Note

Since the question specified the form of the final answer, we need to use the laws of logarithms.

Note

Noticing the pattern in parts **a** and **b** is the key to finding the expression in part **c**.

Note

Part **g** of the question asked for the first few rows of this new triangle, but even without this hint it is a good idea to write a few elements if a general construction like this appears in a question.

Note

Since the command term was 'suggest', you don't have to justify the formulae in parts **g ii** and **g iii**. Nevertheless, can you think of an expression in the form $(a+b)^n$ (where a and b are whole numbers), so that the expansion gives the numbers in the rows of this triangle?

Note

When the words 'tangent' or 'normal' appear in a question involving the graph of a function, the first thing that should come to mind is differentiation.

Using part **b**: $-9 = 2a \cdot 0 - a^2$, so $a = \pm 3$,

hence the equations: $y = 6x - 9$ and $y = -6x - 9$

d

Using part **b**: $0 = 2a \cdot 1 - a^2 = a(2-a)$, so $a = 2$ or $a = 0$,

hence the equations: $y = 0$ and $y = 4x - 4$

e

Using part **b**: $-8 = 2a \cdot 1 - a^2$, so $0 = a^2 - 2a - 8 = (a-4)(a+2)$, so $a = 4$ or $a = -2$,

hence the equations: $y = 8x - 16$ and $y = -4x - 4$

14 a $\dfrac{dy}{dx} = -\dfrac{1}{x^2}$

■ For $x = 1$, gradient: -1, point: $(1, 1)$,
equation of the tangent: $y = -x + 2$

x-intercept: $(2, 0)$, y-intercept: $(0, 2)$

■ For $x = 2$, gradient: $-\dfrac{1}{4}$, point: $\left(2, \dfrac{1}{2}\right)$,

equation of the tangent: $y = -\dfrac{1}{4}x + 1$

x-intercept: $(4, 0)$, y-intercept: $(0, 1)$

■ For $x = 3$, gradient: $-\dfrac{1}{9}$, point: $\left(3, \dfrac{1}{3}\right)$,

equation of the tangent: $y = -\dfrac{1}{9}x + \dfrac{2}{3}$

x-intercept: $(6, 0)$, y-intercept: $\left(0, \dfrac{2}{3}\right)$

b Following the pattern, x-intercept: $(2a, 0)$, y-intercept: $\left(0, \dfrac{2}{a}\right)$

c

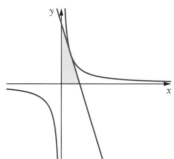

Area: $\dfrac{1}{2} 2a \dfrac{2}{a} = 2$

d Using part **b**, if the y-intercept is $(0, 4)$, then $a = \dfrac{1}{2}$, so the x-intercept is $(1, 0)$

hence the gradient is -4, and the equation is $y = -4x + 4$

e

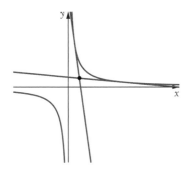

Following the pattern from part **a**, the equation of the tangent line at point $\left(a, \dfrac{1}{a}\right)$ is $y = -\dfrac{1}{a^2}x + \dfrac{2}{a}$.

$$0.6 = -\frac{1}{a^2}0.6 + \frac{2}{a}$$

$$3a^2 = -3 + 10a$$

$$0 = 3a^2 - 10a + 3 = (3a - 1)(a - 3),\ \text{so } a = 3 \text{ or } a = \frac{1}{3}$$

hence the equations are $y = -\dfrac{1}{9}x + \dfrac{2}{3}$ and $y = -9x + 6$

15 a The distance of a point (p, q) from a horizontal line $y = r$ is $|q - r|$.

  i Distance of (a, a^2) from $y = -0.25$ is $a^2 + 0.25$

  Distance of (a, a^2) from $(0, 0.25)$ is $\sqrt{a^2 + (a^2 - 0.25)^2}$, after simplification,

  $$\sqrt{a^2 + a^4 - 0.5a^2 + 0.25^2} = \sqrt{(a^2 + 0.25)^2} = a^2 + 0.25$$

  ii Distance of $(a, 2a^2)$ from $y = -0.125$ is $2a^2 + 0.125$

  Distance of $(a, 2a^2)$ from $(0, 0.125)$ is $\sqrt{a^2 + (2a^2 - 0.125)^2}$, after simplification,

  $$\sqrt{a^2 + 4a^4 - 0.5a^2 + 0.125^2} = \sqrt{(2a^2 + 0.125)^2} = 2a^2 + 0.125$$

  iii Distance of $(a, 4a^2)$ from $y = -0.0625$ is $4a^2 + 0.0625$

  Distance of $(a, 4a^2)$ from $(0, 0.0625)$ is $\sqrt{a^2 + (4a^2 - 0.0625)^2}$, after simplification,

  $$\sqrt{a^2 + 16a^4 - 0.5a^2 + 0.0625^2} = \sqrt{(4a^2 + 0.0625)^2} = 4a^2 + 0.0625$$

b Noticing the pattern, $0.25 = \dfrac{1}{4}$, $0.125 = \dfrac{1}{8}$ and $0.0625 = \dfrac{1}{16}$, for the parabola $y = 3x^2$, the suggested point is $\left(0, \dfrac{1}{12}\right)$ and the line is $y = -\dfrac{1}{12}$.

To check:

Distance of $(a, 3a^2)$ from $y = -\dfrac{1}{12}$ is $3a^2 + \dfrac{1}{12}$

Distance of $(a, 3a^2)$ from $\left(0, \dfrac{1}{12}\right)$ is $\sqrt{a^2 + \left(3a^2 - \dfrac{1}{12}\right)^2}$, after simplification,

$$\sqrt{a^2 + 9a^4 - \frac{1}{2}a^2 + \frac{1}{144}} = \sqrt{\left(3a^2 + \frac{1}{12}\right)^2} = 3a^2 + \frac{1}{12}$$

c Point: $\left(0, \dfrac{1}{4k}\right)$, line: $y = -\dfrac{1}{4k}$

Note

Looking at the diagram, it is clear that from the given point, the tangents are drawn to the part of the graph in the first quadrant. This is confirmed by the calculation.

Note

The distance formula for two points is in the formula booklet, but the distance between a point and a horizontal line is not.

Note

The pattern in the constant only becomes noticeable when it is converted from a decimal to a fraction.

16 a $x \mapsto 0$

   b $x \mapsto e^x$

   c $x \mapsto \cos x,\ x \mapsto x^2,\ x \mapsto \ln|x|,\ x \mapsto e^{-x^2},\ x \mapsto \cos x^2,\ x \mapsto \sin x^2,\ x \mapsto 1$

   d $x \mapsto \sin x,\ x \mapsto x^3,\ x \mapsto \dfrac{1}{x}$

   e

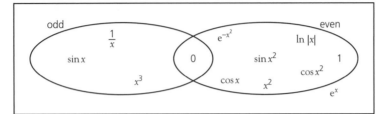

   f   **i**   True, $(f+g)(-x) = f(-x) + g(-x) = -f(x) - g(x) = -(f+g)(x)$

       ii   False, $x \mapsto x$ is odd, but $x \mapsto x + x = 2x$ is not even.

       iii   False, $x \mapsto x$ is odd, but $x \mapsto xx = x^2$ is not odd.

       iv   True, $(fg)(-x) = f(-x)g(-x) = (-f(x))(-g(x)) = (fg)(x)$

       v   False, $x \mapsto x^2$ is even, but $x \mapsto x^2 + x^2 = 2x^2$ is not odd.

       vi   True, $(f+g)(-x) = f(-x) + g(-x) = f(x) + g(x) = (f+g)(x)$

       vii   False, $x \mapsto x^2$ is even, but $x \mapsto x^2 x^2 = x^4$ is not odd.

       viii   True, $(fg)(-x) = f(-x)g(-x) = f(x)g(x) = (fg)(x)$

   g   **i**   False, $x \mapsto x^3$ is odd, but the derivative, $x \mapsto 3x^2$ is not odd.

       ii   True, $\begin{aligned}[t] f'(-x) &= \lim_{h \to 0} \frac{f(-x+h) - f(-x)}{h} = \lim_{h \to 0} \frac{-f(x-h) + f(x)}{h} \\ &= \lim_{-h \to 0} \frac{f(x + (-h)) - f(x)}{-h} = f'(x) \end{aligned}$

       iii   True, $\begin{aligned}[t] f'(-x) &= \lim_{h \to 0} \frac{f(-x+h) - f(-x)}{h} = \lim_{h \to 0} \frac{f(x-h) - f(x)}{h} \\ &= -\lim_{-h \to 0} \frac{f(x + (-h)) - f(x)}{-h} = -f'(x) \end{aligned}$

       iv   False, $x \mapsto x^2$ is even, but the derivative, $x \mapsto 2x$ is not even.

   h   The product of an odd and an even function is odd, since

$$(fg)(-x) = f(-x)g(-x) = (-f(x))g(x) = -(fg)(x)$$

       Since the graph of an odd function is symmetric to the origin, the integral of an odd function over an interval $[-a,\ a]$ is 0.

$$\int_{-1}^{1} \tan x \, dx = 0$$

       $x \mapsto x^3 e^{-x^2}$ is odd, and for $x > 0$, $x^3 e^{-x^2} > 0$, so

$$\int_{-2}^{3} x^3 e^{-x^2} \, dx = \int_{-2}^{2} x^3 e^{-x^2} \, dx + \int_{2}^{3} x^3 e^{-x^2} \, dx = 0 + \int_{2}^{3} x^3 e^{-x^2} \, dx > 0$$

       $x \mapsto x^2 \sin x$ is odd, and for $-\pi < x < 0$, $x^2 \sin x < 0$, so

$$\int_{-3}^{2} x^2 \sin x \, dx = \int_{-2}^{2} x^2 \sin x \, dx + \int_{-3}^{-2} x^2 \sin x \, dx = 0 + \int_{-3}^{-2} x^2 \sin x \, dx < 0$$

       hence the order is

$$\int_{-3}^{2} x^2 \sin x \, dx < \int_{-1}^{1} \tan x \, dx < \int_{-2}^{3} x^3 e^{-x^2} \, dx$$

Note

To show that a statement is true, we need a convincing argument to prove it.

To show that a statement is not true, it is enough to produce a counter-example.

Note

To show a general statement about derivatives, it is usually necessary to go back to the definition.

Note

A graphical approach using the symmetries of odd and even functions can also help. Draw the graph of an odd (or even) function and the tangents to this curve at x and $-x$. What do you notice about these tangents? What can you say about the gradients?

17 a i $\frac{dy}{dx}=2x+4=4$ (since the gradient of $y=4x-1$ is 4) so $x=0$

Note

Parallel lines have the same gradient.

ii $y=0^2+4\cdot0+4=4$

iii Gradient of the normal is $-\frac{1}{4}$, a point on it is (0, 4) so the equation

is $y=-\frac{1}{4}x+4$

Note

The product of the gradients of perpendicular lines is –1.

iv $-\frac{1}{4}x+4=4x-1$, so $x=\frac{20}{17}$ and hence $y=\frac{63}{17}$

the intersection point is $\left(\frac{20}{17},\frac{63}{17}\right)$

v The distance of the closest point on the parabola from the line

vi $\sqrt{\left(\frac{20}{17}\right)^2+\left(\frac{63}{17}-4\right)^2}=\frac{5}{\sqrt{17}}=1.21$

b i For $y=x^2+4x+4$, $\frac{dy}{dx}=2x+4$

At P, the gradient of tangent is $2p+4$, the gradient of the

normal is $\frac{-1}{2p+4}$.

The gradient of PQ is $\frac{(p^2+4p+4)-(4q-3-q^2)}{p-q}$.

Q is on the normal if these two gradients are the same, so

$\frac{-1}{2p+4}=\frac{p^2+4p-4q+q^2+7}{p-q}$

ii For $y=4x-3-x^2$, $\frac{dy}{dx}=4-2x$

The gradient of the tangent at Q is $4-2q$, so

$2p+4=4-2q$, or after simplification $p=-q$

iii Solving the equation system of parts **i** and **ii**,

Note

This is a cubic equation to solve. Graphing calculators have applications to solve it. However, if an equation like this appears on a non-calculator paper, the only way to solve it is to find a root by trial and error. After finding a root, factorise the polynomial and use the quadratic formula to find the other two roots.

$\frac{-1}{4-2q}=\frac{q^2-4q-4q+q^2+7}{-2q}=\frac{2q^2-8q+7}{-2q}$

$2q=8q^2-32q+28-4q^3+16q^2-14q$

$0=4q^3-24q^2+48q-28$

$0=q^3-6q^2+12q-7$

$0=(q-1)(q^2-5q+7)$

Since the quadratic has negative discriminant, the only solution is $q=1$, and hence $p=-1$.

iv P is (–1, 1), Q is (1, 0)

v $PQ=\sqrt{2^2+1^2}=\sqrt{5}$

18 a i $\overrightarrow{AB}=b-a$, $\overrightarrow{AC_1}=\frac{\beta}{\alpha+\beta}(b-a)$

ii $\overrightarrow{OC_1}=\overrightarrow{OA}+\overrightarrow{AC_1}=a+\frac{\beta}{\alpha+\beta}(b-a)=\frac{(\alpha+\beta)a+\beta(b-a)}{\alpha+\beta}=\frac{\alpha a+\beta b}{\alpha+\beta}$

Note

When we add or subtract vectors, or multiply vectors by numbers, we can use algebraic manipulations similar to the ones we use for numbers.

iii $\overrightarrow{OA_1}=\frac{\beta b+\gamma c}{\beta+\gamma}$, $\overrightarrow{OB_1}=\frac{\alpha a+\gamma c}{\alpha+\gamma}$

Note

Note that the notation in the question and in this solution is not precise.
Instead of $\frac{v}{k}$, a more precise notation would be $\frac{1}{k}v$.

b **i** $\overrightarrow{CP} = \dfrac{\alpha a + \beta b + \gamma c}{\alpha + \beta + \gamma} - c = \dfrac{\alpha a + \beta b - (\alpha + \beta)c}{\alpha + \beta + \gamma}$

ii $\overrightarrow{CC_1} = \dfrac{\alpha a + \beta b}{\alpha + \beta} - c = \dfrac{\alpha a + \beta b - (\alpha + \beta)c}{\alpha + \beta}$

iii $(\alpha + \beta)\overrightarrow{CC_1} = \alpha a + \beta b - (\alpha + \beta)c$

$(\alpha + \beta + \gamma)\overrightarrow{CP} = \alpha a + \beta b - (\alpha + \beta)c$, so indeed,

$(\alpha + \beta)\overrightarrow{CC_1} = (\alpha + \beta + \gamma)\overrightarrow{CP}$

iv $(\beta + \gamma)\overrightarrow{AA_1} = (\alpha + \beta + \gamma)\overrightarrow{AP}$, $(\alpha + \gamma)\overrightarrow{BB_1} = (\alpha + \beta + \gamma)\overrightarrow{BP}$

v Since $\overrightarrow{CP} = \dfrac{\alpha + \beta}{\alpha + \beta + \gamma}\,\overrightarrow{CC_1}$, $\overrightarrow{CP}$ and $\overrightarrow{CC_1}$ are parallel vectors, so CP and CC_1 are parallel line segments.

Since C is a common point of these line segments, this means that C, C_1 and P are collinear.

Similarly, A, A_1 and P are also collinear. Also, B, B_1 and P are collinear.

Hence, AA_1, BB_1 and CC_1 all contain the point P.

Note

There are different ways to show that three points, X, Y and Z are collinear. One way is to use vectors to show that XY is parallel to XZ.

19 a $\overrightarrow{CA} = 3\overrightarrow{CP} = 3p$, $\overrightarrow{CB} = 4\overrightarrow{CQ} = 4q$

b **i** $\overrightarrow{QA} = \overrightarrow{QC} + \overrightarrow{CA} = -q + 3p$

$\overrightarrow{QO} = \dfrac{3}{3+x}\overrightarrow{QA} = \dfrac{9p - 3q}{3+x}$

$\overrightarrow{CO} = \overrightarrow{CQ} + \overrightarrow{QO} = q + \dfrac{9p - 3q}{3+x} = \dfrac{9p + xq}{3+x}$

ii $\overrightarrow{PB} = \overrightarrow{PC} + \overrightarrow{CB} = -p + 4q$

$\overrightarrow{PO} = \dfrac{2}{2+y}\overrightarrow{PB} = \dfrac{8q - 2p}{2+y}$

$\overrightarrow{CO} = \overrightarrow{CP} + \overrightarrow{PO} = p + \dfrac{8q - 2p}{2+y} = \dfrac{yp + 8q}{2+y}$

iii $\dfrac{9p + xq}{3+x} = \dfrac{yp + 8q}{2+y}$

$18p + 2xq + 9yp + xyq = 3yp + 24q + xyp + 8xq$

$(18 + 6y - xy)p = (24 + 6x - xy)q$

Since p and q are non-zero, non-parallel vectors, this means that $xy - 6y - 18 = 0$ and $xy - 6x - 24 = 0$.

iv Expressing xy from the two equations in the previous part gives $6y + 18 = 6x + 24$, so $y = x + 1$.

$x(x+1) - 6x - 24 = 0$

$x^2 - 5x - 24 = 0$, so $(x-8)(x+3) = 0$

since $x > 0$, $x = 8$, and hence $y = 8 + 1 = 9$

v $\overrightarrow{CO} = \dfrac{9p + xq}{3+x} = \dfrac{9p + 8q}{11}$

c **i** $\overrightarrow{RA} = \overrightarrow{RC} + \overrightarrow{CA} = -k\overrightarrow{CO} + 3p = -k\dfrac{9p + 8q}{11} + 3p$

$\overrightarrow{RB} = \overrightarrow{RC} + \overrightarrow{CB} = -k\overrightarrow{CO} + 4q = -k\dfrac{9p + 8q}{11} + 4q$

Note

Can you think of a way to prove the claim in part **b v** without working through the previous parts?

In an exam it is sometimes useful to look at the last part of a long question. It is likely that the previous parts (or at least some of them) are there as a guide towards the solution of the last part.

ii $\overrightarrow{RA} = \dfrac{-11}{5}\dfrac{9p+8q}{11} + 3p = \dfrac{-9p-8q+15p}{5} = \dfrac{6p-8q}{5}$

$\overrightarrow{RB} = \dfrac{-11}{5}\dfrac{9p+8q}{11} + 4q = \dfrac{-9p-8q+20q}{5} = \dfrac{12q-9p}{5}$

hence, $3\overrightarrow{RA} = -2\overrightarrow{RB}$, so $\overrightarrow{RA}$ and $\overrightarrow{RB}$ are parallel for $k = \frac{11}{5}$

iii From the calculation of the previous part, $a = 3$, $b = 2$.

iv From the previous part, $\dfrac{AR}{RB} = \dfrac{2}{3}$

also, $\dfrac{CP}{PA} = \dfrac{1}{2}$ and $\dfrac{BQ}{QC} = \dfrac{3}{1}$ are given

so, $\dfrac{CP}{PA}\dfrac{AR}{RB}\dfrac{BQ}{QC} = \dfrac{1}{2}\cdot\dfrac{2}{3}\cdot\dfrac{3}{1} = 1$

> **Note**
>
> IB questions sometimes use the command term 'hence', which means that the connection of the statement to the previous parts of the question needs to be examined.

20 a $f'(x) = 3ax^2 + 2bx + c$, $f''(x) = 6ax + 2b$, so $f''(x) = 0$ for $x = -\dfrac{b}{3a}$

Since $a > 0$, $f''(x) > 0$ for $x < \dfrac{-b}{3a}$ and $f''(x) > 0$ for $x > -\dfrac{b}{3a}$, the

concavity changes only at $\left(-\dfrac{b}{3a}, -\dfrac{b^3}{27a^2} + \dfrac{b^3}{9a^2} - \dfrac{bc}{3a} + d\right)$.

$p = -\dfrac{b}{3a}$, $q = -\dfrac{b^3}{27a^2} + \dfrac{b^3}{9a^2} - \dfrac{bc}{3a} + d$

> **Note**
>
> In an exam, to show that a point is a point of inflexion, we need to check two conditions: the second derivative must be 0 at the x-coordinate of this point, and the second derivative must change sign.

b i $g(x) = a(x+p)^3 + b(x+p)^2 + c(x+p) + d - q$

$= a(x^3 + 3x^2 p + 3xp^2 + p^3) + b(x^2 + 2xp + p^2) + cx + cp + d - q$

$= ax^3 + (3ap+b)x^2 + (3ap^2 + 2bp + c)x + (ap^3 + bp^2 + cp + d - q)$

$= ax^3 + (3a-\dfrac{b}{3a}+b)x^2 + (3a\left(-\dfrac{b}{3a}\right)^2 + 2b-\dfrac{b}{3a} + c)x + (a\left(-\dfrac{b}{3a}\right)^3 + b\left(-\dfrac{b}{3a}\right)^2 + c-\dfrac{b}{3a} + d - q)$

$= ax^3 + \left(c - \dfrac{b^2}{3a}\right)x$

ii $g(-x) = a(-x)^3 + \left(c - \dfrac{b^2}{3a}\right)(-x) = -ax^3 - \left(c - \dfrac{b^2}{3a}\right)x = -g(x)$

iii g is an odd function, the graph is symmetric about the origin.

c i $f(p+x) - q = g(x) = -g(-x) = -(f(-x+p) - q) = q - f(p-x)$

ii Since the graph of g is symmetric about the origin, and the graph

of f is the translation of the graph of g by the vector $\begin{pmatrix} p \\ q \end{pmatrix}$, it is symmetric about the point (p, q).

> **Note**
>
> The equation in part **c i** expresses that the graph of f is symmetric about the point (p, q), so the question in part **c ii** could also be answered by direct reference to part **c i**.

d i $f'(x) = 3ax^2 + 2bx + c = 0$

$x = \dfrac{-2b \pm \sqrt{4b^2 - 12ac}}{6a} = \dfrac{-b \pm \sqrt{b^2 - 3ac}}{3a}$

Since by assumption, $b^2 - 3ac > 0$, there are two distinct points where the tangent line is horizontal.

Since $a > 0$, $\dfrac{-b - \sqrt{b^2 - 3ac}}{3a} < \dfrac{-b}{3a}$ and we already saw that $f''(x)$

is negative if $x < -\dfrac{b}{3a}$, so there is a local maximum here.

> **Note**
>
> We proved here that the graph of a cubic curve is symmetric about a point. We already know that the graph of a quadratic curve has a line of symmetry. Unfortunately, this cannot be generalised further. Higher order polynomial graphs may not have any symmetry at all.

Similary, since $\dfrac{-b+\sqrt{b^2-3ac}}{3a} > -\dfrac{b}{3a}$, so f'' is positive here,

hence there is a local minimum here.

ii The point of inflexion is the centre of symmetry of the graph; the image of the local maximum point must be the local minimum point.

e **i** Using part **d ii**, $\left(\dfrac{1+3}{2}, \dfrac{5+1}{2}\right) = (2, 3)$

ii $(2, 3)$ is the point of inflexion, so $f''(2) = 0$,

hence $6 \cdot 2 + 2b = 0$, so $b = -6$

$(1, 5)$ is a minimum point, so $f'(1) = 0$,

hence $3 + 2b + c = 0$, so $c = 9$

$f(1) = 5$, hence $1 + b + c + d = 5$, so $d = 1$

21 a **i** Graph B

ii $x^3 - x^2 = x^2(x-1)$, graph D

iii Graph A

iv $x^4 - x^3 = x^3(x-1)$, graph E

v $x^4 - 2x^3 + x^2 = x^2(x-1)^2$, graph C

b For graph F: $x \mapsto x^3(x-1)^2$

For graph G: $x \mapsto x^3(x-1)^3$

For graph H: $x \mapsto x^2(x-1)^3$

Note

Look at the difference between, for example, graph D and graph E. Both have a horizontal tangent line at $(0, 0)$, but graph D stays below the x-axis around $(0, 0)$, while graph E crosses the x-axis at the origin.

22 a **i** At $t = 1$, A$(3, 10)$, B$(9, 6)$, so C$(6, 8)$

At $t = 2$, A$(8, 8)$, B$(12, 10)$, so C$(10, 9)$

At $t = 3$, A$(13, 6)$, B$(15, 14)$, so C$(14, 10)$

ii C$(6 + 4(n-1), 8 + (n-1)) = (2 + 4n, 7 + n)$

iii At $t = 10$, A$(48, -8)$, B$(36, 42)$, so C$\left(\dfrac{48+36}{2}, \dfrac{-8+42}{2}\right) = (42, 17)$

The formula gives: $(2 + 4 \cdot 10, 7 + 10) = (42, 17)$

Note

When the command term is 'suggest', then you don't have to justify or prove your formula, just notice a pattern and generalise.

iv $r_C = \dfrac{1}{2}(r_A + r_B) = \dfrac{1}{2}\left[\begin{pmatrix}-2\\12\end{pmatrix} + t\begin{pmatrix}5\\-2\end{pmatrix} + \begin{pmatrix}6\\2\end{pmatrix} + t\begin{pmatrix}3\\4\end{pmatrix}\right]$

$= \dfrac{1}{2}\left[\begin{pmatrix}4\\14\end{pmatrix} + t\begin{pmatrix}8\\2\end{pmatrix}\right] = \begin{pmatrix}2\\7\end{pmatrix} + t\begin{pmatrix}4\\1\end{pmatrix}$

v $v_A = \begin{pmatrix}5\\-2\end{pmatrix}$, $v_B = \begin{pmatrix}3\\4\end{pmatrix}$,

$v_C = \begin{pmatrix}4\\1\end{pmatrix} = \dfrac{1}{2}\left[\begin{pmatrix}5\\2\end{pmatrix} + \begin{pmatrix}3\\4\end{pmatrix}\right] = \dfrac{1}{2}(v_A + v_B)$

Note

Look at the difference between part **a iii** and **a iv**. In part **a iii** you have to 'check' the truth of a statement for a particular t-value. In part **a iv** you need to 'show' a statement. 'Showing' is more than just suggesting or checking; it requires an argument that proves the statement.

b $r_D = \dfrac{1}{2}(r_B + r_C) = \dfrac{1}{2}\left[\begin{pmatrix}6\\2\end{pmatrix} + t\begin{pmatrix}3\\4\end{pmatrix} + \begin{pmatrix}2\\7\end{pmatrix} + t\begin{pmatrix}4\\1\end{pmatrix}\right]$

$= \dfrac{1}{2}\left[\begin{pmatrix}8\\9\end{pmatrix} + t\begin{pmatrix}7\\5\end{pmatrix}\right] = \begin{pmatrix}4\\4.5\end{pmatrix} + t\begin{pmatrix}3.5\\2.7\end{pmatrix}$

Note

In an exam, it would be enough to write the final answer to part **a v** without any working, because of the 'write down' command term used in the question.

c $r_E = \frac{2}{3}r_A + \frac{1}{3}r_B = \frac{2}{3}\left[\begin{pmatrix}-2\\12\end{pmatrix}+t\begin{pmatrix}5\\-2\end{pmatrix}\right] + \frac{1}{3}\left[\begin{pmatrix}6\\2\end{pmatrix}+t\begin{pmatrix}3\\4\end{pmatrix}\right]$

$= \begin{pmatrix}-\frac{4}{3}\\4\end{pmatrix} + t\begin{pmatrix}\frac{10}{3}\\-\frac{4}{3}\end{pmatrix} + \begin{pmatrix}2\\\frac{2}{3}\end{pmatrix} + t\begin{pmatrix}1\\\frac{4}{3}\end{pmatrix} = \begin{pmatrix}\frac{2}{3}\\\frac{14}{3}\end{pmatrix} + t\begin{pmatrix}\frac{13}{3}\\0\end{pmatrix}$

Since the velocity vector has 0 in the second component, the movement is parallel to the x-axis in the positive direction, so due east.

23 a $\overrightarrow{AB} + \overrightarrow{BC} + \overrightarrow{CD} + \overrightarrow{DA} = 0$

$3p + 3q - 3r - 3s = 0$, so $r - p = q - s$

b $\overrightarrow{S_1Q_1} = \overrightarrow{S_1A} + \overrightarrow{AB} + \overrightarrow{BQ_1} = -s + 3p + q = 3p + (r-p) = 2p + r$

c $\overrightarrow{AS_1} + \frac{1}{3}\overrightarrow{S_1Q_1} = s + \frac{1}{3}(2p+r) = \frac{1}{3}(3s + 2p + r)$

similarly to part **b**, $\overrightarrow{P_1R_1} = 2s + q$, so

$\overrightarrow{AP_1} + \frac{1}{3}\overrightarrow{P_1R_1} = p + \frac{1}{3}(2s+q) = \frac{1}{3}(3p + 2s + q)$

$= \frac{1}{3}(3p + 2s + (r - p + s))$

$= \frac{1}{3}(3s + 2p + r)$

$= \overrightarrow{AS_1} + \frac{1}{3}\overrightarrow{S_1Q_1}$

d If $\overrightarrow{AS_1} + \frac{1}{3}\overrightarrow{S_1Q_1} = \overrightarrow{AX}$, then X is on the line segment S_1Q_1.

Since $\overrightarrow{AP_1} + \frac{1}{3}\overrightarrow{P_1R_1}$ is also AX, X is also on the line segment P_1R_1. Hence, X is the intersection of these line segments, which is M.

So $\overrightarrow{AP_1} + \frac{1}{3}\overrightarrow{P_1R_1} = \overrightarrow{AM}$, hence $\overrightarrow{P_1M} = \frac{1}{3}\overrightarrow{P_1R_1}$, so $3P_1M = P_1R_1$.

Similarly, $\overrightarrow{S_1M} = \frac{1}{3}\overrightarrow{S_1Q_1}$, so $3S_1M = S_1Q_1$.

e We already know that $\overrightarrow{AM} = \frac{1}{3}(3s + 2p + r)$.

Similar to the arguments before, N divides S_2Q_2 in the ratio 2 : 1, so

$\overrightarrow{AN} = \overrightarrow{AS_2} + \overrightarrow{S_2N} = 2\overrightarrow{AS_1} + \frac{2}{3}\overrightarrow{S_2Q_2}$

$= 2\overrightarrow{AS_1} + \frac{2}{3}(\overrightarrow{S_2D} + \overrightarrow{DC} + \overrightarrow{CQ_2})$

$= 2s + \frac{2}{3}(s + 3r - q) = \frac{1}{3}(8s + 6r - 2q)$

$\overrightarrow{MN} = \overrightarrow{MA} + \overrightarrow{AN}$

$= \frac{1}{3}(-3s - 2p - r) + \frac{1}{3}(8s + 6r - 2q)$

$= \frac{1}{3}(-2p - 2q + 5r + 5s)$

$= \frac{1}{3}(-2p - 2(r - p + s) + 5r + 5s)$

$= \frac{1}{3}(-2p - 2r + 2p - 2s + 5r + 5s) = \frac{1}{3}(3r + 3s)$

$= \frac{1}{3}(\overrightarrow{AD} + \overrightarrow{DC}) = \frac{1}{3}\overrightarrow{AC}$

Hence MN is parallel to AC (moreover, 3MN = AC).

Note

We use the following properties of vector algebra:

$v + w = w + v$

$\lambda(v + w) = \lambda v + \lambda w$

$\lambda(\mu v) = (\lambda\mu)v$

$(\lambda + \mu)v = \lambda v + \mu v$

Note

In this question, part **d** is the most interesting claim. Parts **a**, **b** and **c** are steps in proving this claim using vectors. Proving this using elementary geometry is not easy. Can you think of a way to do it?

24 a The vertical asymptote is $x = \dfrac{1}{3}$, the horizontal asymptote is $y = \dfrac{1}{3}$, so the graph is symmetric to $y = x$, hence the function is self-inverse.

b The inverse relationship is $x = \dfrac{2y+2}{3y-2}$. Solving for y:

$$3yx - 2x = 2y + 2$$
$$3yx - 2y = 2x + 2$$
$$y(3x - 2) = 2x + 2$$
$$y = \frac{2x+2}{3x-2}$$

c $(f \circ f)(x) = \dfrac{3\dfrac{3x+2}{3x-3}+2}{3\dfrac{3x+2}{3x-3}-3} = \dfrac{(9x+6)+(6x-6)}{(9x+6)-(9x-9)} = \dfrac{15x}{15} = x$

d i The previous examples were all self-inverse. Following the pattern, the suggestion is that for any $d = -a$, ($a \in \mathbb{Z}^+$) the function $x \mapsto \dfrac{ax+2}{3x-a}$ is self-inverse.

ii The inverse relationship is $x = \dfrac{ay+2}{3y-a}$. Solving for y:

$$3yx - ax = ay + 2$$
$$3yx - ay = ax + 2$$
$$y(3x - a) = ax + 2$$
$$y = \frac{ax+2}{3x-a}$$

e i $\dfrac{a\dfrac{ax+b}{cx+d}+b}{c\dfrac{ax+b}{cx+d}+d} = \dfrac{a(ax+b)+b(cx+d)}{c(ax+b)+d(cx+d)}$

$$= \frac{x(a^2+bc)+(ab+bd)}{x(ac+dc)+(cb+d^2)}$$

$A = a^2 + bc$, $B = ab + bd$, $C = ac + dc$, $D = cb + d^2$

ii If $x \mapsto \dfrac{ax+b}{cx+d}$ is self-inverse, then $A = D \neq 0$, $B = 0$ and $C = 0$.

$0 = C = c(a+d)$ implies $a = -d$ (since $c \neq 0$)

If $a = -d$, then $B = b(a + d)$ is also 0

Also, $A = a^2 + bc = (-d)^2 + bc = cb + d^2 = D$,

so $x \mapsto \dfrac{ax+b}{cx+d}$ is self-inverse if $c \neq 0$, $a = -d$ and $a^2 + bc \neq 0$

25 a i $\tan^2 \dfrac{x}{2} + 1 = \sec^2 \dfrac{x}{2} = \dfrac{1}{\cos^2 \dfrac{x}{2}}$, so $\cos^2 \dfrac{x}{2} = \dfrac{1}{1+t^2}$

ii $\cos x = 2\cos^2 \dfrac{x}{2} - 1 = \dfrac{2}{1+t^2} - 1 = \dfrac{2-(1+t^2)}{1+t^2} = \dfrac{1-t^2}{1+t^2}$

iii $\sin x = 2\sin \dfrac{x}{2} \cos \dfrac{x}{2} = 2 \tan \dfrac{x}{2} \cos^2 \dfrac{x}{2} = \dfrac{2t}{1+t^2}$

iv $\tan x = \dfrac{\sin x}{\cos x} = \dfrac{\dfrac{2t}{1+t^2}}{\dfrac{1-t^2}{1+t^2}} = \dfrac{2t}{1-t^2}$

v $t = \tan 120° = -\sqrt{3}$

$\dfrac{1-3}{1+3} = -\dfrac{1}{2} = \cos 240°$

$\dfrac{-2\sqrt{3}}{1+3} = \dfrac{-\sqrt{3}}{2} = \sin 240°$

$\dfrac{-2\sqrt{3}}{1-3} = \sqrt{3} = \tan 240°$

> **Note**
>
> Trigonometric ratios corresponding to special angles may be asked on a non-calculator paper.

b **i** If $\tan\dfrac{x}{2} = t$ and $0 < x < \pi$, then $x = 2\arctan t$,

so $\dfrac{\mathrm{d}x}{\mathrm{d}t} = 2\dfrac{1}{1+t^2} = \dfrac{2}{1+t^2}$.

> **Note**
>
> Although the method of substitution is part of the SL syllabus, these examples are beyond what is usually asked in an SL exam.

ii Replacing $\cos x$ with the expression from part **a ii** and $\mathrm{d}x$ with $\dfrac{2}{1+t^2}\mathrm{d}t$, we get

$\displaystyle\int \dfrac{1}{1+\dfrac{1-t^2}{1+t^2}}\dfrac{2}{1+t^2}\ \mathrm{d}t = \int \dfrac{2}{1+t^2+1-t^2}\ \mathrm{d}t = \int 1\,\mathrm{d}t = t + c,$

so $\displaystyle\int \dfrac{1}{1+\cos x}\mathrm{d}x = \tan\dfrac{x}{2} + c$

iii Using the same substitution, and the expression from part **a iii**, we get

$\displaystyle\int \dfrac{1}{1+\dfrac{2t}{1+t^2}}\dfrac{2}{1+t^2}\mathrm{d}t \quad = \quad \int \dfrac{1}{1+t^2+2t}\ 2\mathrm{d}t$

$= \displaystyle\int 2(1+t)^{-2}\ \mathrm{d}t = \dfrac{-2}{1+t} + c$

so $\displaystyle\int \dfrac{1}{1+\sin x}\mathrm{d}x = \dfrac{-2}{1+\tan\dfrac{x}{2}} + c$

> **Note**
>
> Of course, instead of checking the given answer, the substitution of the previous parts can also work here to find the integral directly.

iv $\dfrac{\mathrm{d}}{\mathrm{d}x}\ln\left(1+\tan\dfrac{x}{2}\right) = \dfrac{1}{1+\tan\dfrac{x}{2}}\dfrac{1}{\cos^2\dfrac{x}{2}}\dfrac{1}{2}$

$= \dfrac{1}{2\cos^2\dfrac{x}{2}+2\sin\dfrac{x}{2}\cos\dfrac{x}{2}}$

$= \dfrac{1}{\cos x+1+\sin x}$

26 a $\quad$ F$\hat{\text{E}}$C $= 180° - 90° - A\hat{\text{E}}$B $= 180° - 90° - (90° - \alpha) = \alpha$

$\quad$ A$\hat{\text{F}}$D $= 180° - 90° - D\hat{\text{A}}$F $= 180° - 90° - (90° - (\alpha+\beta)) = \alpha+\beta$

b $\quad \dfrac{\text{AB}}{\text{AE}} = \cos\alpha$, so $\text{AB} = \cos\alpha$

$\quad \dfrac{\text{BE}}{\text{AE}} = \sin\alpha$, so $\text{BE} = \sin\alpha$

> **Note**
>
> Parts **f** and **h** state the compound angle identities for tangent and sine. Both of these identities can be proved by noticing that on the diagram, AD = BE + EC. The other parts of the question guide you to express AD, BE and EC in terms of α and β. These identities are not part of the SL syllabus, but following these steps, the proof is accessible to both SL and HL students.

c $\dfrac{FE}{AE} = \tan\beta$, so $FE = \tan\beta$

$\dfrac{CE}{FE} = \cos\alpha$, so $CE = \tan\beta\cos\alpha$

d $\dfrac{FC}{FE} = \sin\alpha$, so $FC = \tan\beta\sin\alpha$

e $DF = DC - FC = AB - FC = \cos\alpha - \tan\beta\sin\alpha$

$\dfrac{AD}{DF} = \tan(\alpha+\beta)$, so $AD = (\cos\alpha - \tan\beta\sin\alpha)\tan(\alpha+\beta)$

f $$AD = CB = CE + EB$$

$$(\cos\alpha - \tan\beta\sin\alpha)\tan(\alpha+\beta) = \tan\beta\cos\alpha + \sin\alpha$$

$$\tan(\alpha+\beta) = \frac{\tan\beta\cos\alpha + \sin\alpha}{\cos\alpha - \tan\beta\sin\alpha}$$

$$= \frac{\tan\beta\cos\alpha + \sin\alpha}{\cos\alpha - \tan\beta\sin\alpha}\cdot\frac{\dfrac{1}{\cos\alpha}}{\dfrac{1}{\cos\alpha}}$$

$$= \frac{\tan\beta + \tan\alpha}{1 - \tan\beta\tan\alpha} = \frac{\tan\alpha + \tan\beta}{1 - \tan\alpha\tan\beta}$$

> **Note**
>
> A similar argument can be used to deduce the compound angle formula for cosine, using the fact that $AB = DF + FC$. Can you work this out?

g $\dfrac{AE}{FA} = \cos\beta$, so $FA = \dfrac{1}{\cos\beta}$

$\dfrac{AD}{FA} = \sin(\alpha+\beta)$, so $AD = FA\sin(\alpha+\beta) = \dfrac{\sin(\alpha+\beta)}{\cos\beta}$

h $$AD = CB = CE + EB$$

$$\frac{\sin(\alpha+\beta)}{\cos\beta} = \tan\beta\cos\alpha + \sin\alpha$$

$$\sin(\alpha+\beta) = \cos\beta(\tan\beta\cos\alpha + \sin\alpha)$$

$$= \sin\beta\cos\alpha + \cos\beta\sin\alpha = \sin\alpha\cos\beta + \cos\alpha\sin\beta$$

> **Note**
>
> These trigonometric ratios can also be found using the double angle formulae. Try to work these out. Start with $\cos 15°$.

i $\sin 75° = \sin(30° + 45°) = \sin 30°\cos 45° + \cos 30°\sin 45°$

$$= \frac{1}{2}\frac{\sqrt{2}}{2} + \frac{\sqrt{3}}{2}\frac{\sqrt{2}}{2} = \frac{\sqrt{2}+\sqrt{6}}{4}$$

$$\tan 75° = \tan(30° + 45°) = \frac{\tan 30° + \tan 45°}{1 - \tan 30°\tan 45°}$$

$$= \frac{\dfrac{1}{\sqrt{3}} + 1}{1 - \dfrac{1}{\sqrt{3}}\cdot 1} = \frac{1+\sqrt{3}}{\sqrt{3}-1}$$

$$\cos 75° = \frac{\sin 75°}{\tan 75°}$$

$$= \frac{\sqrt{2}+\sqrt{6}}{4}\cdot\frac{\sqrt{3}-1}{1+\sqrt{3}} = \frac{\sqrt{2}(1+\sqrt{3})}{4}\cdot\frac{\sqrt{3}-1}{1+\sqrt{3}} = \frac{\sqrt{6}-\sqrt{2}}{4}$$

j $\sin 15° = \cos 75° = \dfrac{\sqrt{6}-\sqrt{2}}{4}$

$\cos 15° = \sin 75° = \dfrac{\sqrt{2}+\sqrt{6}}{4}$

$\tan 15° = \dfrac{1}{\tan 75°} = \dfrac{\sqrt{3}-1}{1+\sqrt{3}}$

27 a Because the coin is fair, the probability of five heads appearing first is the same as the probability of five tails. Since they have equal chance of winning, and they paid in the same amount to start the game, yes it is a fair game.

b i

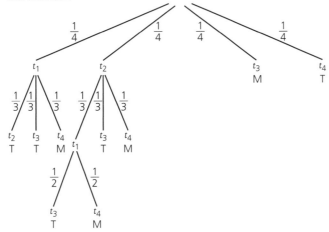

ii $P(\text{Blaise wins}) = \dfrac{1}{2} \cdot \dfrac{1}{2} = \dfrac{1}{4}$

$P(\text{Pierre wins}) = \dfrac{1}{2} \cdot \dfrac{1}{2} + \dfrac{1}{2} = \dfrac{3}{4}$

c To reflect the wining probabilities after this start of the game, they should divide the money in the ratio 3 : 1.

Blaise gets $20 \cdot \dfrac{1}{4} = 5$ écu, and Pierre gets $20 \cdot \dfrac{3}{4} = 15$ écu.

28 a $P(\text{the first number is the largest}) = \dfrac{1}{4}$

b i If the numbers are $t_1 < t_2 < t_3 < t_4$:

- If the first number is t_1, then Martin stops at the second number, and wins if this is t_4, otherwise Tom wins.
- If the first number is t_2, then Martin stops when he sees t_3 or t_4, whichever comes first.
- If the first number is t_3, then Martin wins, because he only stops when he sees t_4.
- If the first number is t_4, then Tom wins, Martin did not keep this number.

ii $P(\text{Martin wins}) = \dfrac{1}{4} \cdot \dfrac{1}{3} + \dfrac{1}{4} \cdot \dfrac{1}{3} \cdot \dfrac{1}{2} + \dfrac{1}{4} \cdot \dfrac{1}{3} + \dfrac{1}{4} = \dfrac{11}{24}$

c There are six equally likely possibilities for the first two numbers: $\{t_1, t_2\}, \{t_1, t_3\}, \{t_1, t_4\}, \{t_2, t_3\}, \{t_2, t_4\}, \{t_3, t_4\}$.

- If the first two numbers include t_4, then Tom wins
- If the first two numbers do not include t_4, but include t_3, then Martin wins (since he stops only when he sees t_4).
- If the first two numbers are t_1 and t_2, then Martin only wins if the next number is t_4.

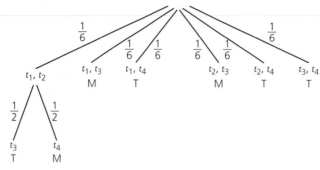

$$P(\text{Martin wins}) = \frac{1}{6} \cdot \frac{1}{2} + \frac{1}{6} + \frac{1}{6} = \frac{5}{12}$$

d $P(\text{the last number is the largest}) = \frac{1}{4}$

e Since $\frac{1}{4} < \frac{5}{12} < \frac{11}{24}$, the optimal strategy for Martin is to let one number go and keep the first one that is larger than this.

29 a $\cos 2kx = 1 - 2\sin^2 kx$, so $\sin^2 kx = \frac{1}{2} - \frac{\cos 2kx}{2}$

$$\int_{-\pi}^{\pi} \sin^2 kx \, dx = \int_{-\pi}^{\pi} \frac{1}{2} - \frac{\cos 2kx}{2} \, dx = \left[\frac{1}{2}x - \frac{\sin 2kx}{4} \right]_{-\pi}^{\pi}$$

$$= \left(\frac{\pi}{2} - \frac{\sin 2k\pi}{4} \right) - \left(\frac{-\pi}{2} - \frac{\sin 2k(-\pi)}{4} \right) = \pi$$

$$\int_{-\pi}^{\pi} \cos^2 kx \, dx = \int_{-\pi}^{\pi} 1 \, dx - \int_{-\pi}^{\pi} \sin^2 kx \, dx = 2\pi - \pi = \pi$$

b i $\int_{-\pi}^{\pi} \sin x \cos x \, dx = \int_{-\pi}^{\pi} \frac{1}{2}\sin 2x \, dx = \left[\frac{-\cos 2x}{4} \right]_{-\pi}^{\pi} = 0$

$\int_{-\pi}^{\pi} \sin 2x \cos 2x \, dx = \int_{-\pi}^{\pi} \frac{1}{2}\sin 4x \, dx = \left[\frac{-\cos 4x}{8} \right]_{-\pi}^{\pi} = 0$

ii Noticing the pattern, $\int_{-\pi}^{\pi} S_k(x) C_k(x) \, dx = 0$

iii $S_n(-x)C_m(-x) = \sin n(-x)\cos m(-x)$

$$= (-\sin nx)\cos mx = -S_n(x)C_m(x)$$

so $S_n C_m$ is indeed an odd function.

Because of the symmetry of the graph of $S_n C_m$, the integral on any interval $[-a, a]$ is 0. Hence $\int_{-\pi}^{\pi} S_n(x)C_m(x) \, dx = 0$.

c i $\cos(\alpha + \beta) = \cos\alpha\cos\beta - \sin\alpha\sin\beta$

$$\cos(\alpha - \beta) = \cos\alpha\cos\beta + \sin\alpha\sin\beta$$

$$\cos(\alpha + \beta) + \cos(\alpha - \beta) = 2\cos\alpha\cos\beta$$

ii We can assume that $n > m$.

$$\int_{-\pi}^{\pi} \cos nx \cos mx \, dx = \int_{-\pi}^{\pi} \frac{1}{2}\cos(n+m)x + \frac{1}{2}\cos(n-m)x \, dx$$

$$= \left[\frac{\sin(n+m)x}{2(n+m)} + \frac{\sin(n-m)x}{2(n-m)} \right]_{-\pi}^{\pi} = 0$$

d From the first two lines of part **c i**,
$2\sin\alpha\sin\beta = \cos(\alpha - \beta) - \cos(\alpha + \beta)$, so

$$\int_{-\pi}^{\pi} \sin nx \sin mx \, dx = \int_{-\pi}^{\pi} \frac{1}{2}\cos(n-m)x - \frac{1}{2}\cos(n+m)x \, dx$$

$$= \left[\frac{\sin(n-m)x}{2(n-m)} - \frac{\sin(n+m)x}{2(n+m)} \right]_{-\pi}^{\pi} = 0$$

e If 2π is a period of a function f, then $\int_{-\pi}^{0} f(x)\,dx = \int_{\pi}^{2\pi} f(x)\,dx$, so adding $\int_{0}^{\pi} f(x)\,dx$ to both sides (and using the periodicity), we get

$$\int_{-\pi}^{\pi} f(x)\,dx = \int_{0}^{2\pi} f(x)\,dx = \int_{2k\pi}^{2(k+1)\pi} f(x)\,dx, \text{ so}$$

Note

A similar argument shows that the integral of any of these functions over any interval $[a,\, a+2\pi]$ is the same as the integral over $[-\pi, \pi]$.

i $\int_{2\pi}^{6\pi} \cos^2(3x)\,dx = \int_{2\pi}^{4\pi} \cos^2(3x)\,dx + \int_{4\pi}^{6\pi} \cos^2(3x)\,dx = 2\pi$

ii $\int_{2\pi}^{6\pi} \cos(3x)\sin(5x)\,dx = 2\int_{-\pi}^{\pi} \cos(3x)\sin(5x)\,dx = 0$

iii $\int_{2\pi}^{6\pi} \cos(3x)\cos(5x)\,dx = 2\int_{-\pi}^{\pi} \cos(3x)\cos(5x)\,dx = 0$

iv $\int_{2\pi}^{6\pi} \sin(3x)\sin(5x)\,dx = 2\int_{-\pi}^{\pi} \sin(3x)\sin(5x)\,dx = 0$

Note

In part **e ii** we calculated the definite integral without finding the antiderivative. Instead we used the symmetry (in part **b iii**) and the periodicity of the function involved.

30 a **i** The acceleration $\dfrac{dv}{dt} = 10 - 0.2v$ is positive for $0 < v < 50$, and negative for $v > 50$. The starting velocity is 0, and there is no reason why the skydiver should slow down during the free-fall part, so $0 \leq v < 50$.

ii $\dfrac{dt}{dv} = \dfrac{1}{10 - 0.2v}$

$$T = \int_{0}^{T} 1\,dt = \int_{0}^{V} \frac{dt}{dv}\,dv = \int_{0}^{V} \frac{1}{10 - 0.2v}\,dv$$

iii $T = \left[\dfrac{\ln(10 - 0.2v)}{-0.2}\right]_{0}^{V} = \dfrac{\ln(10 - 0.2V)}{-0.2} - \dfrac{\ln 10}{-0.2}$

$-0.2t = -\ln 10 + \ln(10 - 0.2v(t))$

$e^{-0.2t} = \dfrac{10 - 0.2v(t)}{10}$

$10e^{-0.2t} = 10 - 0.2v(t)$

$0.2v(t) = 10 - 10e^{-0.2t} = 10(1 - e^{-0.2t})$

$v(t) = 50(1 - e^{-0.2t})$

Note

In part **a iii** the question effectively asks you to solve the differential equation $\dfrac{dv}{dt} = 10 - 0.2v$. For those who study the calculus option, this should be familiar. For the others, guidance is given in part **a ii**. Questions similar to this appear on past papers without help given because, before the 2014 exams, the solution of separable differential equations was on the HL core syllabus.

b **i** $v(60) = 50.0$ m/s

ii The distance travelled is $\int_{0}^{60} 50(1 - e^{-0.2t})\,dt = 2750$ metres

Distance from the ground: $4000 - 2750 = 1250$ metres

c **i** $a = 5, b = 50$

ii $T = \int_{60}^{T+60} 1\,dt = \int_{50}^{V} \frac{dt}{dv}\,dv = \int_{50}^{V} \frac{1}{10 - 2v}\,dv = \int_{V}^{50} \frac{1}{2v - 10}\,dv$

iii $T = \left[\dfrac{\ln(2v - 10)}{2}\right]_{V}^{50} = \dfrac{\ln(90)}{2} - \dfrac{\ln(2V - 10)}{2}$

$2(t - 60) = \ln 90 - \ln(2v(t) - 10)$

$e^{2(t-60)} = \dfrac{90}{2v(t) - 10}$

$2v(t) - 10 = 90e^{-2(t-60)}$

$2v(t) = 10 + 90e^{-2(t-60)}$

$v(t) = 5 + 45e^{-2(t-60)}$

Note

In part **c i** the command term is 'state', so no reasoning is required.

However, $b = 50$ because, when the parachute is opened, the velocity is 50 m/s and, from that point, the skydiver is slowing down. $a = 5$ because for $v > 5$, the acceleration is negative and for $v < 5$ the acceleration is positive.

d $\displaystyle\int_{60}^{T} v(t)\,dt = 1250$

$$[5t + \frac{45e^{-2(t-60)}}{-2}]_{60}^{T} = 1250$$

$$5T - \frac{45}{2}e^{-2(T-60)} - 300 + \frac{45}{2} = 1250$$

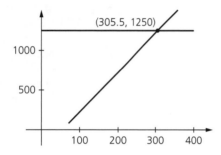

(305.5, 1250)

Using a GDC, the solution is $T = 306$ seconds.

e $v(306) = 5.00$ m/s

Key terms